WORKING WITH
CHALLENGING YOUTH

WORKING WITH CHALLENGING YOUTH

Lessons Learned Along the Way

written by

Brent Richardson, Ed.D.
Xavier University
Cincinnati, OH

BRUNNER-ROUTLEDGE
ALERE FLAMMAM
Taylor & Francis Group

USA	Publishing Office:	BRUNNER-ROUTLEDGE *A member of the Taylor & Francis Group* 325 Chestnut Street Philadelphia, PA 19106 Tel: (215) 625-8900 Fax: (215) 625-2940
	Distribution Center:	BRUNNER-ROUTLEDGE *A member of the Taylor & Francis Group* 7625 Empire Drive Florence, KY 41042 Tel: 1-800-634-7064 Fax: 1-800-248-4724
UK		BRUNNER-ROUTLEDGE *A member of the Taylor & Francis Group* 27 Church Road Hove E. Sussex, BN3 2FA Tel: +44 (0) 1273 207411 Fax: +44 (0) 1273 205612

WORKING WITH CHALLENGING YOUTH: Lessons Learned Along the Way

1 2 3 4 5 6 7 8 9 0

Printed by George H. Buchanan, Philadelphia, PA, 2001

A CIP catalog record for this book is available from the British Library.

⊗ The paper in this publication meets the requirements of the ANSI Standard Z39.48-1984 (Permanence of Paper).

Library of Congress Cataloging-in-Publication Data

Richardson, Brent, 1962–
    Working with challenging youth : lessons learned along the way / written by Brent Richardson.
        p. cm.
    Includes bibliographical references and index.
    ISBN 1-56032-891-6 (alk. paper)
        1. Social work with youth. 2. Problem youth — Counseling of. 3. Counseling.
        I. Title

HV1421.W67 2000
362.7'083—dc21   CIP
                                                                    00-044703

ISBN: 1-56032-891-6 (paper)

This book is dedicated to my children, Carter and Griffin, who challenge me to be a better parent and inspire me to be a better person. You have given me the greatest gift imaginable—the genuine experience of unconditional positive regard.

CONTENTS

Please remember that this is a library book,
and that it belongs only temporarily to each
person who uses it. Be considerate. Do
not write in this, or any, library book.

3   Lessons Learned: Meeting Youth Where They Are—Individually, Developmentally, and Culturally   37

4   Lessons Learned: Finding a Healthy Balance Between Support and Challenge   65

PREFACE

In 1951, Fritz Redl, a pioneer in working with challenging youth, asserted that "there are not enough angels to go around, so ordinary people, like us, with our unique histories choose to work with emotionally disturbed kids" (Long, 1991, p. 44). Fifty years later, this statement still rings true, but the kids are more challenging than ever and halos and wings are still hard to come by. While the frequency and intensity of antisocial and aggressive behavior among youth have increased significantly in the past decade (Long, Morse, & Newman, 1996), human services professionals in schools, community agencies, and residential facilities often find that they have not been adequately prepared to effectively meet the needs of this population. Subsequently, they flock to workshops searching for user friendly, pragmatic strategies. This book is written for human services professionals and other ordinary people who work with or are considering working with challenging youth.

For the past several years, I have been teaching in the graduate counseling program at Xavier University in Cincinnati and conducting workshops and seminars on building and maintaining therapeutic relationships with challenging youth. Before coming to Xavier, I worked with at-risk kids and families as a counselor, therapist, teacher, or administrator in a variety of diverse settings including an agency specializing in treatment foster care, an inner city emergency shelter, a rural high school, a family counseling center, a psychiatric hospital, and a residential school for students with severe learning disabilities and emotional disturbances. These diverse experiences across the continuum of care have prompted me to question the hierarchal pecking order and boundaries that separate the various professions and professionals. Certainly, there are occasions where these distinctions are warranted to help define roles and responsibilities. For example, only psychiatrists can prescribe medications and only specially trained clinicians should attempt interventions such as hypnosis and psychodrama. Nevertheless, there are three practical reasons why overemphasizing the different roles may be counterproductive or artificial for those who regularly interact with challenging youth.

First, successful psychiatrists, foster parents, residential counselors, special education teachers, social workers, therapists, and so forth, tend to share very similar attitudes, beliefs, and even practices for connecting, intervening, and facilitating positive changes with tough kids. Second, as first hand witnesses to the full spectrum of emotions and behaviors, those professionals who spend the most time with challenging youth (i.e., teachers, group home workers, foster parents) have unique insights regarding what works and what does not. The most successful psychiatrists, psychologists, and therapists recognize that there is not an inverse relationship between time spent with children and "real" expertise and work collaboratively with parents and other professionals. Third, and perhaps most important, challenging youth are less likely than other mental health consumers to respect these assigned roles and artificial distinctions (Morse, 1996b). The therapeutic or teachable moment can occur at any time during the day, not just in the confines of a helping professional's office. That's one of the things that makes these kids so challenging. Therefore, everyone who works with these youngsters on a regular basis is thrust into the role of counselor—either by choice or necessity. As Morse noted, "In helping distraught children there really is no division of labor" (p. 140).

Accordingly, this book will use the term counselor to describe a wide array of professionals who regularly interact with challenging youth. Since I am a counselor educator, many of the concepts have been gleaned from theories of counseling and psychotherapy; however, emphasis will be given to strategies most human services and mental health professionals can utilize to build and maintain therapeutic relationships and enhance their effectiveness with tough kids.

For the most part, this book has been written in a narrative, conversational style with limited use of psychological nomenclature to appeal to a wider variety of practitioners in the field. Also, while many of the illustrative examples use adolescents, most of the suggestions in this book are applicable for working with all school age youth.

☐ What Distinguishes Effective Counselors From the Rest?

Since my first job as a residential counselor, I have struggled to identify what distinguishes the really effective counselors from the rest. Why is it that some individuals just seem to have a knack for connecting and intervening with really challenging kids? Why is it that others, no matter how hard they try, seem unable to make the connection? And many more fall somewhere in the middle.

Early on, I was convinced the most distinguishing traits were an appropriate sense of humor and an ability to be both challenging and supportive. I still feel these are near the top of the list, but, over the years, I've expanded my criteria. At first, I also thought this knack was almost entirely innate—either you possessed this gift or you didn't. There were no stores where you could buy the gift and few, if any, places where you could develop the gift.

Since I seldom take a deterministic approach to the world, I worked on softening my stance. I reviewed the research, examined a variety of theoretical perspectives, interviewed effective youth counselors and administrators, and most important, began to pay closer attention to the common traits, attitudes, and behaviors of counselors and other helping professionals who consistently make a difference. I kept asking, "What distinguishes the really effective counselors from the rest?" Answers to that question kept yielding a variety of specific qualities and behaviors; however, each of these tends to fall under the rubric of one or more of the six philosophical principles and beliefs shared by effective helping professionals. These principles are:

1. A therapeutic relationship is an essential ingredient for facilitating positive change with challenging youth.
2. Ongoing helper self-awareness and self-evaluation are critical for building and maintaining therapeutic relationships.
3. To help youth get where they (or you) want to go, you must first meet them where they are—individually, developmentally, and culturally.
4. For relationships to mature, there must be a healthy balance of support and challenge.
5. Problems and solutions are best framed in creative, constructive, and caring ways.
6. Systemic, collaborative, and preventive approaches tend to be more fruitful than isolated or reactive approaches.

☐ Overview of Chapters

In Chapter 1, An Introduction to Challenging Youth, a distinction is made between challenging youth who are often overwhelmed by their feelings and youth with a significant character disorder who are unwilling or unable to offer emotional responses other than anger or excitement. The distinction is important because youth who lack a conscience tend to be more calculating and destructive in their behaviors and may warrant a different professional response than what is described in this book. The first chapter will also identify some of the major theoretical influences for the book, including reality therapy, solution-focused therapy, Mental Research Institute (MRI) brief problem-focused therapy, systems theory, the humanistic philosophy of Carl Rogers and Virginia Satir, as well as the pioneering work of Fritz Redl. Taking an eclectic approach, I draw from these approaches and many others to identify specific considerations and strategies for all professionals who engage in this difficult, but rewarding, work. Empirical and theoretical rationales will be offered to support the assertion that all strategies should reflect an underlying goal of building and maintaining a more therapeutic relationship.

Chapters 2 through 6 are formatted around principles 2–6. Each chapter expands upon these principles and highlights a variety of lessons designed to help counselors incorporate each of these principles into their work with challenging youth. I am not suggesting that these principles are mutually exclusive or that this is an exhaustive list, but I do think these principles capture the essence of what distinguishes the exceptional counselors and human services professionals from the rest.

Certainly, these principles are highly interrelated. In fact, one of the most difficult aspects of writing this book was trying to decide which principle a particular lesson best represented. For instance, many of the lessons that highlight the importance of meeting youth where they are also speak to the importance of finding an appropriate balance between challenge and support, and vice versa. The principles and lessons are not so separate from one another as the unavoidable limitation of writing a book makes them seem to be. Having a separate chapter outlining lessons for framing problems and solutions in creative, constructive and caring ways should not imply that other strategies in the book do not constructively reframe problems. Much of what effective human services professionals do to connect and intervene with challenging youth actually addresses several principles simultaneously.

In Chapter 2, I share eight lessons that highlight the connection between a counselor's self-awareness and his or her ability to build and maintain meaningful relationships. A self-inventory for adults who work with challenging youth is provided as a springboard to encourage reflection about critical self-awareness and relationship issues that are discussed throughout the book. Some other essential skills that are discussed in this chapter include utilizing an appropriate sense of humor, recognizing our own emotional triggers, and learning from our mistakes or past conflict—and then letting go. I propose that these kids are like inkblot tests; they tend to reflect the best and worst in ourselves.

Chapter 3 expands upon the third principle, "To help youth get where they (or you) want to go, you must first meet them where they are—individually, developmentally, and culturally." While this is true for all clients, it is particularly important for working with youngsters. Most of the 12 lessons in this chapter focus on specific considerations and strategies professionals can utilize in the early stages to improve their chances of engaging adolescents. Central themes include recognizing the two basic needs challenging youth struggle to responsibly meet, finding ways to communicate that their perspective is valued, and appreciating ways adolescents are developmentally and culturally unique.

In Chapter 4, I question the dualistic ideology that tends to fuel the debates in western contemporary society regarding "delinquent" youth. I promote the belief that those who possess a unique gift to work with challenging youth offer both support and challenge—often at the same time. I describe situations when confrontation is not only warranted, but expected and desired by tough kids. I demonstrate how the Support, Empathy, Truth (SET) Model can be effectively utilized to keep us grounded and reduce our defenses while also setting limits, reinforcing boundaries, and enforcing consequences. I also discuss how our beliefs regarding control impact our interactions with troubled youth.

Chapter 5, Lessons Learned: Framing Problems and Solutions in More Creative, Constructive, and Caring Ways, promotes the premise that the success of various strategies, regardless of their theoretical framework, lies in the ability of counselors, youth, and families to view the problem in a different light and act accordingly. Specific lessons focus on looking beyond the behavior to avoid escalating the cycle of aggression, focusing on individual and community strengths by paying attention to what we pay attention to, facilitating a process where the youth can evaluate his or her own behavior, and using metaphors and stories to help plant the seeds for change. I also explore educational and psychological labels given to these youth and offer suggestions on how the assessment process can be made more youth and family friendly.

Chapter 6, Lessons Learned: Valuing Systemic, Collaborative, and Preventive Approaches, shares a variety of lessons for promoting a community-wide, collaborative approach for effectively intervening with challenging youth and questions why so many professionals continue to operate in a vacuum despite research that suggests the limited effectiveness of this approach. This chapter highlights the rationale and strategies for collaborating with families, peers, and other professionals. Prevention efforts and advocacy for youth and families will also be discussed.

Chapters 2 through 6 contain 47 lessons, and for each lesson, a number of specific strategies and considerations are offered. This can be overwhelming, particularly for the beginning counselor. In Chapter 7, I encourage the reader to concentrate on the six foundational principles more than the specific techniques.

☐ Recommendations for Reading This Book

I incorporate a number of case vignettes to highlight and illustrate different concepts and principles. Unless permission was otherwise granted, names and identifying details of individuals in the cases have been changed to protect confidentiality.

The vast majority of what I recommend is substantially supported by theory, research, or both; however, some of the lessons and most of the case examples come directly from my own professional experiences. While experience coupled with cognitive reflection have definitely been my best teachers, I need to acknowledge that much of what I think and believe regarding working with challenging youth is based on my own subjective impressions. I hope that over the years, I have grown as a person and as a professional; nevertheless, I do not pretend to have all the answers when it comes to working with challenging youth. I'm still grappling and learning—a work in progress. Subsequently, in reading this book, I would encourage you to focus on what is most meaningful and useful for you.

ACKNOWLEDGMENTS

As I begin to reflect on the magnitude of this project, I am reminded of the many people who have supported, encouraged and inspired me along the way. Without their assistance, this journey could not have been completed.

First, I would like to acknowledge all the youth and families I have worked with for the past 15 years. Their courage, determination, and resilience are truly an inspiration. They are the best teachers I have ever had.

A number of gifted supervisors over the years have taught me numerous lessons along the way. Some of these role models for working with challenging youth include Marietta McCarty, Dave Coslow, Dave Stuckwisch, Donnie Conner, Victoria Foster, and Charles McAdams. Much of what I know and believe about this population can be traced to these individuals. I would also like to thank my fellow practitioners and students who have dedicated their lives to making a difference in the lives of children and adolescents. Their struggles and rewards are chronicled throughout the book.

I would like to express my appreciation to those persons who reviewed earlier versions of this work and ultimately made it better. Special thanks to: Lon Kriner, Xavier University; Robert Wubbolding, author of *Reality Therapy for the 21ˢᵗ Century*; Albert Anderson, Chair, National Youth Advocate Program; Dave Reber, Psychological Services of Danville, KY; Johnston Brendel, Texas A&M–Corpus Christi; Charles R. McAdams, College of William and Mary; Tina Bayer, Adjunct Professor, Xavier University; Tracy Linblad, graduate counseling student, Xavier University; and John Mallery, Catholic Social Services. Also, graduate students in my classes at Xavier University have read drafts of various chapters and provided ongoing feedback and encouragement. Much gratitude to you all.

I would also like to thank Tim Julet, Jill Osawa, and Kim Sauer, editors at Taylor and Francis, for their careful attention to detail and ongoing availability and support.

I owe a huge debt of appreciation to my parents and role models, Emmett and Sylvia Richardson, whose nurturance and guidance have shaped my development.   I am especially appreciative for their undeviating support since my decision to change career paths 15 years ago.

Finally and foremost, I would also like to thank Melanie, my wife, friend, fellow counselor, and first editor for her personal sacrifices, patience, and support throughout this three-year process.

1

CHAPTER

An Introduction to Challenging Youth

☐ What 12 Teenage Boys in a Double Trailer Taught Me About Myself

Some people know from a very early age what they want to be when they grow up. This was not the case for me. I thought I wanted to be a lawyer, but I never really took the time to learn what that meant. In 1985, as I was approaching college graduation, I remained ambivalent. I requested applications to various law schools and one for the Peace Corps. After considerable thought (the Peace Corps application was much thicker than the law school applications), I applied to law school and was accepted. "Whew," I thought, "I can delay this real world bit a little longer." During orientation, all the first year students took a personality inven-tory and were placed in four subgroups. The other three groups had 72, 48, and 20 students. There were two of us in my groupand we were both already questioning our motives and commitment for attending law school. Feeling like the personality inventory confirmed what he already knew, the other individual in my subgroup withdrew the first day of classes, and feeling no pressure to carry the legal torch for our personality type, I withdrew the next day.

Feeling sorry for myself and somewhat disjointed, I retreated to my parents' home for several weeks until my Uncle Billy, who has Down's

Syndrome, started calling me every day and asking, "You got a job yet?" Billy's persistence made me realize three things: 1) I can't stay here and sulk forever; 2) I probably won't get a job if I never apply for one; and 3) No matter what I say, Billy's not going to stop calling.

Knowing that my "accelerated law degree" would probably be of little value in the job market, I decided to look for something that enabled me to work with kids. Or plastics, or sales, whatever—anything to stop the phone calls and recharge my batteries. I checked the classified ads and the first thing I saw was an opening for a residential counselor (translation: live in a double trailer with 12 teenage boys with various learning disabilities and emotional disturbances, work all day long, and make an annual salary of $10,500). I thought, "Perfect, when do I start?"

If you really want to find out about yourself, warts and all (and most of us don't), the double trailer strategy is the way to go. It was one of the most difficult, yet rewarding experiences of my life. There was no where to run, no where to hide. My office was our living room. I couldn't retreat to the suburbs (as I often do now) at the end of a long day. Like it or not, these kids were going to teach me about myself. Much of what I learned was affirming and rewarding. I liked that I was able to remain calm and collected during crises. I liked that for the most part, I enjoyed these kids and my job. However, some of what I learned was not so affirming at the time. I learned that I frustrated myself when confronted with what is often referred to as passive-aggressive behavior by trying to decipher where the youth was coming from, probably because I felt safer and more in control that way. I learned that my sensitivity could be a powerful ally. But I also learned that the vulnerability that derived from that sensitivity coupled with my need to do the right thing could yield considerable self-doubt and second guessing. Although these lessons were difficult to absorb at the time, I look back and am thankful for all the times I overreacted or put my foot in my mouth. Thank God I made so many mistakes because I learned so much. I learned that I have a lot more to learn about troubled youth, and more important, about myself.

☐ Who Are Challenging Youth?

The following are some of the challenging youth who are discussed in this book:

Natasha, an angry 14-year-old Black female who exhibits a wide range of aggressive and indignant behaviors to mask emotional pain, and reinforces both the importance and difficulty of empathic under-standing

Jerry, a sullen 15-year-old White male with a long history of abuse, neglect, and multiple placements, who frequently runs away whenever he becomes emotionally overwhelmed, and illustrates the need to find a healthy balance between support and challenge

Todd, an 11-year-old White male who consistently displays a quick wit and a quicker temper, and reinforces that sometimes laughter is the shortest distance between two people

Joseph, a feisty 12-year-old biracial male who is suspended from school on several occasions for disrupting class and fighting with peers, and demonstrates the value of involving youth in setting goals and de-veloping behavior modification plans

Tyrone, a guarded, confused 15-year-old Black male who reluc-tantly agrees to participate in family therapy after being arrested for breaking and entering, and teaches the relevance of meeting youth where they are, both literally and figuratively

Carlos, an intelligent 15-year-old Hispanic male whose severe learning disability was not diagnosed until he was in the seventh grade, and illustrates that behavior problems or emotional disturbances can be symptoms of an undiagnosed or untreated learning disability

Brandi, a pugnacious 13-year-old White female who consistently challenges her parents, teachers, school administrators, and other au-thority figures, and epitomizes the importance of making a distinction between empathy and agreement

Michael, a spirited 12-year-old Black male who was court ordered to a group home after numerous incidents of cursing school officials, complaints from his parents that they were "at our wit's end," and an arrest for assaulting another student, and shows how analogous stories can be used to help youth begin to make more constructive choices

Mary, a troubled but resilient 11-year-old White female who is given 18 different psychiatric diagnoses in 13 different hospitals, and reinforces that diagnosing children is not an exact science

John, an extremely hyperactive 12-year-old White male who is making tremendous strides after spending much of his childhood in residential treatment due to multiple traumas and uncontrollable, sexu-ally reactive outbursts, and illustrates the value of professional resil-ience and collaboration.

For the most part, I chose to use the adjective challenging to de-scribe a wide variety of children and adolescents who are frequently iden-tified by terms such as "difficult," "troubled," "at-risk," "frustrating," "im-possible," "emotionally-disturbed," "behaviorally-disordered," "oppositionally-defiant," and "conduct-disordered," as well as some less flattering monikers. The term challenging puts the impetus on the relationship between helping professionals and the youth and challenges us adults to adjust our style to meet the needs of the youth.

For the purposes of this book, challenging youth refers to youth, who, for a variety of reasons:

1. experience a wide range of emotions, but often struggle to express and manage these emotions in constructive ways;
2. struggle on a daily basis to responsibly meet their basic needs to a) feel like they belong, and b) feel competent and worthwhile (Glasser, 1965);
3. possess the regrettable ability to elicit from others the opposite of what they need (Tobin, 1991); and
4. seldom seek help from adults voluntarily.

Too many youth have grown up in abusive or otherwise dysfunctional families and have received conflicting messages about what works and what doesn't. One day, they are praised by a parent for fighting with their sibling. The next day, they are beaten or scolded for the same behavior. They are taught not to trust their own judgment or emotions. Additionally, the adult models for many of these youth often have a longstanding pattern of externalizing responsibility and becoming overwhelmed by their own emotions. Understandably, these youth have a difficult time accepting responsibility, managing their emotions, evaluating their own behavior, or believing that adults can help them. These daily internal and external struggles are manifested in a variety of ways in schools, homes, treatment facilities, and so forth.

Throughout much of my professional career, I have worked extensively with children and adolescents who have been the victims of unbearable emotional, physical, and sexual abuse—often by their own parents. However, it would be a mistake to assume that all, or even most, challenging youth come from abusive or dysfunctional homes. Many challenging youth have been raised by supportive, nurturing parents who use appropriate discipline. My oldest son will be 6 years old soon and I recently joked at a workshop that I had 7 more years to be an expert on parenting adolescents. Those of you who are parents know what I mean.

In today's adolescent culture, it seems as though rites of passage take place earlier every year, and our children are exposed to negative lures before they have the cognitive developmental tools to make the best decisions. There are countless temptations and so many ways they can be led astray (i.e., television, music, the internet, drugs, peer pressure). Despite our best efforts, we can't always protect them. Sometimes, it seems like one bad decision, and they begin the downward spiral. Other times, the primary precipitators are more difficult to pinpoint. We've all heard parents describe angelic children who became difficult seemingly overnight.

Although the causes are not always obvious, and, in fact, may be quite different, the term challenging youth purposely describes a wide range of youth who share an inability to manage their emotions, an inability to responsibly meet their needs, and an uncanny ability to locate and activate our emotional triggers. The challenging youth described in this book also possess the capacity to distinguish right from wrong and are able to have some regard for the feelings of others (albeit these traits are not always readily apparent). Because their behavior is seldom what it appears to be, empathic understanding is often the best *first* step in building a therapeutic relationship with these kids (Tobin, 1991).

☐ What About Youth Who Seem to Lack the Capacity to Care About Others?

Mitchell Johnson, Andrew Golden, Eric Harris, Dylan Klebold, and Kip Kinkel are just a handful of severely troubled boys whose shooting rampages in the past few years shattered many families and left the rest of us wondering why and how such tragic incidents could take place in our schools. In an effort to make sense of these senseless tragedies, we point fingers at possible causes such as declining values in American society, inadequate school security, violence in the media, the proliferation of firearms, inadequate or abusive parenting, an overburdened judicial system, and everyone who ignored the numerous warning signs. We rationalize that pinpointing the primary cause will enable us to prevent future massacres, and, to a certain extent, this is true. Although we will be unable to thwart all terrorist actions, we can and should take steps to reduce the number of occurrences and victims. Thus, I applaud these efforts to take preventive measures to improve various systems, strengthen families, and recognize common warning signs such as fascination with weapons, cruelty to animals, and boastful threats of pending violence. However, in an effort to recognize and change societal and familial influences, we must not excuse or forget the primary perpetrators—the boys who pulled the triggers. The vast majority of the millions of youth who have been flooded with violent images in the media, have received inadequate or abusive parenting, or have been exposed to firearms have not chosen to act in such violent ways. What was different about these five boys? Although there are probably many traits and characteristics that make them unique, perhaps the most telling difference appears to be the absence of a con-science—a guiding force which would have prevented them from destroy-ing so many innocent lives.

It is important to recognize that there are some youth, who for a variety of reasons, have misplaced or never developed their conscience. Such youth are typically able to distinguish right from wrong, but their amoral compass guides them to decisions based on what they perceive to be best for them. Rules exist, but rules do not apply to them. Since they have little or no capacity for empathy or sympathy, they view others as objects—as means to an end. While challenging youth are often over-whelmed by their feelings, these youth tend to be unable or unwilling to offer emotional responses other than excitement or anger. They are often described as cool and calculating. These individuals are characterized by their emotional flatness, extreme egocentrism, ambitious mean-spirited pleasure seeking, lack of remorse, unbridled lust for power and control, and little or no desire for change. These youth who truly lack a conscience are more aptly described as sociopaths or psychopaths, or as having a char-acter disorder or antisocial personality disorder (Kellerman, 1999).

Without the capacity to care for others, fear of consequences be-comes the primary deterrent and motivator for good behavior; subse-quently, public safety and security become paramount when working with these kids. While anger and disgust are understandable responses to a youth who seems to lack a conscience, sympathy may be an even more appropri-ate response. How sad it must be to live life without the ability to care for other people (Tobin, 1991).

Experts disagree regarding how many troubled youth can be identi-fied as having a significant character disorder. After years of working di-rectly with severely disturbed youth, Redl and Wineman (1957) asserted that the number of children "without a conscience—the so-called psycho-path" was grossly exaggerated:

> Among all the hundreds of children who were supposed to be without a conscience and with whom we lived quite closely for varying lengths of time, we haven't found one to whom such an exaggerated diagnosis would apply. We admit, though, that we were often tempted to make such a state-ment, about a particular child, especially when we were angry at him, when our middle-class sensitivities were rubbed the wrong way. . . . Whoever follows a child through the totality of a residential life situation, into every nook and cranny of the trivia of the day, is bound to discover that such a concept is an oversimplification which makes no sense. (p. 201)

More recently, professionals such as Magid and McKelvey (1987) have challenged this assessment that psychopathy is rare among youth.

While I agree with Magid and McKelvey that psychopathic youth are a growing concern that needs our full attention, I continue to support Redl and Wineman's contention that this diagnosis is often misapplied and exaggerated. Conduct Disorder, which is characterized by a repetitive and persistent pattern of violating the rights of others, is one of the most frequently diagnosed conditions for adolescents with severe behavior problems. In the majority of individuals, the disorder remits by adulthood (American Psychiatric Association, 1994).

Therefore, despite the seriousness of their offenses, most youth diagnosed with Conduct Disorder are capable of feeling empathy and showing remorse, and are more likely experiencing significant emotional and behavioral difficulties rather than an underlying character disorder. If you are unsure, assume the conscience is merely hidden or underdeveloped, and work to uncover or nurture it. Unfortunately, some of the more severe cases of Conduct Disorder may be an indication that the youth lacks a conscience and is unable to care for or about others. As noted above, these youngsters tend to be more calculating and destructive in their behaviors and may warrant different professional responses than what is described in this book.

☐   Empirical and Theoretical Foundations

In a review of numerous meta-analyses of youth psychotherapy outcome studies covering a wide array of emotional and behavioral disorders, Target and Fonagy (1996) concluded that psychotherapeutic treatments for children and adolescents are often associated with significant improvements. However, there is less agreement regarding the specific types of interventions which produce positive outcomes. Although a number of comparative studies indicated that family therapy and cognitive-behavioral approaches were often most effective in intervening with disruptive youth, the authors reported that conflicting results, contextual differences, and methodological difficulties make it imprudent to conclude that one particular approach is superior for this population.

These conclusions are not surprising. Outcome research on counseling and psychotherapy in general has been conducted for many years; yet, most studies show little or no differential effectiveness for different approaches (Stiles, Shapiro, & Elliott, 1986). The interactive nature and the large number of human variables are only a few of the potential problems in this kind of research (Seligman, 1990). Target and Fonagy (1996) emphasized that there are even more obstacles in conducting systematic research on children and adolescents. For example, youth often are reluctant clients and cannot be assumed to be reliable informants. Further-more, parents and teachers often paint very different pictures when asked to assess the same child. It is also difficult to distinguish spontaneous changes relative to development and changes relative to specific interventions.

However, drawing from my own experiences and observations, common themes from a variety of research and theoretical perspectives, as well as interviews with professionals and challenging youth, I propose that certain helper behaviors, attitudes, and traits are more likely to therapeutically engage youth and facilitate positive change. Specifically, professionals and intervention models that are most successful in connecting and intervening with challenging youth utilize a variety of strategies to incorporate the six philosophical principles and beliefs highlighted in the Preface.

These general principles are more important than any specific techniques. To paraphrase Covey (1990), a technique is the "what to do," a specific application to fit a specific situation. A principle is the "why to do," the foundation upon which techniques are built. For example, different theoretical approaches might suggest vastly different strategies to constructively reframe a family's problems. It's the understanding of why it's important to approach the problem differently or give it a new meaning that gives the technique promise. Again, it has been my experience that successful professionals across the continuum of services (i.e., therapists, residential counselors, foster parents, special education teachers) incorporate these same principles into their work with challenging youth. Some techniques may be unique to the position, but the principles remain fairly consistent.

Karasu (1986) reported that there are more than 400 counseling theories. The majority of counselors can best be described as eclectic (Baruth & Robinson, 1987; Norcross, 1986; Prochaska & Norcross, 1994). Because eclectic counselors tend to believe that techniques associated with no one theory have been adequately developed to help all clients (Baruth & Robinson, 1987), they typically attempt to combine the most applicable components of differing orientations (Corey, 1996; Prochaska & Norcross, 1994).

Several recent authors have recommended using an eclectic framework for working with challenging or difficult youth. Frustrated by treatment approaches which seemed to have little value for this population, Sommers-Flanagan and Sommers-Flanagan (1997) began developing an eclectic model using a variety of behavioral, emotional, and cognitive techniques to make the counseling process more consumer-friendly for tough kids. Goldstein and his colleagues (1987), in developing a comprehensive group counseling model for troubled youth called Aggression Replacement Training asserted that "effective intervention is differential intervention" (p. 8). Selekman (1993), who proposes a solution-focused model for helping challenging youth, also acknowledged the importance of integrating ideas from other approaches. These authors understand that working with creative, impulsive kids may require creative, eclectic strategies. I agree with Frank (1982) that the therapeutic elements of therapeutic approaches are more similar than they are different. If one approach is not working, why not try something else? It is possible to draw from a variety of helping approaches provided the philosophical principles are compatible.

Although I draw from a variety of perspectives and the strategies and considerations I emphasize may be different from others who work with this population (i.e., Selekman, 1993; Sommers-Flanagan & Sommers-Flanagan, 1997), the underlying principles about what helps to facilitate positive change appear to be similar. For instance, each of these authors recommend strategies for constructively reframing problems, balancing support and challenge, and respecting individual and cultural differences. Most importantly, each of the theories and theorists I draw from place considerable importance on the potential healing power of therapeutic relationships.

For decades, it has been a widely held belief that a therapeutic relationship is an essential ingredient for facilitating positive change with challenging youth (Glasser, 1965; Rogers, 1957; Sommers-Flanagan & Sommers-Flanagan, 1997; Trieschman, Whittaker, & Brendtro, 1969). Sarason and Sarason (1996) reviewed a variety of modalities for treating conduct disorder and noted "social supports from one or more close relationships . . . to be one of the principal ways to prevent conduct disorder initially and keep it from developing into a more serious disorder in adulthood" (p. 450). Wehlage and his colleagues (1989) found that the quality of the teacher-student relationship was the primary distinguishing factor for effective schools for at-risk youth. Reporting on a national longitudinal study of over 12,000 adolescents, Resnick and his colleagues (1998) found parent-family connectedness and perceived school connectedness to be the most important protective factors against a variety of risk behaviors. These researchers described challenging youth as "products of disconnection." Van Bockern (1996) warned that the major hurdle in the reclaiming process is to help the child build a new kind of relationship with an adult who can be trusted for support, guidance, and affection. As Yalom (1985) remarked, "It is the relationship that heals" (p. 50). Therefore, every lesson in every chapter should reflect the goal of building and maintaining therapeutic relationships.

In subsequent chapters, a variety of lessons are presented to help the reader clarify and promote the six principles and beliefs identified earlier. Although I draw from a variety of experiences and resources, several theoretical models have been particularly useful in mapping strategies for connecting and intervening with challenging youth: reality therapy, systems theory, humanistic psychology, solution-focused therapy, and MRI brief problem-focused therapy. Another major influence has been the work of Fritz Redl and his colleagues, whose innovative ideas laid much of the groundwork for the treatment of challenging youth. I also borrow important concepts from popular authors such as Stephen Covey and Rabbi Harold Kushner who have focused their writings on human relations in general. Additionally, much of the ideas stem from what I will call pragmatic theory or direct trial and error experience in the field.

Reality Therapy

I probably draw more from reality therapy than any other theoretical approach. Much of the original ideas for reality therapy grew out of Dr. William Glasser's work with delinquent girls at the Ventura School for Girls and are still applicable today. Frustrated with the psychoanalytic model, Glasser developed a theory of human behavior and motivation that was useful for human services professionals and lay persons. Because the cognitive-behavioral ideas can be used by parents, teachers, clergy, residential staff, and other front-line counselors (Corey, 1996; Glasser, 1965), reality therapy is more conducive to collaboration and a systemic framework than many approaches.

Since the publication of *Reality Therapy: A New Approach to Psychiatry* (Glasser, 1965), reality therapy has been taught, studied, and practiced by millions of people. The theory and practice of reality therapy has continued to evolve. Noteworthy contributions to this evolutionary process are Dr. Robert Wubbolding's 1988 book, *Using Reality Therapy*, which helped clarify and expand the practice of reality therapy and Glasser's 1998 book, *Choice Theory: A New Psychology of Personal Freedom*, which further refined the theoretical concepts essential to reality therapy and its underlying theory.

As clinical director of a family services agency, I trained treatment foster parents to use reality therapy and I've used the concepts myself as a residential, school, and clinical counselor. Reality therapy provides an excellent framework for creating the necessary balance between support and challenge for succeeding with tough kids. Since Glasser (1998a) believes that virtually all human problems can be traced to unsatisfying relationships, primary emphasis is placed on establishing and maintaining a warm, caring relationship and helping youth identify what they want.

Furthermore, Glasser (1965) postulated that all youths' behavior is their best attempt to meet one or more of five basic needs. In this book, I discuss how the need for love and belonging and the need for power and achievement are especially critical for many challenging youth. Problems occur when often well meaning adults try to remove what they perceive to be injurious or harmful without considering alternative ways the youth can meet his or her basic needs.

Also central to this approach is the concept that we can only control our own behavior. Believing we can control others, including challenging youth, and believing that others can control us (i.e., "make" us angry), are primary precursors to human misery. Our beliefs regarding who and what we can control greatly impact our approach to working with this population. Furthermore, reality therapy provides a structure to help youth evaluate their own behavior and learn to make more responsible choices. Too often, those of us in the helping profession persist in judging their behavior for them or trying to control challenging youth and coerce compliance. In this book, I highlight and expand upon these elements of the theory and practice that are particularly relevant for working with challenging youth.

Solution-Focused and MRI Brief Problem-Focused Therapies

Two other approaches which evolved largely from therapists' work with families and challenging youth are the solution-focused model developed by deShazer (1985) and his associates at the Brief Family Therapy Center in Milwaukee and the MRI brief problem-focused therapy model developed by Weakland, Jackson, Watzlawick, and Fisch at the Mental Research Institute in Palo Alto, California (Fisch, Weakland, & Segal, 1982). Each of these systems approaches offer a variety of provocative ideas and strategies regarding change and the helping professions. After reading books such as *Keys to Solution in Brief Therapy* (deShazer, 1985) and *The Tactics of Change* (Fisch, Weakland, & Segal, 1982), I began to significantly alter the way I approach and think about challenging youth.

Specifically, I began to view "resistance" as an overused, inaccurate, and counterproductive term. These approaches also gave me more tools to shift my focus to family and youth strengths. I began to explore new ways to constructively reframe problems and recognized that many helpers, myself included, often proposed interventions that were only a slight variation of what had already been unsuccessfully tried. My favorite definition of insanity is "doing the same thing over and over again and expecting different results." Most of us who are in the business of working with challenging youth have experienced temporary insanity. This book explores various ways these concepts and strategies can be utilized by any adult who regularly interacts with tough kids. Once we change the lenses through which we see problems, everything looks different.

Systems Theory

All systems models, including solution-focused and MRI brief therapy, recognize that individuals, particularly children and adolescents need to be viewed within the context of their family, culture, and a larger system. The whole is greater than the sum of the parts. When one member of a family changes or experiences pain, all members will be impacted in some way (Brown & Christensen, 1986; Satir, 1983). Thus, we cannot limit our helping approaches to changing the individual; we must also explore how the youth interacts with other people, particularly his or her family. We must also be attuned to cultural and societal factors that influence his or her development.

The work of Salvador Minuchin has greatly influenced my belief system about what is helpful with this population. Minuchin, like William Glasser, developed structural family therapy in the 1960s after becoming frustrated using Freudian psychoanalytic therapy with juvenile delinquents in residential treatment. He found that children who excelled in residential treatment had difficulty maintaining this progress once they returned to their own homes. He, too, believed that relationships were the key. Like many other systems theorists, Minuchin stressed that symptoms and behaviors are not rooted in inner pathology but in their life circumstances. As an Argentine Jew working with impoverished families, he was at the forefront of recognizing the importance of culture and context in the lives of youth and families (Minuchin & Nichols, 1993). Theoretical foundations and comprehensive empirical studies have implicated family relationships and organization as a primary catalyst for the development and persistence of delinquent behavior (Tolan & Mitchell, 1990). Structural family therapy offers unique ways to conceptualize families struggling with delinquent and antisocial behavior (Fishman, 1988; Minuchin, 1974; Minuchin & Nichols, 1993; Tolan & Mitchell, 1990).

Systems theories teach us that problems are not always what they appear. In Chapter 6, I share a lesson, Appreciate Context: Don't Judge a Kid by His or Her Cover, in which I realized the futility of working with challenging youth without also working with their family and appreciating their culture. Numerous experts and theorists in the field of multicultural counseling have helped me to challenge my beliefs and alter my practices. Perhaps most notably has been Derald Wing Sue, author of numerous books, including *Counseling the Culturally Different: Theory and Practice* (Sue & Sue, 1990).

The Humanistic Teaching and Modeling of Virginia Satir and Carl Rogers

Virginia Satir, although quite different from Minuchin, was another inno-vator in the field of family therapy. She is known less for her specific tech-niques and more for her communication skills, incredible intuition, and ability to facilitate change through genuine connection. "Satir was the pro-totypical nurturing therapist in a field enamored with experience-distant concepts and tricky strategic maneuvers" (Nichols & Schwartz, 1991, p. 277).

Carl Rogers is best known for his research that specified three core conditions necessary for optimal therapeutic relationships: genuineness, unconditional positive regard, and empathic understanding. Since these conditions are fairly easy to understand, they are often written off as "im-portant for beginning counselors." In the next two chapters, I discuss why these conditions are easier to embrace in theory than they are in practice, particularly with this incredibly challenging population.

Watching Satir and Rogers on videotape reminds me how powerful "the basics" can be if you are really gifted. Although Satir and Rogers ad-vocated specific theoretical approaches for helping, I find I'm influenced more by their creative, genuine use of self more than any specific tech-niques.

The Pioneering Work of Fritz Redl and His Followers

Fritz Redl's early works, written with David Wineman [*Children Who Hate* (Redl & Wineman, 1951) and *Controls From Within* (Redl & Wineman, 1952)], revealed a creative mind ahead of his time. His ideas about the treatment, education, and understanding of troubled youth are still rel-evant today (Maier, 1991; Morse, 1991). My experience working in resi-dential facilities supports Redl and Wineman's (1957) assertion that "the surest way of finding out things about children who are hard to know is to live with them" (p. 30). Redl recognized the value of a therapeutic milieu in which frontline youth workers and other paraprofessionals have the most contact and the most impact on the lives of these kids. The therapeu-tic significance of what happens outside the clinicians' office was further developed by some of his followers in the influential book *The Other 23 Hours* (Trieschman, Whittaker, & Brendtro, 1969). Maier (1991) observed that many recent trends such as in-home therapy and expanded residen-tial aftercare programs can trace their roots to the pioneering work of Fritz Redl.

Redl was also influential in highlighting the importance of self-aware-ness and the need to recognize the relationship between our own unique histories and our responses to challenging youth. Nicholas Long's 1991 chapter, What Fritz Redl Taught Me About Aggression: Understanding the Dynamics of Aggression and Counter Aggression in Students and Staff, is one of the best I've read at translating psychodynamic concepts into con-crete strategies that can be understood and utilized by professionals at all levels. Furthermore, Redl was an early advocate for expanding education for child care workers, focusing on prevention efforts, appreciating the influence of context and culture, and working to change systems to more adequately address the needs of challenging youth.

Each of the theorists and theories described in this chapter (as well as others) have greatly informed my belief system and impacted the way I approach challenging youth. While many of these concepts are elaborated upon throughout the book, I emphasize practice more than theory in most of the lessons. For a detailed discussion of the theoretical approaches, I recommend you go directly to the source.

Lessons Learned: Promoting Self-Awareness to Enhance Therapeutic Relationships

☐ Lesson 2.1: Find the Time to Assess Your Own Attitudes, Beliefs, and Behaviors

You are a therapist and Johnny's parents have just called you to schedule an emergency meeting to discuss his recent threat to hang himself. While you are waiting for their arrival, you learn that another client has been arrested for assaulting a store clerk. Meanwhile, an attorney has left several urgent messages on your voice mail.

You are a school counselor and while you are meeting with Darrin, who is making vague threats regarding his homeroom teacher, the principal has asked you to meet with Jane, who is "about to buy herself a one-way ticket home." Meanwhile, the student who was scheduled to meet with you is sharing her frustration with your secretary.

You are a residential counselor, and before the morning's first group session has even started, you've had to separate two students who were on the verge of a physical altercation, you've observed that Billie has been crying and is still visibly shaken, and you've just learned that your co-leader has been called away to handle another crisis.

Professionals who work with challenging youth often feel like busy firefighters. As soon as we put out one fire, two more start across town. Sometimes, the situation dictates that we prioritize and focus our immediate attention on the biggest fire. Once that fire is under control, we become so busy racing around trying to put out other fires, we understandably do not take the time to assess our performance or thoroughly check under the hood. Intervention efforts overshadow prevention efforts.

To paraphrase Steven Covey (1989), we become so focused on what is urgent that we neglect to reflect on what is important. This is particularly true with challenging youth where the "crisis du hour" always seems to find us. Obviously, as ethical professionals, we cannot ignore crisis situations. However, it is equally important that we somehow find the time to step back and look at the big picture—periodically check under the hood of our own fire trucks and honestly assess our own beliefs, attitudes, and behaviors about this incredibly challenging population. We may find our truck is in good working condition and just needs a tune up or we might find that we've sprung a leak and are actually fueling the fires we are trying to put out.

The fact that you are reading this book suggests that you recognize the importance of regularly assessing your own strengths as well as areas that might need improvement. Based on interviews with counselors, administrators, and challenging youth, I developed the following self-inventory (Figure 1) to encourage readers to begin reflecting on important questions which are explored throughout this book. Many of you may have asked these questions long ago before choosing to work with this population. However, it is important that we regularly reassess where we are in regard to these critical questions.

Professionals who are most successful with this population can honestly answer "yes" to most, if not all, of the inventory questions. It is my biased opinion that "no" and "maybe" responses indicate red flag areas which could greatly diminish your effectiveness with challenging youth. It is up to you to 1) agree or disagree with that assessment, and 2) decide if that area is something you are willing and able to change. Furthermore, it is important to note that qualifying language was used to word many of the questions (i.e., in general, for the most part) and that our answers to the questions are not fixed. The qualifying and transformative nature of our answers to these questions will be discussed further in the next lesson.

Additional lessons expand on the qualities and behaviors identified in the inventory as well as other habits of highly successful professionals who work with this very challenging population. In this book, I promote the belief that most, if not all, of these qualities and behaviors can be developed and nurtured. The next lesson focuses on the first three questions—the ones I consider the most important.

1. In general, do you find yourself liking
    challenging youth?   Yes   Maybe   No

2. For the most part, do you enjoy working
    with challenging youth?   Yes   Maybe   No

3. Do you genuinely care about at-risk youth?
    Even the ones whose behavior makes them
    difficult to work with at times? Are you able
    to effectively communicate that you
    really care?   Yes   Maybe   No

4. Do you have a sense of humor? Can you
    appropriately incorporate your sense of
    humor into your work with challenging
    youth?   Yes   Maybe   No

5. For the most part, do you like yourself?   Yes   Maybe   No

6. Can you be yourself with challenging youth?   Yes   Maybe   No

7. Do you possess a cognitive and affective
    appreciation and respect for people who
    are different from you?   Yes   Maybe   No

8. Do you have the time and energy to make
    the necessary commitment to work
    effectively with challenging youth?   Yes   Maybe   No

9. To a large degree, are you aware of your
    own unfinished business? Do you know
    what your own emotional triggers are?   Yes   Maybe   No

10. Are you willing and able to offer both
    support and challenge?   Yes   Maybe   No

11. Are you willing and able to risk trying
    what hasn't been tried?   Yes   Maybe   No

12. Are you willing and able to avoid or lose
    power struggles?   Yes   Maybe   No

13. Are you willing and able to leave your
    office and work with families, peers, and
    other professionals?   Yes   Maybe   No

14. Do you entertain new ideas every day?   Yes   Maybe   No

15. Are you currently effective in working with
    challenging youth? (Or, do you feel you
    can be effective in working with
    challenging youth?)   Yes   Maybe   No

Figure 1. Self-inventory for adults who work with challenging youth.

☐ Lesson 2.2: Find Ways to Meet the Prerequisites

In recent years, farmers have been inundated with new and improved techniques for growing crops. For many farmers, these advancements have greatly increased output and efficiency. Unfortunately, in their excitement to try new seeds, machinery, and techniques, some forgot to take the necessary time to carefully cultivate and nurture the soil. They became so enthralled by the potential of the "new" that they lost sight of the value of the "old," and their harvests suffered. Counselors risk the same fate. As noted in Chapter 1, there are over 400 different counseling theories (Karusu, 1986). Each of these unique approaches recommend a variety of techniques to help promote change. As counselors, we need to regularly remind each other that techniques can only be as strong as the foundation upon which they are built. The relationship between a youth and an adult is the soil that enables techniques to take root (Lazarus & Fay, 1984).

Carl Rogers (1961, 1977), a prominent theorist and researcher, found that genuine, unconditional positive regard is a key ingredient for promoting change in clients of all ages. Unfortunately, the term "unconditional positive regard" is easier to embrace in theory than it is in practice, particularly with challenging youth. Too often, positive regard for the youngster as a person is contingent upon the child engaging in certain behaviors or achieving specific goals. Redl and Wineman (1957) argued long ago that to reverse the destructive spiral of emotionally disturbed youth, love and affection "cannot be made the bargaining tools of educational or even therapeutic motivation, but must be kept tax-free as minimum parts of the youngster's diet, irrespective of the problems of deservedness" (p. 303). Glasser (1998a) asserted that one of the keys to working with tough kids is to treat them well no matter how they treat you. "Establishing trust means that there is nothing the children can say or do that will persuade you to reject them" (p. 211). Each of these authors reiterated that this is easier said than done. These concepts are fundamental for all helping professionals (Patterson, 1996) and should not be dismissed as only for beginning counselors. In fact, when we find ourselves struggling with this population, *all* of us should start with the basics by searching our soul for honest answers to the following three questions:

1. In general, do I find myself *liking* challenging youth?
2. For the most part, do I *enjoy working with* challenging youth?
3. Do I *genuinely care* about at-risk youth—even the ones whose behavior makes them difficult to work with at times? More importantly, am I able to effectively communicate that I care?

I firmly believe that only when we answer "yes" to these questions can we begin to maximize our potential to work with this incredibly challenging population. Morse (1996c) asserted that caring for challenging youth is "the single most central matter at the core of helping" (p. 105). He noted that while most professionals do care, obstacles such as struggling for control and focusing on symptom behaviors sometimes make communicating this caring quite difficult. The real "task is to communicate our caring to the youngster so that she or he feels cared about" (Morse, 1996c, p. 108). Youth who sense that their counselors do not like or respect them are less likely to "listen to the therapist, utilize the therapist's recommendations, choose to continue with counseling, benefit from its process, or like or respect the counselor in return" (Sommers-Flanagan & Sommers-Flanagan, 1997, p. 34). If you can answer "yes" to these three questions, it will be *much* easier to develop other skills and effectively implement specific interventions.

During workshops, I often joke:

Kids who have been exposed to a lot of B.S. inevitably develop their own sophisticated B.S. detectors. These devices look like a tiny freckle, are barely visible to the human eye, and are located just behind the left ear.

I say this to make the important point that *challenging youth possess a unique capacity to recognize hypocrisy.* Subsequently, professionals who work with challenging youth should heed the advice of Dr. Sidney Simon, "If you are a plum, no matter how hard you try, you will never be anything but a second-rate banana. What's more, in a vain attempt to be a banana, you lose your sense of plumness" (Simon, 1988, p. 75). Connecting with troubled youth requires that we adapt our style and flex our approaches. However, connecting with these kids has nothing to do with pretending to be someone we are not (Minuchin & Nichols, 1993). Kids know. They can tell if we are genuine and sincere in our approach.

Rogers (1961) used the term congruent to refer to an "accurate matching of experience with awareness," someone who consistently presents as genuine, "not a facade, or a role, or a pretense" (p. 282). He asserted that congruence was the most important of all the relationship variables. When I interviewed many effective counselors, administrators, and challenging youth, they echoed Roger's sentiments. When asked, "What distinguishes the really effective counselors from the rest?" two recurrent themes emerged: 1) those who are real or genuine and 2) those who are able to communicate that they *really* care.

Gary, a therapist my agency works with, definitely comes to mind. He immediately comes across as sincere, not at all phony; the kids know right away that he really cares. He doesn't try to rush into the therapy; he tries to really understand where they're coming from—get into their world. Humor is a big part of that for Gary. But the humor works because the kids know he really cares.

—Bob Newingham, Adolescent Therapist,
Baptist Children's Home

You know, I've been in seven different foster homes so I've seen lots of shrinks and social workers. Some of them were pretty cool, but most of 'em, you could tell, they were just punching the clock. I don't blame them; If I was them I would probably do the same thing, but Lisa's different. When I tell her something, she's really listening. But what I like best is she ain't bogus. She's real. I know she's going to shoot straight with me. I don't know how I do it, but I can usually tell right away if they're real or not.

—Keisha, age 13

Again, these three questions ("In general, do I like challenging youth?" "For the most part, do I enjoy working with challenging youth?" "Do I genuinely care about at-risk youth?") were purposely worded using qualifying language because, of course, it is not possible for us to like every kid we work with or always enjoy our work. As human beings, we are going to have bad days and there are going to be some kids whom we allow to rub us the wrong way. Furthermore, to affirm the "realness" of the relationship, it may be necessary to let them know we are disappointed, concerned, irritated, or angry. Nevertheless, we should be cognizant of Fritz Redl's advice, "There is a difference between having feelings and being had by your feelings" (cited in Long, 1991, p. 51). We want to let them know what we are feeling while simultaneously communicating our genuine concern for their well-being. It is time to worry when our negative perceptions and angry or aggressive feelings predominate and begin to jeopardize our willingness and ability to build and maintain meaningful relationships.

It is important that, in general, we enjoy our work and are able to find something to like about every youngster. We are apt to ignore client strengths and allow our personal feelings to jeopardize and sabotage our effectiveness with kids we dislike. If we are not careful, self-centered goals such as winning power struggles may supersede more therapeutic goals such as teaching responsibility and facilitating self-evaluation with these kids. I have yet to meet a really effective helping professional whose overall impression of challenging youth was negative. While there have been some people who have been able to get the youth to do what they wanted, their ability to elicit compliance should not be confused with making a real difference in youths' lives.

Many professionals begin their careers by answering "yes" to these questions, but over the years find themselves struggling to really like or care about these kids. They begin to dread going to work. Most of us who have been in the field for an extended period can remember times when our negativism and cynicism peaked as optimism and enthusiasm began to wane. However, I have worked with many good people who found out too late that tough kids were not their cup of tea. Watching these teachers, counselors, residential workers, and others grasping for technique straws while struggling to like or genuinely care about these kids reminds me of what Sisyphus must have felt like pushing his rock up the mountain. It is a painful exercise in futility. For these professionals, it may be in their best interest to put the rock down and find another line of work. Those professionals who recognize a need to take proactive steps to change their negative perceptions can often do so. In future lessons, I share a variety of warning signs and specific strategies for altering our perceptions and improving our relationships.

☐ Lesson 2.3: Challenging Youth Are Like Inkblot Tests

When I need to learn how a teacher perceives his ability to reach a troubled child, I ask him to fill out a behavior rating on that child. This rating is effective in helping me understand the teacher. Sometimes I also learn about the child.

—L. Tobin (1991, p. 65)

If you really want to learn about challenging kids, observe and listen. Observe and listen to the kids. If you want to learn about the professionals who work with these kids, observe and listen. Observe and listen to how they interact with tough kids, what they say about them during clinical staffings, what they focus on when they complete behavior checklists, or what they write for case narratives. The details may tell us about the youngsters, but the themes that emerge often tell us more about ourselves. Challenging youth often serve as inkblot tests for the professionals who work with them. Seldom are we unaffected. They reflect the best and worst in ourselves.

We all have emotional triggers, and youth, particularly challenging youth, possess an uncanny ability to locate and push these buttons. If we operate under the assumption that the preceding statement is true, we are more likely to:

1. be ourselves,
2. avoid lose/lose power struggles, and
3. take more proactive steps to educate ourselves regarding our unfinished business.

Nicholas Long (1991), who was trained by Fritz Redl and has significant experience working with challenging youth in residential settings, shared a story that illustrates the relationship between a professional's current perception of a conflict and his or her own unique history. Long was supervising Patricia, a graduate student, who was becoming increasingly upset by the behavior of Jerome, a 12-year-old boy who appeared to be taking pleasure from teasing and intimidating Inez, a 7-year-old girl.

Patricia adamantly stated, "Behavior like Jerome's should never happen in a therapeutic school. It's not fair to Inez, and Jerome shouldn't get away with his verbal abuse. He needs to be taught a lesson!"

Dr. Long agreed that the behavior needed to be changed, but also inquired whether the incident had a personal meaning to Patricia.

Initially, she seemed puzzled and responded "No," but a short time later said, "Oh my God, it reminds me of what my older brother used to do to me when my parents weren't home" (Long, 1991, p. 46).

Again, we all have emotional triggers and tough kids have an uncanny ability to locate and activate them. Much of what we feel and think about crying, expressing anger, bullying behavior, aggression, and so forth is related to our own early experiences and models. Think about it. Few of us like to see one child bully another. But those who are most likely to overreact are likely to do so because of something from their own early history. Perhaps they were picked on by an older sibling. Or perhaps they were the older sibling and abhor that part of themselves.

If we, as professionals, are able to recognize this connection between our own histories and our emotional responses to certain behaviors, we are more likely to offer a rational, helpful response to the bullying youth (Long, 1991). One thing is certain: If we work long enough with challenging kids, our hot buttons will be revealed to us in one way or another. We could learn about our emotional triggers in other jobs or interpersonal situations; however, few individuals possess the pinpoint accuracy of challenging youth. This is one of many reasons we should *choose* to avoid power struggles with an angry kid. Most adults have limits, while many children, when pushed to the brink, will go for the heart of our deepest insecurities.

Ideally, we want to do whatever we can to locate as many of our own buttons as possible before we begin this challenging work. Covey (1989) defined responsibility as "the ability to choose your response" (p. 71). He has observed that highly proactive people are more likely to make decisions based on conscious choice than unconscious emotional conditioning. This self-awareness of emotional processes certainly increases our chances of remaining objective and responding responsibly. A more objective understanding of our own needs and feelings enables us to focus our attention on the needs and feelings of the youth. For instance, we need to say "yes" to acknowledging our feelings, but also "no" to the overt or covert expression of these feelings in behaviors that are hurtful or counterproductive (Long, 1991). This awareness is a crucial step. If I recognize and own my counter aggressive feelings toward Joey, it will be easier to compartmentalize these feelings and choose to explore the needs that are being masked by Joey's aggressive feelings and behavior. I can also choose to work on my own issues at another time through reflection, counseling, supervision, or other means.

While awareness is a crucial first step, insight alone is seldom sufficient. If we stop at awareness, the process may be more frustrating than educational. We need to use this insight to begin to make necessary changes in ourselves so we can choose to respond in a therapeutic manner. We must also remember that it is easier to find something when we are looking for it. The following are several recommendations regarding where and how to look for your emotional triggers:

1. Make this a conscious process. Take the time to step back before, during, or after both positive and negative interactions. Ask yourself, "What about me led me to respond this way?" "Is this way of responding that I am choosing (or chose) helping or hurting this relationship?" Is it helping me grow? Is it helping the youth grow?"
2. Regularly solicit feedback and consultation from colleagues and supervisors.
3. Read and reflect on books that might help you with your emotional triggers.
4. Consider seeking professional help. Discuss with a counselor how your unique history may be impacting the choices you are making today. While I am not an advocate of mandatory counseling for counselors and other human services professionals, I tend to worry about those professionals who won't even entertain the idea of counseling for themselves. What does that say about their perception of themselves, their clients, and their chosen profession?

☐ Lesson 2.4: Be Aware of Your Emotional Triggers and Remember You Are Human

There are not enough angels to go around, so ordinary people, like us, with our unique histories choose to work with emotionally disturbed kids.
—Fritz Redl

None of us can check our personalities and histories at the door. They will inevitably emerge in some form or another. Before we can work through our unfinished business, we need to know what our history is and how it manifests itself interpersonally. In Chapter 1, I shared some of what I learned about myself while working with teenage boys in my first job after college. Over the years, a variety of challenging youth have continued to peel back the layers of my rather thick onion and shed light on my own unfinished business. With this increased self-awareness and subsequent increased other-awareness, I feel I am now more apt to recognize my emotional triggers and choose more therapeutic responses during conflict. While I would hope to continue to become more self-aware and grow in my ability to show compassion and avoid power struggles, complete control is a goal that is not only unachievable, but undesirable. Perhaps if we were a descendent of Spock (the Vulcan, not the doctor), we could prevent our emotional buttons from ever being pushed; however, sacrificing genuineness for perfection is rarely a worthy trade.

During that first year as a residential counselor, I remember one particular lose/lose power struggle that reaffirmed my humanness. I was angry when disciplining Eric, a 13-year-old boy, and made a disparaging comment in front of his peers. Feeling hurt and angry, Eric turned up his tracking device and went for my jugular, "No wonder nobody likes you." I pretended to be unaffected, but after a break in the action, I cried in my room. In that brief moment, Eric taught me two painful lessons about myself: 1) I needed to be liked more than I knew, and 2) there might be kids who didn't like me. His five little words packed quite a wallop. I thought about it and realized I had developed this need to be liked a long time ago. Fortunately, over the years, I have been able to reduce and reframe this need. I'm sure I'll never completely extinguish my need to be liked, nor do I want to. (I hope you're enjoying the book so far.)

Being real, however, doesn't mean that we need to express every fleeting thought and emotion. It means that we own all parts of ourselves—the so-called positive and negative. It means allowing ourselves to sometimes feel aggressive, angry, or hurt. But we must find appropriate venues to express these emotions. Again, there is a difference between having feelings and being had by your feelings. Unfortunately, this distinction has been lost on some professionals. At one end of the spectrum, there are those who deny most all negative emotions and, at the other end, there are those who feel the need to constantly vent their frustrations. Both of these types of professionals pose a greater risk of emotionally or physically harming troubled and troubling youth. Those who wear their emotions on their sleeves are likely to eventually cross that fine line and lash out in destructive ways. Those who continue to deny these feelings may harm the youth in more unconscious or indirect ways through inappropriate humor or insensitive comments.

Professionals who work with challenging youth, particularly those in the trenches, need appropriate channels to vent their feelings and frustrations; however, it is important that we strike a healthy balance. We need to learn to recognize the difference between the occasional need to vent and a pattern of negativism and complaining. We can make this distinction by looking at the results. Venting is helping us only if we actually *vent* our pent-up feelings. If this process only increases our negativity or frustration, we may want to try a different strategy. It has been my experience that of all the precursors for professional burnout, a pattern of unproductive venting in the copy room, at lunch breaks, at clinical staffings, or wherever is often the most foreboding. So, periodically gauge your feelings and coping skills, and seek out positive models.

It is important to remember that we will never discover all of our buttons or finish all our business. Even the most self-actualized humans such as the Dalai Lama are not completely void of emotional triggers. The growth process should be viewed as consistent movement along a continuum, not complete amelioration of all our buttons (Frankl, 1963; Kottler & Hazler, 1996; Miller, Wagner, Britton, & Gridley, 1998). We are all works in progress. In his highly insightful and sensitive 1991 book, *What Do You Do With a Child Like This? Inside the Lives of Troubled Children*, L. Tobin, an educational specialist who has worked extensively with challenging youth, eloquently described the importance of appreciating and reframing self-revelations and lessons learned along the way:

I have learned that the child who evokes my anger is a gift to me. He embodies the unresolved issues I carry at the time: rebellion, anger, selfishness, self-doubt—the hurt within me. As I work with this child I am invited to confront the passion of our shared struggle. I can respond or attempt to avoid it. But this child will force the issue—that is the gift. . . . Somehow, from somewhere, I must find the strength to overcome my struggle and embrace this particular child . . . for he is the child within me. (Tobin, 1991, p. 34)

Professionals who are able to identify and own their emotional scars will not only be in a better position to demonstrate compassion for challenging youth but also recognize the subjective nature and possible harmful ramifications of their responses (Miller, Wagner, Britton, & Gridley, 1998). Several upcoming lessons discuss the importance of empathic understanding. However, in order to understand the phenomenological world of a child, it is imperative that we have some understanding of our own.

☐ Lesson 2.5: "Laughter Is the Shortest Distance Between Two People" (Victor Borge)

Consistently failing to find the humor in potentially humorous situations and circumstances is another major warning signal that burnout could be on the horizon. Working with challenging youth can be very demanding at times. Many of these kids are trying to make sense out of a variety of highly charged emotional stressors. Professionals who work with them often become the recipients of intense feelings and acting-out behavior. Youngsters need to be held accountable; however, if we choose to take ourselves too seriously and fail to find humor in potentially humorous situations, we place ourselves at risk for both overreacting and burnout. We need to be diligent and sincere in our approaches; however, we do not want to take ourselves or our jobs too seriously.

Mitchell (1998) joked that angels can fly because they take themselves lightly. I have not seen a study that relates having fun to low job success. In fact, appropriate humor has been proven as a successful strategy for engaging challenging youth (Johns & Carr, 1995; Redl & Wineman, 1957; Selekman, 1993; Sommers-Flanagan & Sommers-Flanagan, 1997). Humor, when used effectively, has the potential to enhance empathy and help the youth see the counselor as more genuine and human (Kuhlman, 1984; Pierce, 1985). Furthermore, as the following case demonstrates, appropriate humor can help thwart potential power struggles.

During my first year as a residential counselor, Todd, an 11-year-old boy notorious for both his quick wit and quicker temper, reinforced the power of humor. Those of us working on Sundays would take the kids to church. We tried to position ourselves next to the more challenging youth. One particular Sunday, I sat to the left of Todd. He had a habit of making mountains out of mole hills, and reluctantly agreed to a program that required him to carry a behavioral card. Each day was divided into 11 sections and he could earn four points for each section. Whenever he needed a reminder, we would ask for his card and take off one point for that time period. (Looking back, this strategy may have led us to overlook his positive behaviors and over focus on Todd's misbehaviors.) Todd had such a difficult time controlling his temper that simple reminders often escalated into major conflicts.

During the sermon, Todd smacked the kid in front of him and I whispered, "Todd, I need to see your card." While Todd was reaching in his pocket, I had to turn to my right to two other boys who were on the brink of causing a scene.

When I turned back around Todd said, "Oh yeah, you wanted to see my card." He then opened his hand, revealed a hundred little pieces of paper which used to be his card, sprinkled the pieces on my head, and said, "Here, Brent, sign this!"

I was able to quickly recognize two possible responses. First, I could get angry and immediately reprimand Todd which almost certainly would have led to further conflict. Or I could recognize both the creativity and the humor in Todd's choice and laugh with him. I chose to find the humor in Todd's misbehavior (it really was quite funny).

I started laughing and said, "That's a good one, Todd." The situation did not escalate further, and Todd later accepted his consequence for destroying his card and mistaking my head for a trash receptacle.

Redl and Wineman (1952) described this process long ago as tension-decontamination through humor. These authors discussed a number of incidents at a cottage for severely disturbed boys in which humor was used as a diversionary tactic to thwart tantrums or physical aggression. Tobin (1991) noted that humor has a way of defusing conflict, disarming aggressors, and drawing people closer. Selekman (1993) asserted that humor is an effective way to distance youth from their immediate concerns and heal those in pain. Albert Ellis, the father of cognitive-behavioral therapy, is a master at using humor to help clients laugh at themselves and their problems. If the youth is feeling overwhelmed, it may be important to distract him or her; however, we should also remember that humor is a common defense mechanism that prevents people from addressing important concerns (Haig, 1986).

In this line of work, there's too much big stuff to sweat the small stuff. Laugh at yourself. Laugh at funny situations. Laugh *with* children and adolescents, not *at* them. Also, appreciate the difference between humor that hurts and humor that heals. Humor that hurts is often sarcastic, caustic, and serves to push people away from one another. Humor that heals is sensitive, good natured, tends to help diffuse difficult situations, and brings people closer together.

Certainly, we need to have more tools in our toolbag to be effective with challenging youth; however, I've never seen one successful counselor or teacher who lacked an appropriate sense of humor. A sense of humor is an absolute requirement for long term success with this population. There are no exceptions.

☐ Lesson 2.6: Learn From Unsuccessful Interventions or Past Conflict—And Then Let Go

Two things are certain for those of us who work with challenging youth: 1) We will make mistakes, and 2) We will experience conflict. It is essential that we learn from these experiences and remember the old adage, "Those who do not learn from history are destined to repeat it." One of Fritz Redl's greatest contributions to the field was his ability to learn from his mistakes and encourage others to muster the courage to do the same (Maier, 1991; Nicholson, 1991). Wubbolding (1988) emphasized that the ability to self-evaluate is essential to personal growth of all human beings. Children and adolescents need to learn to assess for themselves whether or not their behavior is helping them get what they want. However, self-evaluation is a two-way street. Not only does the youth need to evaluate his or her own behavior, we need to regularly monitor and evaluate ourselves (Wubbolding, 1996). Again, we need to explore our role in the relationship. What are we doing to promote positive change and what are we doing that might not be helping?

The following are just a few questions all professionals can ask to self-evaluate their own behavior:

1. Have I established a trusting, caring relationship with this youth? What can I do to enhance the relationship? Am I listening intently and empathically?
2. Am I trying an intervention that has already been tried? Was it helpful then? How can I make it different this time? Are there any "out of the box" ideas which have not been considered?
3. Did the youth evaluate their own behavior or did someone else (i.e., me, parents)?
4. Is the behavior plan addressing his or her needs? Who has primary ownership for this plan?
5. How can I reframe the behavior so that I can be more helpful? How can I be more flexible and less resistant?

While our professional growth is dependent on our ability to reflect on and learn from our experiences, our professional survival is largely dependent on our ability to normalize and let go of these experiences. In his 1984 book, *Way of the Peaceful Warrior: A Book that Changes Lives,* Dan Millman shared the following story to illustrate the importance of letting go:

> Two monks, one old, one very young, walked along a path in a rain forest, on their way back to a monastery in Japan. They came upon a lovely woman who stood helplessly at the edge of a muddy, fast-flowing stream. Seeing her predicament, the older monk swept her up in his strong arms and carried her across. She smiled at him, her arms around his neck, until he put her gently down on the other side. Thanking him, she bowed, and the monks continued on their way in silence. As they neared the gates the young monk could no longer contain himself. "How could you carry a beautiful woman in your arms? Such behavior does not seem proper for a priest." The old monk looked at his companion, replying, "I left her back there. Are you still carrying her?" (Millman, 1984, p. 172)

Continuing to carry past conflict and unsuccessful interventions decreases future effectiveness and increases the likelihood of burnout. Kushner (1996) stressed the importance of following the lead of young children in our approach to past conflict and power struggles. He observed that sometimes, letting go simply means choosing happiness over righteousness. Unlike many of us adults, young children can be enthralled in conflict one moment and playing cheerfully the next. They can make this choice because they possess three extraordinary gifts:

1. the ability to forget
2. the ability to stay in the moment
3. the ability to choose happiness over righteousness

Some professionals, such as successful lawyers, football cornerbacks, and youth counselors have developed and refined these abilities out of necessity. Good lawyers view conflict as a necessary part of their job. Therefore, they are less likely to take it personally and more likely to let go. Cornerbacks play one of the most difficult positions in the National Football League. Not only do they have to cover the team's fastest player, the slightest error in judgment can result in a touchdown for the other team. I once heard a football coach say the three most important qualities of an NFL cornerback are speed, confidence, and a short memory. Good cornerbacks know that mistakes will happen. They also know that dwelling on mistakes impacts confidence which impacts performance. They recognize the importance of being a quick study and moving on. Professionals who are gifted in working with the population of challenging youth possess these same qualities and abilities. They are quick on their feet and have the ability to make confident decisions, learn from their mistakes, and move on.

Professionals who are able to reframe past conflict and unsuccessful interventions as helpful feedback rather than some personal failure greatly enhance their chance of professional success and survival. Unfortunately, striking a balance between healthy reflection and unhealthy immersion is easier said than done. Again, ongoing consultation is essential for professionals who work with tough kids. Supervisors and colleagues can help us recognize when we are harboring resentment, holding grudges, or dwelling on past mistakes.

☐ Lesson 2.7: Look for Ways You Are Making a Difference

When I worked with foster parents, we often shared the following story of the young boy rescuing the starfish on the beach to remind them to focus on ways they were making a difference:

> A young boy was walking along the beach in the middle of a sweltering, summer day. As the tide was retreating, he noticed thousands of starfish washed up on the dry sand. As the boy began throwing starfish back into the ocean, a man was passing by, and said, "Son, look how many there are—you'll never make a difference." Smiling, the boy looked at the starfish in his hand, threw it into the ocean, and declared "I'll make a difference to that one." (source unknown)

Sometimes, like starfish stranded on the dry sand, the plight of troubled youth seems so overwhelming, we become paralyzed by the magnitude of the task. We tell ourselves, "I'm only one person, what can I do? I wouldn't know where to start." Chances are, if you are reading this book, you have already reached the starting point and cleared this hurdle. You have already discovered an avenue for making an impact with troubled youth.

Unfortunately, change is often a slow process (Corey, 1996; Meier & Davis, 1997), particularly with challenging youth. Certainly, we want to maintain high expectations for ourselves, kids, and families; however, we must also remember that it is normal to experience setbacks and pitfalls. Change can also be very fragile and so-called failures can be so gut-wrenching and disturbing that it is easy to fall into the "why bother trap." The following are just two examples in which these lessons have been reinforced over the years.

Seven years ago, as a family therapist, I worked extensively with Anthony Jones (fictitious name) and his family. Anthony was 14 years old, experimenting with drugs, skipping school, and associating with known gang members. With the help of many professionals (i.e., teachers, coaches, minister), and the perseverance of his family, Anthony made drastic changes. I followed up with the family a year after termination from counseling and found that Anthony was continuing to make strides in all areas of his life. He was communicating better at home, passing all his classes at school, and excelling in basketball. Several months ago, a colleague at the counseling center sent me a copy of an article in the local newspaper beginning, "Anthony Jones, 21 years old, was arrested last night for felonious wounding with a firearm. . ."

As a treatment foster care program, we were often asked to transition youngsters from long-term residential or psychiatric placements back to the community. Sarah, a girl with an extensive history of emotional, physical, and sexual abuse had spent much of her first ten years in and out of various institutions. We used individualized team approaches to improve the chances of long-term success. Sarah's team included Sarah, her social worker, case manager, therapist, special education teachers, and most importantly, two supportive *and* firm foster parents. For two years, Sarah experienced only minor setbacks. Her overall improvement was remarkable. Then one day, at age 12, she was arrested for sexually assaulting a 7-year-old neighbor.

It would be easy to get demoralized when youth like Anthony and Sarah, who have finally begun to make positive choices and sample life's rewards, commit criminal, injurious acts. While we don't want to become desensitized to tragic incidents or fail to learn from our experiences or mistakes, we also do not want to let these events become so overwhelming that we fail to acknowledge significant ways we are making a difference in the lives of troubled youth. Sometimes we need to focus on the opportunities Anthony and Sarah were given to turn things around. Or the progress other kids continue to make. In short, we need to periodically reflect on ways we are making a difference in the lives of challenging youth.

People tend to think that burnout results most often from never taking time off or blurring social and professional responsibilities. Certainly over extending ourselves does sometimes lead to burnout with this population; however, it is more likely to result from a persistent feeling that we are not making a difference. Do not let negative events or people rob you of the idealism that propelled you into the field. If you find yourself bogged down thinking about the starfish that wash back up on the beach, take a moment to remember the starfish you've helped back to the ocean (and others that are waiting for your assistance).

☐ Lesson 2.8: Embody What You Teach, and Teach Only What You Have Embodied (Millman, 1984)

Consider the following story about Mahatma Gandhi:

> A mother brought her young son to Mahatma Gandhi. She begged, "Please, Mahatma. Tell my son to stop eating sugar."
> Gandhi paused, then said, "bring your son back in two weeks."
> Puzzled, the woman thanked him and said she would do as he had asked.
> Two weeks later, she returned with her son. Gandhi looked the youngster in the eye and said, "Stop eating sugar."
> Grateful but bewildered, the woman asked, "Why did you tell me to bring him back in two weeks? You could have told him the same thing then."
> Gandhi replied, "Two weeks ago, I was eating sugar." (Millman, 1984, p. 185)

Because much of an adolescent's behavior is developmentally geared toward emulating high status peers and deviating from social norms, we have a tendency to underestimate the potential influence we have as adult role models (Sommers-Flanagan & Sommers-Flanagan, 1997; Wallbridge & Osachuk, 1995). A number of researchers and practitioners have asserted that the behaviors of significant adults may be the most important factor influencing adolescent identity development (Bandura, 1974; Bienert & Schneider, 1993; Wallbridge & Osachuk, 1995). As helping professionals, we are constantly being watched and evaluated by adolescents for clues on how to act as an emerging adult. These youngsters are exploring different identities and they will use adults they identify with as their templates. Even angry or unyielding kids tend to pay attention to how we act and may use this information later (Wallbridge & Osachuk, 1995). Subsequently, we should try to follow Gandhi's lead and embody what we teach, and only teach what we embody.

Helping professionals have a responsibility to serve as positive role models for challenging youth. Adults perceived as role models are likely to be those who are able to both act in a professional manner *and* relate on a personal level. This can be a delicate balance. In an effort to connect with tough kids on a personal level, some neophyte counselors try too hard to blend in with their adolescent clients and be accepted as a contemporary. Often, their efforts to gain respect produce the opposite effect. Other counselors try so hard to maintain a professional stance, they may be perceived as aloof and unable or unwilling to relate to adolescent concerns or problems. Wallbridge and Osachuk (1995) advised that "somewhere in the middle of the continuum you will find grounds for a relationship with the adolescent, while maintaining your professional stance" (p. 212).

In addition, effective professionals (similar to effective parents) who demonstrate integrity and respect, show interest in youth and youth activities, and enjoy their time with kids are most likely to be viewed as positive role models (Sommers-Flanagan & Sommers-Flanagan, 1997). Challenging youth are also desperately searching for role models who convey appreciation and respect for their diverse worldviews, opinions, beliefs, experiences, values, dress, and so forth. The preceding statement should not be misinterpreted to imply that professionals can or should convey a relativistic, anything goes attitude. In fact, a number of authors have asserted that it is not possible to have a helping approach void of values (Corey, Corey, & Callanan, 1993; Sommers-Flanagan & Sommers-Flanagan, 1997). When we try to cultivate the youth's self concept, promote more responsible social behavior, teach anger management skills, or improve relationships with family members, we are inevitably expressing our values.

Corey, Corey, and Callanan (1993) cautioned helping professionals against taking either of two extreme positions when it comes to expressing their own values. On the one extreme are those who hold definite and absolute beliefs and see their role as having youth adopt their positions and values. On the other extreme are counselors who try so hard to remain neutral, they risk rendering themselves immobile by their unwillingness to ever take a position. One of the most important roles of helping professionals who work with troubled youngsters is to promote moral development and encourage value clarification. Youth want counselors who are honest and genuine; however, they do not want someone who believes they have all the answers. Any conversation that resembles a lecture will often be tuned out. Challenging youngsters are more likely to reflect on their own values when:

1. they are consistently exposed to prosocial behaviors or values (i.e., being fair, resolving conflict peacefully, listening empathically, not abusing drugs or alcohol);
2. they are challenged to honestly evaluate their values and decide for themselves what changes to make; and

3. they are allowed to experience natural and logical consequences and encouraged to make the connection between these consequences and their poor decisions.

We should also strive to be responsible and ethical models for others in the profession. As helping professionals, it is imperative that we familiarize ourselves with our professional organization's code of ethics. Professional organizations such as the American Counseling Association, the American Psychological Association, and the National Association of Social Workers have revised their ethical codes in recent years to adjust to increasingly complex ethical and legal dilemmas (Okun, 1997). Although all ethical codes are unique to the profession, most are based on five fundamental ethical principles: 1) respect autonomy, 2) do no harm, 3) benefit others, 4) be just and fair, and 5) be faithful and responsible (Kitchener, 1988). A supervisor once remarked that "ethical behavior is what we do when no one is watching." Subsequently, we may want to ask ourselves questions such as "Would I want my behavior to be shown on television or used in a training video?" or "Would I want to be treated this way if I were the youth and/or family?"

We also have an obligation to educate ourselves regarding state and local laws so that we can give reasoned, informed consideration to the situations that may present themselves in day-to-day practice (Anderson, 1996). It is particularly important that we develop a sense of right and wrong as it relates to the treatment of minors. It is beyond the scope of this book to fully discuss all of the ethical and legal issues which might arise when working with minors; however, here are just a few questions you may want to investigate:

Can minors consent to treatment without parental consent?
Can minors consent to treatment without parental knowledge?
What are the limits of confidentiality in counseling with minors?
What does informed consent consist of in working with minors?
What are the reporting procedures for suspected child abuse?
What are the procedures for hospitalizing a minor?

These can be difficult questions to answer because laws vary from state to state and institution to institution, and state certification and licensing requirements impose different obligations on professionals (Anderson, 1996). Ethical and legal issues are becoming increasingly complicated and complex, and it is impossible to avoid them. Those who strive to behave in ways consistent with ethical codes and laws, have a clear sense of their own values, and regularly seek consultation from colleagues are less likely to break the law or behave unethically (Okun, 1997). Excellent resources include your professional organization's code of ethics, *ACA Ethical Standards Casebook* (Herlihy & Corey, 1996), *Issues and Ethics in the Helping Professions* (Corey, Corey, & Callanan, 1993), and *The Counselor and the Law* (Anderson, 1996).

Lessons Learned: Meeting Youth Where They Are—Individually, Developmentally, and Culturally

☐ Lesson 3.1: Remember What Uniform(s) You Wore

> As they balance their checkbooks, pay their mortgages, sip their coffee, answer their voice mail, and attend marriage enhancement seminars, there is no doubt that most social workers, counselors, and therapists have daily experiences very different from those of their young clients, clients who are busily bumming cigarettes, skipping classes, and reading comic books. (Sommers-Flanagan & Sommers-Flanagan, 1997, p. 4).

Why do many adolescents request younger counselors and teachers? Their perception, although sometimes mistaken, is that older counselors (anyone ten years older than they are) have forgotten what it was like to be a teenager. They feel we try to force feed adult solutions that are not yet relevant for them. They feel we do not understand the culture of adolescence. We do this by dismissing a youth's feelings by using terms such as puppy love or failing to remember what it was like to feel everyone was looking at us all the time. Perhaps most importantly, they feel we have forgotten how important it was to fit in—to belong. We're worried about goals while they are focused on roles. Long range goals (i.e., college) are important, but they'll always be secondary for youth who feel they do not belong (Glasser, 1972). No wonder there are so many impasses.

In his 1993 book, *Family Healing* (written with Mike Nichols), Salvador Minuchin shared a moving story about Keith, a teenager, and his father, Carter, who had reached such an impasse. During the session, the metaphorical expression of poor communication in the family happened to be a disagreement over Keith's desire to wear torn jeans. After the father and his son debated for several minutes, Minuchin offered the following observations:

> You see, this was a perfectly good conversation between two cultures. You and your son belong to two cultures that see things differently. It happens that in this crazy culture in which these kids live, ragged pants are in and dressy pants are out. We are old-timers, we don't understand that. He needs to be able to do something to explain that to you. But Peggy (mom) is the translator. So they go to her. Meanwhile you remain the square peg and cannot enter. (Minuchin & Nichols, 1993, p. 186)

Later in the session, Minuchin facilitated a process in which Keith could explain to his dad why he wears torn jeans:

> It's kind of like it shows that you don't have anything to prove. That you know you're not any better than anyone else. Because you see all these kids always bragging about their Jordaches or whatever. But me and this little society I hang around in—my friends—we just can't stand kids who like to shut out people because they're not as good as them. . . . (Minuchin & Nichols, 1993, p. 187)

After Carter began to listen closely and communicate an understanding of where his son was coming from, Minuchin asked: "Carter, what was your uniform when you were fifteen? How did you show that you belonged?" After a long pause, Carter faced his son and responded in a sad tone, "I didn't. I didn't belong. I didn't belong in the way that you belong. So I don't understand."

Carter's admission that he didn't understand was probably one of the most understanding things he had said to his son in a long time. It also shed some light for both of them on Carter's conflicted feelings and motivation.

It is important to remember that youth from any particular time period or any given peer group belong to a subculture all their own (Sommers-Flanagan & Sommers-Flanagan, 1997); subsequently, it is impossible to fully comprehend the specific nature of their trials and tribulations. However, certain basic needs transcend these generation gaps. For instance, the need to belong is universal (Glasser, 1965). Working with challenging youth, it is not so important that we remember whether we belonged as a child or adolescent, but rather how important it was, and is, to connect with others and feel like we belong.

☐ Lesson 3.2: Challenging Youth Struggle on a Daily Basis to Meet Two Basic Needs

Every youth's behavior is their best attempt at that time to meet one or more of the following five basic needs common to all humankind: survival, love and belonging, power and achievement, fun, and freedom (Glasser, 1965). The concept of teaching responsibility was central to Glasser's early writing. He defined responsibility as "the ability to fulfill one's needs, and to do so in a way that does not deprive others of the ability to fulfill their needs" (Glasser, 1965, p. 15). Consequently, kids who are acting irresponsibly are doing so because they are unable to meet their needs in a way that does not restrict the need-fulfilling behaviors of others. Problems tend to be exasperated when adults, trying to meet their own needs, attempt to either force compliance or intervene in other ways that are not need-fulfilling for the youth. What follows is a series of tit-for-tat responses until the unmet needs of the adult and youth become buried in a cycle of conflict and power struggles. Neither party can recognize their own needs, much less the needs of others. They just know they are not getting what they want. Subsequently, they focus much of their energies distributing unhealthy doses of blame.

The importance of each of the needs varies for every youth depending on his or her culture, experiences, situation, and personality. For instance, survival may be paramount for a kid who has found himself living on the street while another youth whose survival needs are being met may have other needs which are more prominent. An inability to meet any of the five basic needs can lead to problems for all humans; however, I have found the need for love and belonging and the need for power and achievement to be particularly crucial for many challenging youth. It is rare to find a challenging youth who does not struggle on a daily basis to responsibly meet these two needs. Youngsters, particularly adolescents, need to feel connected to others. In fact, they base their own identity and self-esteem on their sense of belonging and connectedness as well as on their sense of achievement. If given the choice between having a positive identity and negative identity, virtually all youngsters would choose positive identity. However, when they feel they've been given the choice between negative identity and no identity, they will choose negative identity—every time.

An identity crisis occurs when well-meaning parents and professionals try to remove what they perceive to be injurious or harmful (for example, gangs, social drinking, or drug use) without considering alternative ways the youth can meet his or her basic needs. Or when the adults rush into focusing on long-term goals (i.e., college) when the youth is still trying to establish his or her own roles (identity). Again, for a youngster who struggles daily with identity and belonging issues, a discussion focusing on long-term goals will seldom be heard. Effective intervention meets youth where they are. Gangs and negative peer groups are frequently desperate attempts by challenging youth to meet this basic human need to belong (Brendtro & Brokenleg, 1996). All youth need to feel like they belong, and feel like they are good at something. Adults often try to supplant gangs and negative peer groups through punishment, jail, or other means of removing the youth from the situation. Jung (1934) recognized long ago that "despite any amount of understanding, crooked habits do not disappear until replaced by other habits" (p. 52). Logical and natural consequences are necessary to teach responsible behavior; however, unless culturally relevant options are provided that help meet the youth's need for belonging and achievement, we are seldom helping the youth learn, grow, and develop. Also, any benefit to society is short-lived. In an interview with Leon Bing for her 1991 book, *Do or Die*, about youth gangs in Los Angeles, A.C. Jones, an African-American correction officer, eloquently described a jailed, inner city kid struggling to meet his needs for belonging and power:

> What do you think happened when that kid there first began to seek out his masculinity? What happened when he first tried to assert himself? If he lived in any other community but Watts there would be legitimate ways to express these feelings. Little League. Pop Warner. But if you're a black kid living in Watts, those options have been removed. . . . But you're at that prepubescent age, and you have all those aggressive tendencies and no legitimate way to get rid of them. And that's when the gang comes along, and the gang offers everything those legitimate organizations do. The gang serves emotional needs. You feel wanted. You feel welcome. You feel important. And there is discipline and there are rules. . . . The very fact that a kid is in a gang means something is missing. (Bing, 1991, pp. 12–13)

Not all kids who end up in gangs take the path described by Mr. Jones, but many adolescents who are in gangs or negative peer groups do so because they perceive those options to be their best outlet to feel competent and connected. Any alternative must consider these needs. We also should not underestimate the strength of these bonds. Challenging youth are understandably going to be skeptical about any new path as well as scared of ramifications of perceived dissing (disrespecting) friends or fellow gang members.

In summary, we all have five basic needs. We all strive to meet these needs in responsible and irresponsible manners. With challenging youth, look beyond the behavior. Pay particular attention to how the youth is meeting his or her need for love and belonging (identity) and power and achievement (esteem). Try to ascertain what needs are being met responsibly and what needs are either not being met or being met irresponsibly. What can we do as helpers to increase the chances the need will be met responsibly?

☐ Lesson 3.3: Recognize and Appreciate Ways Adolescents Are Developmentally Unique

The previous two lessons discussed challenging youth's struggle to develop and maintain a connected and competent sense of self. Adolescence, in particular, is a time of numerous physical, cognitive, emotional, social, and personal changes which impact identity development. It is a time of sorting and searching—sorting through the intense changes and searching for answers to *big* questions such as "Who am I?" and "Where do I fit in?" While most youth can navigate these changing tides and new freedoms without experiencing major turmoil, already troubled youth often find this transition period overwhelming and rife with strife and confusion. Their searches tend to yield more questions and frustrations. Subsequently, their behavior becomes more erratic, contemptuous, rebellious, and challenging.

To truly connect with challenging youth, we must try to see the world through their eyes and appreciate some of the daily "damned if I do, damned if I don't" paradoxes that arise when American culture collides with adolescent development. While it is beyond the scope of this book to discuss all of these developmental dilemmas, the following excerpts represent some of what these youth might say if they could step outside themselves and begin to make sense out of the bombardment of mixed messages and double binds we call adolescence:

> I need to begin to separate from my parents and other adults; yet I need these adults to help me through this transitional period. You can't help me,

but please show me you want to (Gurian, 1998). I really need guidance from trusting adults, but I also need to convince you that I am independent and self-assured. Much of what you tell me makes sense, and deep down, I appreciate it. Well, sometimes I do. Of course, as a teenager, I'm developmentally bound to share this appreciation only on very special occasions, so you better look close or you might miss it.

I have so much on my mind, I need to be alone to sort things out. I feel like there is a constant Jeopardy game going on in my head. And the topic is always me! I can come up with the questions (i.e., Who am I? Why am I here? What can I do? What do I believe? Should I drink? What is sex? What happens when I die? What in the world is happening to my body? What do I wear?), but the answers—I don't know. I need the freedom and space to find my own answers. I need privacy to sort things out. I also need structure to keep me grounded. I would greatly appreciate it if you would provide me with structure and rules so I feel safer, but also I may choose to break some rules. Can we talk? I mean, can I talk and maybe you can like listen?

I know what you're thinking. Adolescents are selfish. Well, I read somewhere that this is more likely a developmental phase than a personality trait. I'm not really narcissistic; I'm just searching and sorting. How am I supposed to feel good about myself unless I take the necessary time to get to know me? I haven't experienced this much change since the first two years of my life. Doesn't it make sense that I would be monitoring these changes closely and assuming others were doing likewise? Didn't you? Well, it's not easy having everyone look at me all the time—checking out how I talk and walk. What's weird is the more I care what people think the more I pretend I don't. Sometimes, I spend an hour trying to figure out what clothes best communicate that I don't care what I look like. Why is that?

It's tough being a teenage boy. Much of the time, I feel sad or agitated or something. Actually, I don't know what I'm feeling. I just know something's bugging me and I don't know why. If I was a girl, I could talk about my feelings, cry, or reach out in some other way. Try to figure things out. Unfortunately, my biology (low prolactin and high testosterone) and acculturation (real men don't cry) make it harder for me to recognize and express my feelings. Also, like most guys, I don't see pain as a potential bonding agent that keeps me from making emotional connections that would help me feel better (Gurian, 1998). I have an idea. Since I can't figure out what's bugging me, I'll yell or kick something or act out in some way to release the tension quickly. I won't give much thought to consequences, and I'll direct much of my intense feelings at the closest and safest adults. Timber. Then I'll pretend I really like myself and make people think I have high self-esteem. No one will ever know. Will they?

It's tough being a teenage girl. There are so many mixed messages. Be beautiful, but beauty is only skin deep. Be sexy, but not sexual. Be honest, but don't hurt anyone's feelings. Be independent, but be nice. Be smart, but not so smart that you threaten boys (Pipher, 1994). There seem to be so many unwritten rules. We're damned if we do and damned if we don't. I see what's considered pretty in magazines and on T.V. and it's really hard to get there. And even if I could, would that be a good thing? My best friend is really attractive and she's considered a dumb slut. What's weird is that she's really smart and has never had sex. And the unattractive girls don't stand a chance. I used to think I was really smart. Now, I don't know if I am. I don't know if I want to be. So much of who I am, or who I thought I was, seems to be drifting away. Is this person I am becoming the new me or a false front? I don't know. I do know that I am confused. I wish I didn't worry so much about what I ate or how I looked. Sometimes, I just wish I could scream rather than pushing everything inside. Thanks for listening. Did that sound okay?

I read that on average, puberty occurs six years earlier than it did in 1850 (Gurian, 1998). Plus, we're exposed to so many sexual images so soon. Our brains aren't evolving as fast as our bodies or technology. How can we be expected to make such important choices? Everyone is telling me something different. I'm really scared. Who should I listen to?

I'm an average teenager. The television is on in my house 2,714 minutes a week (Gurian, 1998) and I spend about four minutes a week engaged in meaningful, uninterrupted conversation with my parents. Who do I listen to?

I hate how everyone expects me to act and dress a certain way—conform to the norm. Well, that's not me. I have to be myself. I'm going to dress the way I want to dress and act the way I want to act. Hey, what is the rebellion dress code these days? Trench coats? All black? Size 60 waist pants?

One of the most important parts of the sorting process is putting things in the proper baskets. Having the freedom to make more choices and form opinions as a teenager is both exciting and scary. Thank goodness, the developmental fairy recognized this and only gave me two baskets—the really good basket and the really bad basket. I may appear apathetic, but actually, I'm not indifferent about much. These are the best of times and the worst of times. Most of my world, including you (and me), is divided into really good and really bad. Let's see, which basket should I put you in today?

These excerpts are just a sampling of some of the developmental hurdles faced by today's youth. As helping professionals, we need to remember that these differences must be respected and considered, not belittled or minimized, when attempting to build or maintain therapeutic relationships. In short, we must meet youth where they are—developmentally. It is also important to recognize that most challenging youth are trying to figure out these "Who am I" questions while simultaneously strug-gling to cope with a multitude of other stressors (i.e., a learning disability, abusive adults, school failure, an uncertain tomorrow) that tend to stunt development and raise the bar.

☐ Lesson 3.4: Recognize and Appreciate Racial and Cultural Differences

Adolescents have different developmental needs than adults. It also is im-portant to recognize and appreciate racial and cultural differences of these youth and their families. In our elementary history classes, many of us were taught that cultural and ethnic differences have slowly dissolved over the past few centuries in a vast melting pot. More and more theorists have begun to advocate a model of cultural pluralism as an alternative to the melting pot theory.

> Cultural pluralism is often likened to a cultural stew; the various ingredients are mixed together, but rather than melting into a single mass, the compo-nents remain intact and distinguishable while contributing to a whole that is richer than its parts alone. (Atkinson, Morten, & Sue, 1993, p. 10)

Julian Bond (1999), Executive Director of the NAACP shared that people frequently tell him, "When I see you, I just see a man, I don't see color." He identified two concerns with this often-used expression: "First, it sounds disingenuous, and second, it fails to acknowledge an important part of who I am."

From an early age, many of us have also been taught that either you are a racist or you are color blind. Considering the number of people in America who report they are color blind, it is amazing how many people (approximately 98.5%) marry someone from their own race (Hardy, 1996). Although there are exceptions, most of us really do recognize when some-one is racially, ethnically, or otherwise culturally different from ourselves. Pretending we do not see color is often counterproductive. By not acknowl-edging the racial and cultural identity of a youth and his or her family, we may be unwittingly denying an important part of who they are and there-fore limiting the connection we make with them (Hardy, 1996; Pederson, 1988; Sue & Sue, 1990).

African-American counselor educator and diversity lecturer Ken Hardy (1996) exclaimed, "Admitting we see color does not mean we see one group as inferior!" Unfortunately, many of us have been conditioned to place a negative value on someone or something that is culturally different from ourselves. For example, most of us have heard (or said), "the British drive on the wrong side of the road," when, in reality, they drive on the left side of the road (Weaver, 1990). Again, self-awareness is the first step to other-awareness and a prerequisite for developing multicultural competence (Pederson, 1988; Richardson & Molinaro, 1996). It is important that we have a sense of our own cultural identity and examine our biases, prejudices, and beliefs about persons who are both similar and different from ourselves.

I grew up in a small, predominantly White town in rural Virginia and attended a small, predominantly White undergraduate college in a neighboring town. Nevertheless, I felt that I had been exposed to healthy role models and considered myself sensitive to the oppression and racism faced by many minorities in America. Looking back, I probably had some cognitive understanding but limited affective appreciation.

Several years after graduating, I worked as a counselor at a runaway shelter and a high school, each with a large percentage of African-American students. Operating from a color blind perspective (so I thought), seldom did I initiate the subject of race—not wanting to alienate, misinterpret, or "break any egg shells." Although I felt I developed good rapport with many of the students and families, I can see now how trust could have been strengthened by realizing that cultural heritage was often an issue whether I spoke to it or not. I'm not suggesting that cultural or racial identity needs to become the topic of conversation for every cross-cultural interaction. However, it has been my experience that longer term relationships (counseling, friendship, supervision), have been enhanced by such discussions if: 1) they are approached with the goals of improved understanding, communication, and appreciation, and 2) we remember that as humans, we tend to be more alike than different.

I do not want to imply that these discussions be limited to race. Other potential "elephants" in the counseling room include ethnicity, religion, sexual orientation, age, geography, and socioeconomics. All of these are important ingredients for understanding the whole person and meeting them where they are. Cultural and developmental differences are particularly important when we consider our work with adolescents because, in many ways, adolescence is a separate culture in itself. By acknowledging and discussing important developmental and cultural differences, we may uncover hidden obstacles, gain a greater appreciation of how adolescents see the world, and strengthen our relationships.

There is an old Yiddish saying, "To a worm in horseradish, the whole world is horseradish" (Kushner, 1986). I wrote the following story about Willy the Worm as an ice breaker to encourage 5th and 6th grade students to talk about racial and cultural differences:

Hi, my name is Willy. I'm a green worm. I was born in this very jar of horse-radish and I've lived here ever since. My mother says she's been around, whatever that means. Something about there being other places worms live—like ketchup and mustard and dirt. She says she liked the people in some of those places. Mom says that sometimes those people don't act right, but it's not their fault. They really don't know any better. My uncle told me some bad things about worms who live in those places, particularly dirt. The dirt worms sound kind of mean. He says they were colored red and looked kind of funny. And slithered sort of sideways. My brother says one time he went into some mustard, and the worms all stared at him. It seems strange to think that there are other places to live. I'm sure it all looks and feels pretty much the same. Besides, I like it here. One time, a brown worm named Billy came through our town. He was different but I accepted him nonetheless. I took the time to tell him about our town and the right way to do things around here. He couldn't stay. Said he had to get back for some reason I don't remember. I feel kind of sad for worms like Billy, not getting a chance to live in a jar like this.

Cultural encapsulation was a term coined by Wrenn in 1962 to describe individuals like Willy the worm. Although Willy knows other places exist, his exposure has been very limited and biased. Willy doesn't think of himself as encapsulated. He believes he sees the world as it is. It makes sense that he sees his worldview as *the* worldview. He doesn't really know any other way. Also, perspectives of other worm cultures that have been shared with him didn't sound too inviting. He is very comfortable in his horseradish world and has never felt motivated to venture out into other worlds.

I am not proposing that, as helping professionals, we need to become cultural anthropologists. Yet, many prominent professionals have under-scored the importance of learning as much as possible about the primary cultural groups we work with (Hardy, 1996; Pederson, 1988; Sue & Sue, 1990). For example, when working with the elderly, one should become versed regarding strengths, problems, and resources that tend to be ger-mane to this population. Similarly, when working with inner city kids or specific social cliques, one should try to understand and appreciate their unique experiences and worldviews as much as possible.

We may realize that the more we learn, the less we really know. What we "know" is good for kids and families may not be so. Consider the following excerpts from fictional counseling summaries:

Jim is a 17-year-old male who has been seen by this counselor for a total of six individual sessions. Jim has been invested in his therapy and has talked openly about current and past family concerns. He has consistently demon-strated a willingness to take positive risks during the sessions, and on several occasions, this risk taking has produced cathartic expression of emotions and subsequent insight into the nature of his problems. Overall, Jim's attitude has been very positive toward therapy and he has shown tremendous progress. . . .

Tim is a 16-year-old male who has been seen by this counselor for a total of six individual sessions. Tim has remained very guarded throughout therapy and has been reluctant to discuss any personal or family concerns. His responses to questions are often brief, superficial, and impassive. His answers also suggest limited capacity for independent thought and an overdependence on family members for a high school senior. Furthermore, he appears to have very little insight into the nature of his problems. Overall, his attitude toward therapy has been negative and resistant. . . .

What were your first impressions of Jim and Tim? Would you view Tim differently if you learned that he was a member of a minority group that had experienced significant oppression in the U.S. and that the counselor was racially different? What if Tim was White and you learned Tim had responded honestly to a social worker's questions when he was 11-years-old and was subsequently removed from his home against his will? What if you learned Jim had told his best friend "I know how the system works. I tell them what they want to hear, the judge gives me a lecture, and I'm free to go. Been there, done that"? What if you learned that Jim would be ostracized or beaten if his social clique or gang learned that he had shared information with the counselor? What if either had been female? Can you think of other factors which might impact your perceptions (i.e., your race, your experiences)?

Sue and Sue (1991) point out that is not unusual for counselors to view clients in terms of their level of insight, individual autonomy, self-disclosure, and expression of feelings. These are often seen as barometers of psychological health as well as counselee motivation. Are these appropriate indicators? Well, it depends. Not everyone sees the world in the same light. There are many cultural groups that tend to view some of these traits as counterproductive or countercultural. Furthermore, each youth's unique history will impact his or her perception of these concepts.

It is important to recognize that our own beliefs about mental health and normalcy have been culture-based and value-based, and others may see things differently. For instance, insight can be a valuable intermediate process, but not always. First, there is no assurance that insight or expression of feelings will lead to behavioral change. Second, as Maslow (1954) suggested long ago, individuals who struggle with daily survival issues may view insight as a luxury reserved for persons who have the time for self-exploration. Third, some cultural groups may view insight as self-indulgence at the expense of the family unit. Similarly, counselors may mistakenly view culturally normal concerns about privacy and respect for family as resistance, guardedness, or dependent behavior. Different cultures also have varying norms regarding when it is appropriate to share personal information with others. Also, reluctance to trust on the part of many minority youth may be a rational, understandable response to experiences of racism (Sue & Sue, 1990). The concepts listed in the brief case comparisons above represent only a few of the possible values which may be culture-based.

The majority of counseling theories taught in America were developed by White European and European-American men. Subsequently, it only makes sense that these theories would reflect their worldviews and values. Hence, elements of particular theoretical frameworks regarding human behavior and change may be inappropriate or need to be adapted to meet the needs of females or non-Whites. On the other hand, just because the individual is female or a member of a minority group, we should not assume that a particular approach is appropriate or inappropriate. Each individual's receptiveness to particular approaches will be influenced by their gender, age, developmental level, personality, and familial, social, and political experiences, as well as a variety of other cultural factors. Because there is no cookbook formula, we need to constantly examine our assumptions and regularly check in with the youth and families we work with to determine if we are on the right track. Regardless of our theoretical approach, adaptability and flexibility are essential ingredients.

☐ Lesson 3.5: Recognize and Appreciate Within Group Differences

People who have had very limited exposure to other cultures or groups of people sometimes make false generalizations based on a few interactions. They succumb to faulty reasoning often described in Logic 101 classes:

> I knew two blue guys at work.
> Both blue guys were lazy.
> Therefore, all blue people are lazy.

> I knew a kid with a nose ring.
> He was always smoking pot and skipping school.
> Therefore, all kids with nose rings smoke pot and skip school.

I worked for one year with 20 exchange students from Japan. I learned many things from these students. First, I learned a great deal about life in Japan and Japanese customs and manners. Second, I learned that because of the deference to authority and emotional restraint (displayed by most, but not all), I needed to adjust my style of communication to decipher what they really wanted or needed. Third, and most importantly, in working with a group this large, I was able to discard many stereotypes and recognize individual differences among the students.

I now have many friends and acquaintances who are gay and lesbian and have worked with many gay and lesbian students. However, this was not the case until after I was in graduate school. It would have been easy (and I probably did) to form my own beliefs and stereotypes based on very limited information and interactions. Increased exposure has not only enabled me to recognize some common strengths and concerns of this population, but also has reinforced the importance of appreciating and recognizing individual differences. Without this exposure, I might have made the false assumption that there is greater uniformity of attitudes and beliefs among minorities than there are for members of the dominant culture (Atkinson, Morten, & Sue, 1993).

Although it is important to be cognizant of traditions and differences between cultural groups (i.e., value of extended family, significance of particular holidays, common coping skills, tendencies regarding child rearing, tendencies regarding styles of communication, beliefs about death and mourning), we need to try to avoid stereotyping groups by assuming that all members possess certain beliefs, traits, or attitudes (Atkinson et al., 1993; Lee & Richardson, 1991; Pederson, 1988; Sue & Sue, 1990).

For this reason, I am reluctant to embrace the trend to emphasize culture-specific techniques in my classes. For instance, I would not want to make express recommendations regarding eye contact and culture X. Those who emphasize culture-specific techniques almost invariably include a disclaimer regarding stereotyping, but too often the disclaimer gets lost, and the lesson is distorted. The student may only remember, "Don't try to make eye contact with him, he's a member of X culture." I would prefer to teach people that there tend to be cultural as well as individual variations regarding eye contact, and we should be wary of our own assumptions. For instance, a youth who is reluctant to make eye contact may be showing disrespect; however, there are a plethora of other possibilities to explain this behavior. Avoiding eye contact may be a cultural norm to actually demonstrate respect, or it may reveal a lack of social skills, embarrassment, or perhaps an understandable distrust of authority figures or members of the establishment.

Another reason I steer clear of overemphasizing specific cross-cultural techniques is because I do not want to overshadow the importance of the nature of the relationship between the youth and the helping profes-sional. As an educator, I sometimes find that conveying the importance of learning cultural customs, norms, and tendencies while trying to avoid creating or reinforcing stereotypes can be a delicate balancing act. The students who are able to draw this distinction tend to be the ones who have a clear sense of their own cultural identity as well as a general appre-ciation for differences. Ken Hardy (1996) once remarked, "If I'm in touch with my racial self, my class self, my gender self, etc., I don't need to know every nuance of this mythical other. . . . Too much of a cookbook ap-proach breeds rigidity and limits flexibility."

☐   Lesson 3.6: Adapt Rather Than Adopt

When Alex was referred by his teacher, she described him as "impossible to reach," and "totally apathetic about school." She requested that I "talk to him and make him care about school." I knew very little about Alex. When questioned further, his teacher said he was a big fan of the heavy metal band Metallica, and he was capable of doing grade level work. We also discussed what had been attempted thus far to motivate Alex (lec-tures, threats, pleas, failing grades, and calls home). These traditional at-tempts to motivate Alex had proved futile for the most part. Subsequently, I knew I needed to resist the common temptation to dress up what had already been done in psychological clothing. It also made sense to start where he was—not where others wanted him to be. Youth understand-ably "resist efforts to change them by people they feel don't understand and accept them" (Minuchin & Nichols, 1993, p. 41). Although Alex and I are both White, we live in two very different cultures. Rather than de-manding youth adapt to our culture, it is often better to adjust our style and work within their culture (Sue & Sue, 1990).

I read through a few magazines, asked around, and gained enough familiarity with the band to engage Alex in an intelligent conversation about Metallica. During our first several interviews, Alex talked about why he loved the band and his dream of being a musician. He described how heavy metal music gave him a voice to express his anger and frustration. Feeling disconnected at school and home, he found validation through his music. During the third session, he brought his guitar in and gave me a brief demonstration (unplugged). While talking about these things and sharing his music, his speech became more pronounced and his affect much brighter. Alex seemed shocked that an adult wanted to discuss music with him. Since I did not have detailed knowledge of Metallica, I mostly asked questions and listened. This seemed to be a pivotal point in strengthening my relationship with Alex. He appreciated that I both took the time to demonstrate some respect and understanding of an important part of his culture and that I did not pretend to be a big fan of the band. Wallbridge and Osachuk (1995) asserted that "it is enough to know the name of the heavy metal band on your client's shirt; you do not need to be wearing the shirt yourself" (p. 212). That is the difference between adapting to the culture and trying to adopt the culture. Building therapeutic relationships has nothing to do with pretending to be who we are not (Minuchin & Nichols, 1993). We have to be ourselves. Otherwise, the youth's B.S. detector goes off and the relationship suffers.

When I first started counseling, I might have considered those first three sessions with Alex as unproductive and thus unprofessional. I probably would have rushed in and focused on his primary presenting problem—his poor motivation in school. However, experience has taught me that Alex's sense of disconnection with school and school authorities was longstanding and fairly entrenched, and thus, the *real* presenting problem. I knew I needed to adapt my own style and perceptions so that I could enter his world. I viewed Metallica as an entry point. Only after we began to develop a trusting and caring relationship largely through Alex's love of music were we able to focus on other issues. In subsequent sessions, Alex was able to identify his own reasons for improving his grades and together we worked on a concrete plan. Alex raised his grades from mostly "Fs" to all "As," went on to be the class valedictorian, and later won a Grammy Award. Just kidding—that's the movie version. Alex did raise his grades from mostly "Fs" to all "Cs" and one "D" and eventually graduated from high school. Actually, all gains are relative, and relatively speaking, Alex's improvement was considerable.

As discussed in Chapter 2, kids know. They know when an adult doesn't care enough to understand their world. They also know when we are pretending to be someone we are not in an effort to make a connection. Adapting involves flexibility—adjusting your style to fit the needs of the family, using language that is clear and understandable, learning about the youth's culture, agreeing to meet with the family in their home, including members of extended families in the sessions, and so on.

☐ Lesson 3.7: Meet Youth Where They Are, Both Literally and Figuratively

I will always remember Tyrone J., a 15-year-old African-American male who reluctantly agreed to accompany his father, a local businessman, to family counseling. On the surface, Tyrone presented as guarded, sullen, and angry. Numerous clues, including the fact that he came regularly, suggested more pain than anger. Of course, I didn't need to be Sherlock Holmes to figure that out. Behind almost every angry kid is considerable emotional pain (Tobin, 1991). Also, his suspicions about me as another member of the establishment made sense considering his experiences. Historically, people of color have received inadequate or inappropriate mental health services (Lee & Richardson, 1991; Sue & Sue, 1990). In fact, if Tyrone had trusted me earlier than he did, I might have considered this irrational or phony.

Although his father expressed concern about Tyrone's failing grades at school and increased withdrawal in the home, one particular incident precipitated the referral—an upcoming court date for grand larceny. It was September and Tyrone had been arrested in March for breaking into a neighbor's house and stealing approximately $200 worth of coins. The wheels of justice were moving characteristically slow, and he was not scheduled for trial until November.

After three sessions, Tyrone understandably remained guarded and said very little. He complained about having to come, but he always came. My main goal during the first few sessions was to understand the family's perspective so that we could begin to make a connection. Yet because of the upcoming court date, I began to feel the need to quicken the pace. My supervisor asked me about Tyrone's strengths and interests and suggested I play basketball with him. I must admit there was a part of me that wanted to say, "Hey, I'm not a camp counselor anymore, I'm a *therapist,* damn it." Also, while I understood and agreed with the rationale for this suggestion, it seemed contrary to what I had been taught about maintaining roles, avoiding dual relationships, and being professional. I shared these concerns, and I don't remember exactly what she said but it included the word "hogwash." Fortunately, I was working at a college counseling center and didn't have to include billable hours and managed care into the equation. So I called Tyrone's father before the next session and told him what I wanted to do. He supported the idea and I challenged Tyrone to several games of H-O-R-S-E. Both Tyrone and his father shared later that these games were pivotal in tipping the scales of trust, and more importantly, in showing a level of commitment and concern beyond what they expected.

Despite overwhelming evidence that supported Tyrone's guilt and increased level of trust, he understandably maintained his innocence. There was a big part of me that wanted to challenge Tyrone and have him immediately acknowledge his crime and accept responsibility for his actions. However, I had a sense that he was not ready. I also knew that challenging him on this issue might reframe his behavior from self-preservation to lying, and I felt this would be counterproductive. And besides, on several occasions, he hinted at implied admission of guilt. This was the best he could do at this stage.

Several weeks before court, I helped prepare Tyrone for his court appearance. He had been before the judge on two previous occasions and his attitude and behavior had bordered on contempt. However, I felt that I could facilitate a discussion in which he would realize such behavior was not getting him what he wanted. After offering what I felt was empathy for his position, I tried several ways to frame this "face-losing" behavior in a different light. Tyrone wasn't biting and we reached a temporary impasse. I thought more about the so-called empathy I was offering and realized it was merely lip service, a means to my end. So I tried harder. As I tried my best to put myself in his shoes, I began to develop a deeper understanding of what he was telling me. In essence, he was saying, "I would rather spend one year behind bars than one minute sucking up to this White guy in a black robe. I don't have much. What I do have is who I am." In Tyrone's mind, acting respectfully (at least what I deemed respectfully) would be to lose face, and without face, Tyrone felt he would lose the two types of respect which were most important to him: self-respect and peer-respect.

Only after I was able to convey some understanding for his dilemma, were we able to move forward. Only then was he able to reframe this behavior from disrespecting himself to helping himself. And then, it was a series of compromises. "I'll wear a nice shirt and tuck it in—but no tie. I'll say 'Yes sir'—but no 'your honor' crap. I'll sit up, but only when it's my turn. I'll stand when he enters, but I'm not looking at him." We did some role plays and Tyrone followed through in court. He was found guilty and given probation and community service, both of which he fulfilled. Tyrone and his father continued to come regularly for several months until we mutually agreed on termination. He began to accept more responsibility for his behavior and get involved in various prosocial activities. He even admitted responsibility for the burglary. All success is relative. I felt that Tyrone was beginning to succeed. And I appreciate the lessons he taught me. Tyrone was a wonderful teacher and two lessons stand out: 1) meet kids where they are literally, and 2) meet kids where they are figuratively.

☐ Lesson 3.8: Empathic Understanding Is the Key to Reaching Troubled Youth—But It's No Easy Task

Okun (1997) defined empathy as "understanding another person's emotions and feelings from that person's frame of reference" (p. 10). Early research by prominent counseling theorists Carl Rogers (1957) and Robert Carkhuff (1969) found empathy to be one of the most significant factors in stimulating positive change in clients. Steven Covey (1989), renowned author and lecturer, asserted that the principle, "Seek first to understand, then to be understood" is the single most important principle in the field of interpersonal relationships. I agree and I can think of no better advice for professionals who work with challenging youth. To meet youth where they are, we must not assume we know the directions. We must ask *and* listen.

As an externally oriented society, we often have difficulty seeing things from someone else's perspective. We tend to assume that our frame of reference is the only frame of reference (Patterson, 1974). Someone once joked, "There tend to be two primary forms of communication in America: Talking and waiting to talk." While I find that statement very funny, the inherent truth that makes it funny is also very sad. These two forms of communication were on public display during the impeachment hearings of President Clinton. On both sides of the aisle, everyone had a perspective they could not wait to share. They were so focused on scripting their response, there was no room to really hear or entertain any new perspectives.

Professionals who choose to work with challenging youth do not possess some magic potion that makes us more empathic than the rest of humankind. Ironically, for many, the word has been used so often it has lost its meaning; people have become desensitized. Sometimes we need to relearn and personalize the meaning of empathy. Remember that it does not just occur—it requires considerable effort and intentionality, particularly with challenging youth. To truly empathize, we need to suspend judgment and stay in the moment—be fully present.

In fact, an early review of the literature by Rogers (1961) revealed that the most important predictor of understanding another's feelings and meaning was essentially an attitude of desiring to understand. My own experience with challenging youth has supported these findings. When I've been able to convey some understanding of what the youth is feeling or thinking, I have been more likely to engage them therapeutically. Too often, I have been able to trace problems in our relationship to incidents in which I thought I was being empathic, but I was really just going through the motions or presenting my own agenda.

While empathic understanding is an essential first step in reaching troubled youth, it is easier said than done. Natasha, who was 14 years old when I met her, was one of many kids who has reinforced this point. Her predominant mood was angry and indignant, her behavior was often aggressive and destructive, and her motivation appeared completely self-serving. She seemed totally oblivious or uncaring to both peers and adults. Although I knew her extensive history of abuse and displacement, I found it hard to look past her wide array of in your face, acting-out behaviors. Her complete disregard for others made it hard to be in the same room with Natasha. At least, those were my perceptions of her. Dave, my supervisor, was able to look beyond the bravado and respectfully communicate to Natasha some of the pain she was feeling. In short, he was able to empathize with Natasha. Subsequently, he was able to use this caring and understanding to help Natasha begin to understand (and care!) how her behavior was affecting others. Only after considerable consultation and reflection was I able to begin to look beyond this surface behavior and see Natasha's disguised pleas for help.

We are often asked to develop meaningful relationships with youth who have experienced severe abuse, neglect, and rejection. These youth have learned to view conflict in simple, self-serving terms and bring with them intense emotional pain manifested in feelings of mistrust, abandonment, rage, confusion, and low self-esteem. Feeling and communicating empathy can be an enormous challenge for all of us who work with these kids, particularly professionals such as teachers, residential counselors, and foster parents who share these struggles day in and day out. Nevertheless, as the professionals and the adults, it is our responsibility to take the initiative to demonstrate and model empathic responses (Long, 1991; Richardson, 1996; Sommers-Flanagan & Sommers-Flanagan, 1996). Many troubled youths are like Natasha; they have grown up in a world without empathy. Because they have not been exposed to positive responses and examples, they are unable to be empathic toward others. By offering empathic responses, we may be giving them what they need today and tomorrow— they feel understood today and learn to understand tomorrow (Richardson, 1996).

Certainly, making a difference in the lives of these youth requires more than empathic listening. At the same time, I believe it is easy to get so caught up in complicated genograms, paradoxical techniques, or psychological jargon, that we lose sight of the basics. If you find yourself having a hard time connecting with a challenging youth, quit talking and start listening. Remember, meaningful relationships develop from warm, friendly, accepting, and nonjudgmental attitudes conveyed through active, empathic listening (Rogers, 1961; Wubbolding, 1988). The next several lessons will discuss common roadblocks for empathizing and connecting with challenging youth.

☐ Lesson 3.9: Learn About the Car Before Tinkering With the Engine: Avoid Premature Problem-Solving

Think about the last time you had a really bad day at work. Were you frustrated by the difficulty of completing a task? Or perhaps you felt you were treated poorly by a colleague or supervisor? Close your eyes and try to remember what you were feeling? Was it anger, frustration, hurt, or something else?

If you are like most of us, you probably went home and shared your version of what happened to a spouse, friend, or significant other.

I've surveyed my counseling classes using this same scenario and asked them, "What response did you get?" and "What were you hoping for?" The most typical response to the first question was some variation of problem-solving (i.e., "Have you ever tried . . . ?" or "Next time, you should . . . ") In your situation, did the people you talked to attempt to help solve your problem for you? Were you even looking for a solution? Chances are, you weren't. Based on personal experience and consistent responses from my students, I would venture a guess that you were merely looking for a confidant with whom you could share your story and express what you were feeling. And hopefully, they would listen and communicate some level of understanding of how difficult your day was.

Now think about the last time you interacted with a kid who was having a really bad day. What were they feeling? How did they communicate these feelings? What response did you give them?

If so many of us are looking for an empathic listener (at least in the beginning), why do we find expert problem-solvers? Are the people that make up our support system trying to be unsupportive? I doubt it. In fact, even those of us in the "listening professions" who are aware that premature problem-solving is a primary roadblock to effective communication (Gordon, 1978), often find ourselves jumping the gun with those close to us. Most of us have been conditioned from an early age that the best way to assist another is to offer advice or problem-solve. At the risk of stereotyping, this is particularly true for us males. It makes us feel like we are doing something. Helping others solve problems is how we show we care.

Unfortunately, and somewhat ironically, these attempts to help often have the opposite effect. We send the message that we don't care enough to really listen and try to understand. In essence, we are unwittingly communicating the following:

> Although you have been struggling with this problem for some time, I have come up with several simple and appropriate solutions.

Another reason we tend to rush in too quickly to try and solve the problem is our own discomfort with hearing the youth's story of pain and frustration. Regardless of our motivation, these premature responses will likely frustrate the youth or serve to transfer responsibility for the problem from the youth to the counselor (Young, 1998). Even if we solve the problem, we may be reinforcing a sense of learned helplessness rather than equipping them to solve future problems.

Listening feels too easy. It is a common myth that listening is easy. In a recent television interview, a reporter described how a disabled veteran was able to connect with other persons with disabilities, "One of the most important things he does is also the simplest—he listens." Important, yes. Simple, no. The passive or selective listening many of us tend to use is relatively simple. However, active, empathic listening is a learned behavior that requires considerable, conscious effort—particularly with youth we perceive as hostile, aggressive, or otherwise challenging.

Really listening requires appropriate eye contact and body language. It requires that we suspend judgment. And perhaps most difficult (at least for me), it requires that we be quiet and really focus as we listen to both the content and meaning of what is being said. Sometimes with challenging youth, these obstacles are compounded. Often, the appropriate course of action or solution to their problem seems so obvious, we cannot wait to offer advice or share our perspective. We are often so eager to teach, we neglect to take the time to learn. Thus, except in the classroom, we should "seek first to learn, then seek to teach."

Helping youth problem-solve is a crucial component in helping relationships. However, prerequisites to helping another problem-solve include:

1. taking the time to fully understand the problem from the eyes and heart of the youth (Covey, 1989; Meier & Davis, 1997), and
2. taking the time to hear what has already been tried before we start helping to generate alternative behaviors (deShazer, 1985).

☐ Lesson 3.10: Admitting We Don't Understand Is Sometimes the Most Understanding and Validating Statement We Can Make

Remember that pain is always an individual experience. I've seen many counselors tell troubled youth, "I know how you feel, I've been there." You may have experienced similar life circumstances as a youth. These experiences may get you off the starting blocks faster because troubled youth may find it easier connecting with someone who they believe "has been there." But remember, no matter what, you haven't been there. You experienced something similar—not the same. Even if you were abused, were addicted to drugs, or suffered parallel misfortunes as the youth you are working with, your experience was different. What you felt may be different from what they felt. What worked for you may not work for them. And certainly the context of the situation was different (Sommers-Flanagan & Sommers-Flanagan, 1997). Along the same lines, no two kids' experiences are the same. Every experience is unique. We can only see the world through our own eyes. Subsequently, every interpretation involves some degree of prejudging or projecting from our own experiences. Empathic responses are responses that keep these to a minimum.

> From the child's perspective, most adults are clueless regarding what it is like to be a youth struggling with contemporary issues. In essence, statements that young clients make (e.g., "You don't know how I feel or what I think") are true. Adults will find themselves making little progress if they try to convince children otherwise. (Sommers-Flanagan & Sommers-Flanagan, 1997, p. 10)

Sometimes, meeting youngsters where they are means telling them we are having trouble following them. In other words, it's okay to say, "I don't understand." Several times, I can remember kids telling me, "Man, you don't understand." It was really tempting to start lining up my arguments to convince them how much I understood what they were feeling, where they were coming from, and what they were experiencing. On more than one occasion, I've taken this path and found it quite thorny.

I've made stronger connections when I've responded by saying something like, "You know, you're right. I don't understand. I probably never will understand completely. Only you can fully understand what you've experienced and how you are feeling, but I would like to learn more. Can you help me to understand better?" The famous psychotherapist Carl Jung (1934) warned helpers that "nothing is more unbearable for the patient than to always be understood" (p. 11). Jung recognized the futility in pretending to accomplish the impossible. Again, sometimes admitting we don't understand is the most understanding and validating statement we can make. Additionally, allowing youth to retell their story provides an opportunity for them to hear it again, put it in perspective, and maybe even realize things they've forgotten or overlooked. If we "understand" right off the bat, we deny them this opportunity to better understand themselves.

☐ Lesson 3.11: Invite Participation—Identify and Name the Real Experts

Many challenging youth have seen a variety of mental health professionals. To keep from repeating past failures, go to the real expert—the kid. Take the time to ask them about their past treatment experiences. Selekman (1993) asserted that placing young clients in the expert position, we open the door for them to tell us how we can best help them. In addition to helping us appreciate the youth's perceptions, we are also sending the message that we respect their opinion and want to work collaboratively. Some possible questions include:

> "You have seen many therapists before me, what do you suppose they missed with you?"
> "What should a new therapist do with you that will make a difference?"
> "If I were to work with a teenager just like you, what advice would you give me to help him (her) out?" (Selekman, 1993, p. 99)

Goal-setting is an essential aspect of any successful therapeutic endeavor. It has been recommended (Selekman, 1993; Sommers-Flanagan & Sommers-Flanagan, 1997; Wubbolding, 1988) that we first ask the youth about his or her ideas regarding specific goals. If parents or other professionals voice their opinions first, the youth may be reluctant to say anything or may be overly influenced by the adults. Parents and professionals tend to voice their list of goals regardless of whether they are asked to share first, or in the middle (Sommers-Flanagan & Sommers-Flanagan, 1997).

Over the years, I have attended numerous meetings to coordinate services and help youth set specific, attainable goals. Typically, these meetings are held two to four times a year and are called Individualized Education Plan (IEP) meetings in schools and Treatment or Service Plan meetings in social service agencies. Since all of the primary service providers are invited, these meetings can be very effective tools for getting everyone on the same page.

Several years ago, I was invited to a middle school IEP meeting for Joseph, a 12-year-old boy in our treatment foster care program. Since Joseph had been suspended several times in the past month, the meeting, led by the principal, focused on a new behavior modification program. Due to car troubles (okay, a speeding ticket), I arrived late and Joseph was sitting outside. The large conference room was overcrowded. There were five teachers, the principal, a vice principal, the school counselor, the school psychologist, and Joseph's foster mother. They were concluding their discussion regarding appropriate behavior goals and strategies for Joseph. The school psychologist (who admitted she had never met Joseph) seemed to have the most ideas for what might work. I apologized for being late and asked, "Should Joseph be in here?" The psychologist informed me that it was easier to come to a consensus without Joseph and when they had decided the best course of action, he would be invited in. Needless to say, when Joseph was informed of the new plan, he assumed little or no ownership.

I should note that the majority of school and agency personnel are very conscientious about inviting and involving youth in such meetings. While the meeting I described above is the exception, too often, youth are excluded in more subtle ways. For instance, it is more common for a youth to be invited, but then forgotten. Either their perspectives are not sought or the conversation is so laden with acronyms and professional talk, that the youth understandably tunes out. Again, if we want cooperation, we need to invite participation.

We also need to be sensitive to how the youth perceives this meeting. We must remember that while these meetings may be commonplace to professionals, they can be very threatening to children. Sometimes, in an attempt to involve all the players, it is easy to unwittingly intimidate the youth through sheer numbers. We need to take time to prepare the youth for such meetings, periodically gauge his or her reactions, and adjust the meetings accordingly. Also, there may be times in which it is best to exclude younger children from frank discussions about certain issues such as custody considerations or a family member's sexual trauma. However, we should keep in mind that when youth are asked to step out of the room while a certain topic is discussed, the meaning the youth is inventing may be more damaging than what is actually said.

In addition, first impressions are critical for building relationships and laying the groundwork for positive experiences. It is critical that we remember that most challenging youth who come to a counselor are not doing so voluntarily. While it is important to greet and involve the parents, we may want to first acknowledge the youth and send the message that we have been looking forward to seeing them and are interested in their perspectives (Sommers-Flanagan & Sommers-Flanagan, 1997). I've frequently used the strategy of sarcastic empathy described by Sommers-Flanagan and Sommers-Flanagan, "Wow, it must have been hard to drag your parents in here." This statement indirectly reflects empathy with the youth that they do not want to be here, but also shows them we have a sense of humor. Whatever strategies we use, we want to communicate that we understand that the first few minutes are the most important for setting the tone and building relationships.

I've never seen the power of first impressions more apparent than in my work with foster children and school personnel. Unfortunately, due to a shortage in qualified foster parents, these kids frequently had to live in a family outside their community. Since many had a history of educational and behavioral difficulties and were forced to move in the middle of the semester, the most difficult transition was often adjusting to a new school. To protect themselves from another disappointment, some of these challenging youth wore a facade of indifference and aggravation. But underneath this protective armor were scared, confused children. What happened during their first 15 minutes in the new school greatly affected their attitude and overall experience. Fortunately, most of the counselors (or principals or teachers or secretaries) sensed their apprehension and recognized the importance of first impressions. In short, as ambassadors for the school, they made the youth feel welcome. However, on several occasions, I witnessed various adults convey through words or deeds that the student was not welcome, did not belong, or were jumping on an already "full plate." While these professionals are often overwhelmed with their work load, it is unfortunate that youth whose plates are truly running over, have to experience one more indignity. While these messages may have been unintentional, they were heard loud and clear.

☐ Lesson 3.12: The Past Is History, But Don't Dismiss It

Most of the primary theoretical influences I draw from (reality therapy, structural family therapy, solution-focused therapy) place primary emphasis on current relationships and behaviors. Minuchin asserted that "anything in the family's history that is relevant will show up in their interactions" (Minuchin & Nichols, 1993, p. 45). Solution-focused therapists generally only explore the past to identify and build on past successes (deShazer, 1985). Although Glasser has traditionally placed little therapeutic value in exploring the past, he has been misquoted as saying the past plays little role in who we are today (Glasser, 1998b). In fact, Glasser (1984) acknowledged that we are all inevitably products of our past. However, he has chosen to focus reality therapy on areas in which the youth has direct control. These theorists contend that while the problem may be related to past events, it can only "be" in the present. Youth have no control over their abusive past; they do have some control over how that is impacting them today.

Unfortunately, it has been my experience that this message is often misconstrued and misapplied when working with youth. The counselor, in an effort to focus on the changeable now, inadvertently communicates to the youth that they do not care about the past. Kids, like all of us, need to share their stories. The process of this exchange is often more therapeutic than the content. They need to know that the person who is trying to understand them knows where they are coming from (or at least wants to know). Unfortunately, there is no cookbook formula to tell counselors how much is enough and how much is too much. Certainly, we don't want to become so indulgent in the past that we reinforce negative self-fulfilling prophecies. A colleague once recommended that "we can look, just don't stare." I sometimes tell youth and families, "The past is a good place to visit, but we don't want to stay too long."

I firmly believe that most problems are best addressed by focusing our attention on the present; however, there are problems that require a deeper look. For instance, most professionals who work with juvenile sex offenders have found it helpful for these youth to gain a better understanding of their own abuse before they can begin to empathize with their victims and begin to heal. Additionally, it may be necessary to revisit the past to help validate previous coping mechanisms and evaluate whether these behaviors are still helpful. For example, revisiting her childhood may help a 17-year-old girl not only realize that dissociative behaviors were necessary for a seven-year-old to survive unbearable abuse, but also see how these behaviors may no longer be effective. The past may be a valuable place to find past successes. Youngsters and families who have been on a downward spiral for several years may need to look to their past to remember times when they felt a sense of achievement or togetherness. As helpers, we are most effective if we don't repeat what has failed in the past. We may ask the youth and his or her parents, "You've been to many counselors. What was helpful?" Or we may ask, "Tell me about a time when the family wasn't experiencing this problem. What were you doing differently?" These questions explore the past to more effectively intervene in the present. The past is history but we don't want to dismiss it. To meet youth where they are, we sometimes need to return to where they've been.

Lessons Learned: Finding a Healthy Balance Between Support and Challenge

☐ Lesson 4.1: Avoid the Dualistic Trap: You Do Not Have to Choose Between Drill Sergeant and Doormat

All this talk about caring and empathy just doesn't cut it in the real world. I work with tough kids every day and you have to lay down the law or they will walk all over you.

—overheard at counseling conference

Kreisman and Straus (1989) observed that Western contemporary society tends to promote the kind of dualistic ideology demonstrated by the conference participant. We like to label and compartmentalize our world into neat, tidy packages. We yearn for a time when right and wrong were more easily defined—where the good guys wore white hats and were always good and the bad guys wore black hats and were always bad. In reality, these simpler times were never so simple, except maybe within the confines of television and movie screens. We have been conditioned to create mythical polarities to see people and their problems more clearly than they really are. Either you are a gutless, bleeding heart liberal, or a heartless, staunch conservative. Either you try to empathize and support the helpless victim or challenge and confront the malevolent delinquent. Often, those unwilling to take a polar position are considered wishy-washy or apathetic. Yet, invariably, those who possess a unique gift to work with challenging youth know that you have to offer both support and challenge—often at the same time.

> Clearly, the therapist must be prepared to be many different people to adolescent clients in order to meet their various needs. Sometimes you must be hard (e.g., setting limits, establishing rules), sometimes soft (e.g., being supportive and understanding), and sometimes both at once. These divergent roles can be quite complicated to manage, especially given that one of your overriding goals is to be consistent. (Wallbridge & Osachuk, 1995, p. 215)

Recently, the Washington State Supreme Court mandated that all youth be educated, even those incarcerated with felony convictions. Many legislators, arguing that prisons were designed to punish criminals, lobbied against the Supreme Court's decision. I must admit that I struggle to find the logic behind these legislators' rationale for opposing education. Even if you are a tough disciplinarian, the reality of the situation is that these kids will eventually be back in society. Without some minimal education, Washington would be closing the door on many socially sanctioned options and virtually guaranteeing the release of more embittered future criminals. Surely these legislators do not believe future youngsters will no longer view prison as a deterrent and therefore commit more felonies because they know they will be educated in prison.

Joseph Marshall and Jack Jacqua are cofounders of the highly successful Omega Boys Club in San Francisco. Their tireless work has helped numerous inner city, African-American youth channel their talents and energies away from a life of gang-banging and drug dealing. In order to maximize their effectiveness, they have had to wear many hats: counselor, teacher, activist, mentor, surrogate father. They have received numerous accolades from national and local community and civic organizations. Their efforts are chronicled in the book *Street Soldiers* (Marshall & Wheeler, 1996). In reading their stories, several things are clear. Their work is a mission, not a job. They really believe in what they are doing and the youngsters they are helping. They possess a unique ability to understand and empathize with the daily struggles these kids face *and* they can be very tough and demanding when these adolescents act irresponsibly. About his colleague, Joe Marshall wrote:

> He, by contrast, was there to lend an ear. But at the same time, Jack was much more than a well-meaning sympathizer. He helped the kids with their homework, he hooked them up with basketball and track teams, he gave them lunch money out of his pocket, and if they broke their promises or the law, he gave them hell. He expected as much from them as he gave them, and that was an arrangement they could understand. (p. 40)

Professionals like Jack know that his confrontations would not be successful if the youth didn't know that he genuinely cared. The fact that he is willing to take risks to identify and challenge discrepancies further demonstrates his investment.

However, those professionals who cannot tolerate any acting out behavior and demand that youth submit to their will "during their watch," often confuse fear for respect. Many of us have been taught that fear is a prerequisite for respect, but more often, if fear is the primary motivator, the adults are simply reinforcing what the kid already thought they knew— the world is cluttered with hostile, threatening adults.

These professionals may confuse discipline with abuse of power. Many convince themselves their way is the only way—the end justifies the means. But what is the end? A hurt, angry, blaming, irresponsible kid who does what you say for most of the wrong reasons? When these youngsters are presented with a "safer" adult, they are likely to displace and unload an array of pent-up emotions. Long-term process goals such as autonomy, responsibility, empathy, and self-esteem will have been sacrificed for the short-term goal of compliance—all to achieve order, which is short-lived, and respect, which is contrived. Basketball coaches such as Dean Smith, Skip Prosser, and Roy Williams, and helping professionals such as Joseph Marshall and Jack Jacqua, to name just a few, have repeatedly proven it's not an either/or proposition. We can and should be both supportive and confrontive. Unfortunately, the public persona of a few have helped create the following commonly held myth: To motivate and gain the respect of challenging students, you have to be a drill sergeant. This was not true in the "good ol days" and it's not true now. Drill sergeants are needed in the military (and possibly with violent offenders) where fear can be used to save lives; however, with most challenging youth, fear will not teach responsibility. It will merely reinforce the youth's perception of a hostile, uncaring world where might makes right.

☐ Lesson 4.2: Reframe Confrontations as a Way to Develop Closer, More Genuine Relationships

Many of us have been taught that confrontation is a dirty word and that confrontations should be avoided at all costs or used only as a last resort. Patterson (1974) observed that the word itself tends to connote aggressiveness or face-to-face conflict. Graduate students in my Group Process class often report that confrontation is one of the counseling skills that sparks the most consternation and apprehension. Furthermore, while many verbalize a cognitive appreciation of the importance of acknowledging and addressing conflict, they still find themselves avoiding these growth opportunities out of habit, fear, or uncertainty.

The following interaction reflects a fairly common belief that really good relationships are void of conflict and confrontation. Mark, a 26-year-old White male, was a previous client who was now struggling with his marriage and beginning to have fantasies of reuniting with a previous girlfriend. I felt that we had developed a trusting working relationship when Mark presented the following:

Mark: We dated for over a year and never disagreed about anything or had a confrontation of any sort. It was so nice, there was never any conflict.

BR: Mark, I want to help you sort out your feelings. Is it safe to say that you are very apprehensive and frustrated with your current relationship? (empathy)

Mark: Yeah, that's a fair assessment.

BR: What was your girlfriend's name?

Mark: Melissa.

BR: I may be totally off base here, but it sounds like if you and Melissa never had any conflict, then either your relationship never matured beyond a superficial level, or understandably, you are not remembering everything about your relationship with Melissa. What do you think? (tentative confrontation)

In the above scenario, I attempted to communicate support and empathy, as well as confront Mark about the perceived incongruency in his statements. Initially, Mark became somewhat agitated and defended his position. Based on his reaction, I sensed that Mark had heard my point. I had struck a cord and I felt this was the time to seek greater understanding of his feelings and position. During the next session, Mark said that he had given it more thought and felt there was some truth to what I said.

There are two main reasons why I share this interaction: 1) to demonstrate a qualified or tentative confrontation, and 2) to communicate my belief that a successful relationship void of conflict, or at least the occasional need for confrontation, is either superficial or an aberration. Additionally, relationships (including those between helping professionals and challenging kids) that disintegrate under challenge are based on a false sense of connection.

If we view timely and effective confrontations as an opportunity to use caring, honest feedback to develop closer, more genuine relationships with youngsters (Corey & Corey, 1997), we are more likely to engage in approach—rather than avoidance—reactions (Okun, 1997). Nevertheless, we need to make sure that we put the horse (support and empathy) before—or at least beside—the cart (confrontation). But again, just because someone is supportive and empathic does not imply that they are not challenging, tough, and firm also. In fact, confronting or recognizing and communicating discrepancies in a youth's verbalizations and behavior requires empathic understanding (Patterson, 1974).

The art of effective confrontation is a prerequisite for succeeding with challenging youth. They expect it and want it from those professionals they feel close to. Confrontation is a way of reaffirming the realness of the relationship. It is a way to communicate that we care enough to hold them to their end of the bargain. Professionals who tolerate chaos and are unwilling to challenge youth when necessary will be seen as incompetent or uncaring (Morse, 1996c). If a trusting relationship has been established with the youth, a confrontation communicates that you care enough to confront behavior rather than ignore unpleasant or difficult aspects which may impede growth (Hutchins & Vaught, 1997).

In essence, effective confrontations with challenging youth communicate much of the following:

I like you.

I care about you.

I expect a lot from you.

Here are my boundaries and expectations for this relationship.

Expecting or accepting less would be the ultimate sign of disrespect.

☐ Lesson 4.3: Recognize Times and Situations When Confrontations May Be Warranted

Timing is one of the most important considerations when deciding to confront challenging youth (Hutchins & Vaught, 1997). So, when is the best time to first challenge or confront challenging youth? Whenever possible, try to be able to answer "yes" to the following two questions first:

1. Have I communicated that I care about him or her? (Remember, few of us subscribe to a guaranteed delivery service; successful communication involves both sending and receiving.)
2. Have I developed a working relationship with this youth?

Often, challenging youth will test limits and challenge us from day one. That is what makes them challenging—they tend to forget Gloria Vanderbilt's suggestion, "If you must be difficult, don't forget your manners and protocol." Although communicating that we care and taking the time to develop a relationship are essential goals, those who work with this population know that we can't always wait to accomplish these goals before confronting a youth. They also know that when necessary, confrontation and limit setting, delivered in a firm and caring manner, can enhance and expedite the relationship-building process.

How much should you confront a challenging youth? Use the amount of support as a gauge. It is rarely helpful if you are confronting more than you are supporting (Meier & Davis, 1997). If you feel the need to be more confrontational, make sure there is a healthy balance of support. Of course, if you are supportive while confrontational, this question is really moot.

Here are some questions to consider when confronting:

1. How can I do this in a way that's clear, firm, and supportive?
2. What do I hope to accomplish?
3. What needs am I trying to meet?
4. Whose needs am I trying to meet?
5. What can I do to avoid responses that typically are not helpful (i.e., lecturing, arguing, yelling, blaming, sarcasm)?
6. Is there a way to facilitate a process in which the youth recognizes that his or her behavior is not helping?
7. Would it be better to meet with the youth away from his or her peers?

If possible, wait until you are able to answer these questions. When this is not possible, learn about yourself by asking these questions after you've had time to reflect back on a confrontation.

Some Situations Where Effective Confrontations Will Be Helpful

In the following examples, A = adult and Y = youth.

1. When you hear a discrepancy between the youth's goals and their behavior (Hutchins & Vaught, 1997; Patterson, 1974; Young, 1998).

A. Chris, I hear you've been skipping your algebra and history classes. Do you want to tell me about it?

Y: Those classes are stupid. Besides, I go most of the time. I sometimes get detoured after lunch.

A: I bet it is difficult at times to make yourself go. However, I'm a little confused. You've told me several times that you want to play on the softball team this Spring. Is that still true?

Y: Yeah, I'd like to.

A: So you want to play softball. And you need to pass those courses to be able to play softball. What are you going to do?

The preceding example highlights another reason for encouraging youth to tell you what they want and to share their goals for the future. If goals are elicited from adolescents rather than presented to them, they will assume more ownership. This information can be recalled to identify discrepancies between current behavior and stated goals. Subsequently, these types of confrontations can lead to serious discussions about what that person really wants to do and specific ways to take action (Hutchins & Vaught, 1997; Wubbolding, 1988).

2. When you see a discrepancy between the youth's verbal and nonverbal behavior (Meier & Davis, 1997; Rogers, 1961; Young, 1998).

Y: I really don't care anymore. He doesn't bother me one bit.

A: I hear you saying you're not mad at your dad anymore; yet, you're clenching your teeth and making a fist.

In his influential book, *On Becoming a Person*, Carl Rogers (1961) discusses the importance of congruence for all human beings. For Rogers, congruence means that whatever feeling or attitude one is experiencing would be matched by awareness of that attitude. Discrepancies between verbal and nonverbal behavior is one of the leading indicators of incongruence. It is the responsibility of counselors to observe these indicators in both themselves and their clients. Sensitive confrontations regarding verbal and nonverbal discrepancies can lead to increased awareness of particular behaviors and issues.

3. When you hear a discrepancy between two conflicting statements (Hutchins & Vaught, 1997; Okun, 1997; Young, 1998).

Y: That m–f–. He's always doing something to get under my skin. Every day, he thinks he can tell me what's up. I've had it up to here with him. He doesn't bother me anymore. He's nothing to me.

A: I may have misunderstood what you said because I'm hearing two different things. On the one hand, I'm hearing that this guy is getting on your last nerve, and on the other hand, I hear you saying that you are choosing not to let what he does effect you anymore. Help me out.

The qualified, tentative nature of the above confrontation is intended to reduce the defensiveness of the youth. Patterson (1974) stressed that more tentative confrontations are generally warranted in the early stages. It has been my experience that when you begin by saying something like, "I might be totally off base here, but . . ." the youth is less likely to challenge the confrontation. And if he or she does, the challenge will probably be less forceful.

4. When you feel it is important to challenge the sincerity of a statement or action (Okun, 1997; Patterson, 1974).

Y: I definitely learned my lesson this time. I hope to get out of this hospital soon so I can show everyone I'm through with booze.

A: You keep telling everyone in the group that you want to stop drinking, but to be honest, I think you are playing games with us. I don't think you have any intention of stopping. You're just telling us what we want to hear.

Often, when a relationship has been established, more specific and direct confrontations may be warranted (Patterson, 1974). Your overall attitude toward the youngster is more important that what you say or how you act during any one confrontation. It is often necessary to be very confrontive with kids struggling with substance abuse, sexual offending, and other problems in which denial predominates. With adolescents I have developed a relationship with, my confrontation is often much more direct and less tentative (i.e., "Nobody's buying this crap." "If you're going to snow me, at least be original."). It's worth repeating that I seldom take such a direct, confrontational approach unless a positive, supportive, and trusting relationship has already been established.

5. When it is necessary to reinforce consequences, boundaries, or limits.
6. When a youth's behavior or emotions begin to escalate.

The next three lessons will address specific considerations and strategies for responding to situations described in #5 and #6.

☐ Lesson 4.4: Empathic Understanding Does Not Mean Agreeing With or Excusing Unacceptable Behavior

I recently reviewed a taped session of a counseling intern who, in his eagerness to make a connection with Brandi, a 13-year-old girl, appeared to confuse empathy with agreement. Brandi was referred by her principal for repeated problems with her teachers and for violations of school rules. She immediately began sharing how her teachers were rude and mean, the principal was unfair because she would not let her wear a spiked necklace, and her parents were too strict. Rather than saying something like, "So you feel many authority figures in your life are treating you unfairly," the intern replied, "You're right, it sounds like they're not being very fair to you." There is a subtle, but important distinction between the two responses. The first response communicates empathy. After the counselor communicated empathic understanding of what Brandi felt everyone else should be doing differently, he could then explore what Brandi could do differently to make things better for herself. The second response communicates agreement and may even win a fan, but it's likely to only fuel the fire and make things worse for not only the teacher, principal, and parents, but also Brandi.

In my first year as a school counselor, students would often come to my office complaining they had been mistreated by a teacher. I wanted to convey a sense of trust to both the students and the teachers. I found myself evaluating their choices rather than empathizing with their predicament and facilitating a process in which they could evaluate their own choices. In short, I fell in the common trap described by Meier and Davis (1997) of confusing empathy (understanding their emotions and feelings from their frame of reference) with taking sides or agreement (approving of their choice or behavior). Over the years, I learned I could even empathize with persons I didn't necessarily agree with by using statements such as "Sounds like you feel Mrs. Cook is picking on you and you want things to change." Or, even when I couldn't muster empathy, I could at least validate their perspective (i.e., "I bet it feels that way").

We want to communicate to kids that we are on their side without also communicating that we are against someone else. We do not want to provide fuel for the fire the next time they get in an argument with a parent, teacher, or other authority figure. Sommers-Flanagan and Sommers-Flanagan (1997) offer several helpful principles to keep in mind. First, empathic responses should be aimed at the feelings, not the behavior. Second, we should use the youth's own negative language, rather than providing innovative and profane language alternatives.

The authors of the highly successful book, *Tough Love* (York, York, & Wachtel, 1982) expressed their frustration when they wrote: "We have been encouraged to 'understand' these psychological developmental principles and been told that our understanding will solve everything. In fact, if we all take the latest 'parenting' courses our understanding will *prevent* everything" (p. 26).

Several of the lessons in the previous chapter focused on the value of empathic understanding. It is my belief that confrontations are more successful with kids who feel like they have been heard. Furthermore, taking the time to see the problem from the youth's perspective or appreciate the mitigating factors (i.e., stressors, low self-concept) increases our chances of choosing a rational response based on choice rather than a reactive response stemming from emotional overload. While empathizing is a valuable tool, I do not want to imply that understanding in itself will solve or prevent problems. Nor does communicating an understanding of the youth's feelings and his or her perception of the problem mean we are also excusing or allowing unacceptable behavior.

Professionals who fail to set boundaries or enforce limits in an effort to increase their attractiveness to the youth with whom they work often find that this approach backfires. Because they have difficulty controlling their own emotions and behaviors, challenging youth often look to adults to provide external control when warranted and will view the counselor who fails to provide this structure as frightened or inadequate (Trieschman,

Whittaker, & Brendtro, 1969). Also, professionals who set limits but fail to follow through with expected consequences not only weaken their status but create an insecure environment that invites misbehaviors (Johns & Carr, 1995).

When natural and logical consequences are necessary, the youth is most likely to recognize his or her poor choice, accept responsibility, and alter future behavior if the consequences are presented with empathy, not anger (Cline & Fay, 1990). There are several reasons for this, some of which are obvious.

First, we want to model self-control. Human beings are not born with an inherent ability to manage their anger effectively. In fact, Goleman (1995) reported that while young males can readily access anger, they often have tremendous difficulty managing it. The primary way we learn is by watching others. Many challenging youth have been taught a wide array of maladaptive responses. As helping professionals, we are in a unique position to model more adaptive responses for managing anger.

Second, empathy is both a prerequisite for advanced moral development and a learned behavior. Children who are exposed to empathic responses are more likely to learn how to show empathy themselves (Bandura • & Walters, 1960). Until youth learn to put themselves in someone else's shoes, they will not be able to engage in more advanced moral reasoning (Hoffman, 1976).

Third, most youngsters (like most adults) can really only focus on one thing at a time. If the consequence is presented with anger, the youth will focus on the anger rather than their poor choice. Sometimes, to affirm our humanness, we may want the youth to recognize that his or her behavior can "generate" anger in others. If that is our goal, we want to 1) be careful not to show our anger in hurtful or destructive ways, and 2) remember that additional goals such as teaching responsibility will probably be diluted when our message is delivered with anger. Think back to a time when you were a kid and a parent or another adult lost their temper after you did something wrong. Maybe they yelled at you and sent you to your room. It is unlikely you went to your room and thought, "Gosh, I really made a poor choice this time. I'm so glad that my parents yelled at me so I can learn from my terrible mistake." You were probably too busy plotting your revenge or mumbling obscenities.

Subsequently, before deciding on a consequence for a youth we should (if possible) decide whether our primary goal is to teach responsibility or to let him or her know that we are angry. The next lesson highlights a three-step strategy that balances both support and challenge to reinforce consequences, boundaries, and limits while diffusing potential power struggles.

☐ Lesson 4.5: Use the SET Model to Diffuse Potential Power Struggles

In their 1989 book, *I Hate You—Don't Leave Me*, Jerold Kreisman and Hal Straus recommended using a three-step, structured approach called SET (Support, Empathy, Truth) in communicating with clients diagnosed with Borderline Personality Disorder. This approach was developed by the staff at the Comprehensive Treatment Unit of Saint John's Mercy Medical Center in St. Louis. This model can be adapted to help us deal with a variety of people we consider difficult or challenging, particularly youth who make unreasonable demands or struggle to express their emotions in constructive ways. The structure can help keep us grounded and reduce our own defenses while also addressing the plethora of emotions of troubled youth (i.e., fear, loneliness, feelings of being misunderstood, helplessness, and loss of control). Additionally, we can use the steps to set limits, reinforce boundaries, and enforce consequences.

Step 1: Communicate Support

The first stage of the model, "S" stands for Support. Most of us, whether we are emotionally disturbed or not, have moments in which we feel unsupported and alone. Challenging youth have more than their share of these moments. Their lifeboat is slowly sinking, and, from their perspective, no one seems to care—particularly us adults. It feels as though we are either ignoring their plight, truly unaware of their pain, or too wrapped up in our own struggles to care. Often these perceptions are inaccurate. However, it is incumbent upon us as professionals to continue to present evidence to justify a new perspective. Subsequently, it is often a good starting point to offer a personal statement of concern—but only if we mean it. Don't forget, kids know.

> "Jerry, I really care about you and right now, I'm very concerned." (Support)

Many challenging youth are unaccustomed to legitimate statements of personal concern. Therefore, they may dismiss your statement or challenge it. If we offer a genuine statement of concern, it will often be appreciated and remembered even when their initial reaction suggests otherwise.

Step 2: Empathize With or Validate the Youth's Position

After we have offered support, it is important that we attempt to communicate some understanding of the youth's position and what he or she is feeling. Several lessons in the previous chapter highlighted the importance of "E," or Empathy. The best time to "seek first to understand and then be understood" (Covey, 1989) is when we feel the need to be confrontive. Again, confrontation and empathy are *not* two mutually exclusive terms—they can go together. It's fairly simple to validate or empathize with someone who is feeling or thinking the same things we are. It's extremely difficult to empathize with someone who is currently challenging us or making unreasonable demands. Thus, after we have offered a statement of support, we need to focus our energy on really listening and understanding the youth's feelings and perspective. Then we try to communicate this understanding in a fairly brief, empathic, or validating statement.

"It sounds like you're pretty frustrated with this whole situation." (Empathy)

"If I were in your position, I would probably feel a little frustrated myself." (Validation)

Refer to the previous chapter for additional reminders and strategies regarding empathizing with challenging youth. But for the purposes of using the SET model with escalating youth, it is recommended that the empathic statement be brief and to the point.

Step 3: Reinforce the Reality or the Truth of the Situation

The last step in the SET process is "T" which represents Truth (or reality). Again, just because we understand a youth's behavior does not mean we excuse it. We are not helping anyone if we deny the reality of living in a world with problems, consequences, and limitations. Rescuing and excusing kids may serve to confuse them. The cartoon character Bart Simpson repeatedly begs his parents for something whenever he is told "No." Because this behavior has worked in the past, he has been taught that begging is a rational response. It is typically easier for the professional or parent to take the easy way out than it is to hold firm and teach responsibility. We need to find ways to reaffirm the youth's worthiness and also clearly communicate our expectations. When we challenge or confront kids, it is important we communicate that we accept them as they are *and* want them to improve. We need to explain that while we understand there are many paths to the same problems and other factors and people may have contributed to a challenging youth's situation, it is almost always easier to change his or her own behavior than someone else's. An effective Truth statement communicates what we can and cannot do as helpers, and that ultimately, the youth is responsible. The SET model is one structured way to show concern and understanding while teaching and modeling responsibility.

How We Present the Truth Statement Is Critical

We want to communicate the reality of the situation without using sarcasm or trying to one up the youth. We may have to remind ourselves that the statement is designed primarily to meet the youth's needs. It may be necessary to communicate our own needs regarding boundaries, limits, and expectations; nevertheless, we should be careful not to confuse these with our needs for power or vindication. This point cannot be overstated. It is a major differentiator between productive and counterproductive helping professionals.

The following are examples of appropriate and inappropriate Truth statements:

1. Appropriate: "If you do choose to run away, I will have to call the police."
   Inappropriate: "I forbid you to leave this house." (baiting and unenforceable)

2. Appropriate: "These are the rules and I will expect you to follow them."
   Inappropriate: "It's my way or the highway, buster." (reactive, baiting)

3. Appropriate: "That chair you are sitting on cost $75 and will need to be replaced if it is broken."
   Inappropriate: "This is my office. You break that chair and you pay for it!" (baiting, more punitive and more likely to sour the relationship)

4. Appropriate: "I want to help you and there's only so much I can do for you. I can. . . . What are you going to do?"
   Inappropriate: "When are you going to start doing some things for yourself?" (baiting)

5. Appropriate: "I'm having trouble following you. Please slow down so I can try to help you."

   Inappropriate: "No one can help you when you are ranting and raving like this." (I messages are more disarming)

Note that the tone and body language you use are often more important than the actual words. Remember, our goal is to communicate the reality of the situation and hopefully deescalate the crisis.

Case Example Using the SET Model of Confrontation

Jerry is a 15-year-old White male. When he was 7, his parents told him they were going to the store and never returned. Although they were never located, they closed their bank account and it is believed that they moved to Florida. Jerry stayed in an emergency foster home for several months until an aunt reluctantly took custody. Two years later, several neighbors filed a complaint of abuse and neglect with Child Protective Services. Jerry was often left alone for days and beaten severely by the aunt and her boyfriend—both of whom struggled with polysubstance abuse. He was removed from her home and placed in an emergency shelter. Over the next five years, Jerry lived in six different foster homes. His anger and depression intensified and he was placed in a residential treatment facility for two months. Jerry demonstrated significant improvement and was subsequently discharged to a treatment foster care program with experienced, resilient foster parents, Mr. and Mrs. Cook.

For the first three weeks, Jerry was a model citizen, but soon thereafter, he became more and more challenging. Whenever Jerry would be given a consequence, he would threaten to run away. Despite their skills and experience, Mr. and Mrs. Cook found themselves conflicted and frustrated, particularly over his runaway behavior.

There were several instances in which Mr. Cook went to block the door and physical altercations almost occurred. Mr. Cook would order Jerry not to leave the house and Jerry would yell, "You can't make me do anything!"

While Mr. Cook felt sucked into counterproductive power struggles, Mrs. Cook often found herself feeling sorry for Jerry. She was apt to reduce or forsake the consequences whenever Jerry made comments such as "You're just like everyone else, you don't care" or "Do whatever you want. There's no way you can hurt me anymore than anyone else."

Fortunately, the Cooks recognized two things: 1) as Jerry's foster parents and primary treatment agents, it was imperative they work together, and 2) what they were doing was not working, so they solicited recommendations from their counselor. They reviewed the SET approach and role-played several possible situations. They also talked about how easy it is to feel pity considering Jerry's history and anger considering Jerry's behavior and attitude. They recognized how these responses were not helping Jerry and practiced ways to avoid these emotional traps.

Several days later, Jerry presented the Cooks with an opportunity to practice the SET approach. Jerry became very angry when the Cooks matter-of-factly reminded him of their agreement.

Jerry: I've finished my homework for the weekend. Can I go skating tonight?

Mr. C: Jerry, I'm glad you've already done your homework for the whole weekend. You've been working really hard the last couple of hours. I knew you could do it. Jerry, I know you are going to be very upset, but on Monday, we agreed with your proposition that if you completed your homework each day this week, you could go skating on Friday. Your weekly progress report states that Monday was the only day in which you did so; therefore, we're going to keep our end of the bargain. I was really hoping you would be able to do it (nonsarcastic), and I bet you will next week.

Jerry: That's not fair.

Mr. C: I bet it feels that way.

Jerry: You're just like all the rest of them. Nobody wants me to have any fun. If you treat people like prisoners, they act like prisoners. Well, I'm nobody's prisoner. I'm out of here. And I'm not coming back. You can't stop me.

(Jerry begins walking toward the door.)

Mrs. C: Jerry, you are right, we can't stop you. I care about you and what happens to you. I can tell you're frustrated and angry about not being able to go skating. I hope you'll be able to go next week.

Jerry: I'm leaving and you can't stop me.

Mr. C: That's true Jerry. We care about you and hope you choose not to run away, but it is your choice. If you make that choice, we will be required to file a police report.

Case Analysis

Jerry chose not to run and sulked in his room. And the Cooks should be commended for their skilled use of the SET approach. They stayed calm and resisted engaging in counterproductive responses such as arguing, lecturing, or making provocative statements such as the popular, but seldom helpful, "Life's not fair." It is important to make Truth statements clear and succinct. Anything longer becomes a lecture which, at best, is tuned out. They also resisted the temptation to convince Jerry how ludicrous some of his statements were. Jerry knows he made the choice. There's a difference between pointing this out and brow beating him with it.

At that point, a rational argument would likely have just made him more irrational. The Cooks also validated Jerry's power and ability to choose to run away. Many troubled youth are more likely to run away after they have been forbidden not to. Feeling powerless, this becomes their best attempt to exert some power over their lives. Parents and helping professionals often fall victim to the trap of forbidding teenagers to drink, have sex, whatever. This is both dualistic and irrational. They reason, "To be a responsible adult, I have to say no, and saying no means over my dead body." Unless we have a 24-hour secret service escort when we forbid them, we are writing a check with our mouth that our body can't cash. We also may be fueling the fire. There is a difference between forbidding something and telling someone they will be breaking a serious rule and will face serious consequences if they make that choice. It's much more than semantics. By acknowledging Jerry's power, the Cooks lessen or eliminate his need for power.

The SET method has been successfully utilized in intervening with both challenging youth and adults who are making unreasonable demands. The next lesson will elaborate on the importance of understanding the nature of control.

☐ Lesson 4.6: Trying to Control Challenging Youth Is Like Teaching a Pig to Sing. It Wastes Your Time and Annoys the Pig

Our beliefs about the statement, "We can only control our own behavior" have significant ramifications for how we interact with challenging youth.

Unfortunately, believing we can control and change others is so embedded in human behavior and relationships, we often don't recognize how futile it is (Glasser, 1998a). Our rational selves may acknowledge that we cannot control others; nonetheless, in the heat of the moment, we revert to habitual, reactive behaviors despite their past ineffectiveness. This is a common pitfall for those of us who work with the challenging youth population. Not only do we assume too much power in controlling tough kids (i.e., "You will not smoke pot." or "You will listen to what I have to say."), but we often give them too much power in controlling us (i.e., "He makes me so mad."; "You forced me to respond that way."). We show disrespect both to ourselves and to challenging youth when we fail to acknowledge that as human beings, we make choices.

Research on peer-group processes indicates that empowering youth has a reciprocal effect. Programs that respect the autonomy of youth tend to have more youth who are receptive to the legitimate authority of adults. Ironically, these programs that recognize the limitations of control tended to be better controlled since the youth shared and supported the treatment goals of the staff (Brendtro & Brokenleg, 1996). These philosophies regarding control are relevant in any setting with challenging youth.

In his book, *Choice Theory*, Glasser (1998a) asserted that believing we can control others, including challenging youth, and believing that others control us are two of the primary precursors to human misery. These beliefs dismantle the therapeutic process by perpetuating destructive cycles and unrealistic expectations. Subsequently, in areas where change is desired, there are two general solutions: 1) change what *you want*, or 2) change *your approach* to getting what you want. Glasser (1998a) used this philosophy to describe why friendships often work and more intimate relationships do not. "Unlike lovers or even many family members, good friends can keep their friendship going for a lifetime because they do not indulge in the fantasies of ownership" (p. 36).

To further illustrate the nature of control, Glasser extends the meaning of behavior beyond traditional action behaviors. Our total behavior is made up of four components: actions, thoughts, feelings, and physiology. Each of these components always accompanies the other three components. We have direct control over our actions and thoughts and indirect control over our feelings and physiology. Therefore, we want to focus most of our energies on the areas in which we have the most direct control.

Glasser (1998a) used a car metaphor to explain this theory of total behavior. The front two wheels (acting and thinking) are the only wheels we have direct control over. Although, as we steer the car, we are inevitably impacting the direction of the back two wheels (feeling and physiology). Therefore, we have direct or indirect control over our thoughts, actions, feelings, and physiology. Wubbolding (1988) extended the analogy to compare our feelings to the warning lights of a car. When the lights go on (i.e., we feel sad), it tells us that we need to change our thinking or actions in order to make the light go off. Because of its emphasis on actions and thoughts, reality therapy is often misrepresented as an approach that ignores the role our feelings play. Glasser (1998b) asserted that "all behavior is an attempt to feel better; we never attempt to accomplish something so we will feel worse." Subsequently, most reality therapists pay close attention to a youth's feelings; however, they are more likely to try to help the youth feel better by facilitating a process that encourages better acting or thinking which in turn improves feelings. Skilled practitioners are also flexible in their application; they recognize there may be times where the youth needs to share his or her stories and feelings. How much direct attention we give to feelings is dependent upon the situation and the preferred style of the counselor. However, it is has been my experience that taking the necessary time to convey some empathic understanding is usually the best first step. We are then less likely to encounter misunderstandings down the road and more likely to engage youth in honest assessments of whether their thoughts and behaviors are helping them get what they want.

Lesson 4.7: Empathize With Those Who Are Oppressed, Fight to Change Oppressive Systems and People, and Continue to Have High Expectations for Youth Who Have Been Oppressed

A combination of biological, cognitive, social, and familial factors determine each youth's perception of reality and view of the world. When we work with challenging youth and families, it is essential we remember that their experiences, opportunities, and developmental concerns are invariably different from our own. Subsequently, we need to resist the common urge to change people who have perfectly good reasons (at least to them) not to change. Unless of course, our goal is to hear ourselves talk while kids tune us out. If that is the case, then rigid conversion tactics are certainly the way to go.

Developmental movement first requires that we sit still long enough to begin to comprehend where the youth is before we can start to help him or her determine where he or she wants to go. Often, we can only *begin* to understand how different a kid's worldview is from our own. For example, there is no way for me to ever fully appreciate the covert and overt racism that young African-American males in American society face every day. In Leon Bing's 1991 book *Do or Die*, a powerful book about Los

Angeles gangs, she interviews A. C. Jones, an African-American correction officer at Camp Kilpatrick. He offered the following assessment:

> It goes further than those kids simply being perceived as American kids. These are African-American kids and they're dealing with the added aspect of disenfranchisement that goes along with that. These kids are black in America. Every time a 17-year-old black male walks into a mall, a liquor store, or a market, every time he buys a ticket to an Eddie Murphy movie, he knows that every person who sees him is viewing him as a menace. . . . I'll tell you something—I grew up here, I was a Marine, I have an education and a nice family, I'm a peace officer . . . but every time I walk through the parking lot of a shopping center I see older white women clutch their purses closer to their sides. I hear a clicking of a car door lock as I move past. And that's a haunting thing. Now, you start feeling that when you're nine, ten years old, then by the time you're 14 or 15, you've got to figure that you're unwanted. That nobody likes you. Even though you may be hearing in history class that everybody loves you, that you can be all you can be. . . . Well, it sounds pretty but it's just not true. (p. 11)

It is imperative that we don't project our own experiences and opportunities onto the kids we work with. Their challenges, struggles, and support systems are different from our own. Again, empathic understanding is a good starting point. For example, we need to understand how inner city life affects young African-Americans' growth and development. Although there are certainly inherent benefits in living in the inner city, these teens also confront demands and expectations as well as risks and temptations that are more numerous and complex than their middle class, suburban counterparts. Research has consistently demonstrated a connection between multiple, intense stressors and an individual's chances of displaying maladaptive behaviors (Compas, 1987; Johnson, 1986; Trent & Artiles, 1995). Most kids can be all they can be; however, if you add ten extra hurdles along the way, it makes sense that more kids will be unable to finish the race. We must not forget that the efforts required to reach the finish line may be quite different.

We must also find ways to empathize with the oppression without expecting less from the oppressed. Back to the importance of balance. We can and should do it all. We can empathize with oppression, fight to change oppressive systems and people, and continue to have high expectations for youngsters who have been oppressed. It does not need to be an either–or proposition. There is a difference between explanations and excuses—between having feelings and being had by our feelings. We need to ask ourselves, "How will I communicate that the past does not equal the future without discounting or disrespecting current or past struggles?"

Many children and adolescents have experienced failure so often, they learn to expect it. Learned helplessness and persistent feelings of powerlessness become breeding grounds for low self-esteem in many troubled youth. Believing they do not deserve better, they find themselves stuck in the mud, reluctant to even hope for positive change, much less attempt it. We want to be careful not to create a negative, self-fulfilling prophecy for at-risk youth, excusing them from acting responsibly and teaching them they will not succeed. As helping professionals, we need to promote culturally sensitive interventions and programs that enhance self-confidence, foster resiliency, and lessen helper dependency (Rak & Patterson, 1996).

As a beginning counselor, I viewed myself as very much an action-oriented, problem-solver. Looking back, I can think of many times in which I was unwittingly paternalistic, particularly with the at-risk students who came to see me often and I knew well. While I felt this action-oriented style appealed to these students, I sometimes failed to recognize the difference between helping and directing. I fought too many battles for students rather than teaching them effective ways to fight these battles for themselves. While the counselor's goal should be to make himself unnecessary, I was making myself a crucial cog in future problem-solving. Although the short term problem was often solved and my ego was often stroked, my enabling behavior may have contributed to more irresponsible behavior and feelings of learned helplessness. The following case illustrates how difficult it is sometimes to know where to draw the line.

Tracy, a White 17-year-old senior with above-average grades, needed only a few credits to graduate, but she quit coming to school in March after a painful break up with her boyfriend, with whom she had shared an apartment. She was now temporarily living rent-free with a friend. Her parents had moved to another state and could not be reached. After nearly a month of absences, myself, a teacher, and several friends were able to convince her to return to school and make the necessary strides to graduate. She dropped the courses that were not required and her schedule was rearranged so that she only had to come in the mornings for the last two months. She refused to see a therapist, but periodically met with me to talk about finishing school and coping with the recent break up. For the first several weeks, Tracy attended every day and made up much of the work she had missed. During the rest of the year, she missed one or two days each week but convinced most of her teachers (often with my help) to allow her to make up the work. Several times during the last month of school, I would call her at home and convince her to return. Tracy barely graduated that Spring (perhaps only with the help of sensitive teachers using "new math"), went on to cosmetology school a year later, and last I heard, was a successful hairdresser. At the time, I was very proud of how I helped Tracy. Since that time, I have vacillated.

Beauchamp and Childress (1983) defined paternalism as the "claim that beneficence should take precedence over autonomy" (p. 169). These authors argued that if one is incapable of exercising one's autonomy, paternalism may be justified in order to help or prevent the person from harming him- or herself. In cases of suicide or other instances where there is a clear and present danger, the answer seems clear. However, with adolescents such as Tracy, I'm not sure. Considering the multiple stressors and her maturity level, was Tracy incapable? Was keeping her from dropping out of school preventing her from harming herself? Would she have learned more if we had held firmer on our expectations? Did we send the wrong messages? Does the end justify the means? Was I overly paternalistic or taking the necessary steps to help a student in need? More than ten years later, the answers are still not clear to me.

I can think of several instances where I look back and know that my paternalistic behavior was not helpful. I was not expecting enough from the students I was helping. Over the years, I gained a greater understanding of the importance of balancing support and challenge, allowing natural and logical consequences, and facilitating a process where the student could make his or her own choices. I do not have any magical formula to make this distinction any less blurred. However, some questions we may want to consider include:

1. Have I communicated an empathic understanding of this youth's or family's situation?

2. Am I recognizing and utilizing the strengths of the youth, family, or community?

3. How will I communicate that the past does not equal the future without discounting or disrespecting current or past struggles?

4. Is my way of helping making the youth or the family more or less dependent on me? Do I see this changing in the foreseeable future?

Lessons Learned: Framing Problems and Solutions in More Creative, Constructive, and Caring Ways

☐ Lesson 5.1: All Effective Counselors Appreciate the Power of Reframing

> What distinguishes a master therapist from a journeyman is the former's greater skill at reframing things.
>
> —P. Barker (1994, pp. 220–221)

During my first job as a residential counselor, the school custodian introduced me to the power of reframing. I was walking down the hall during classes and saw Joe surveying a fresh pile of papers thrown on the floor.

I remarked, "As soon as you finish cleaning, they just throw more down. They should be more respectful."

Joe smiled, picked up a piece of paper, and responded, "I don't see it as disrespect. I see it as job security." Joe was a very good-natured man.

Many people look at aggressive youth and assume they are void of conscience, character-disordered, or simply "bad apples" that need to be discarded. While those views may be understandable at times, they seldom foster positive change. Counselors who are gifted at connecting and intervening with challenging youth possess both the creativity and compassion to see these youth and their struggles differently than most adults. Borrowing a phrase frequently heard in business seminars, they exercise out of the box thinking. They do not assume that the popular way of viewing problems is the only way. The following are two examples of how Tobin (1991) chose to view common themes in uncommon ways:

> There is something to be admired about children who can stand up to you and tell you what they think. It is a raw courage that, when channeled and nurtured, will serve them well. They will do all right in life, eventually. I don't worry about them. (p. 11)

> Troubled kids are more sensitive than other kids, although it may not seem that way. Most truly intuitive adults have this sensitivity. Troubled children sense and feel beyond their ability to understand—though someday they will; someday this sensitivity will serve them well. (p. 15)

Is Tobin's perspective the correct perspective? Who knows? Reality is much more subjective than we like to believe. Watzlawick (1976) stressed that "the most dangerous delusion of all is that there is only one reality" (p. xi). There is no one way to view problems; rather, our understanding depends on our particular point of view (Barker, 1994). Similarly, there is no one path toward problem resolution. This may explain why a number of diverse theoretical models have proven to be effective with this population. Constructionists suggest that reality is what we make it. I am in favor of constructing a reality that offers the most promise for helping youth, their families, and the professionals who work with them view the problem and solution(s) in a more constructive, optimistic light.

Reframing is the name often given to this process of changing the meaning of something (Barker, 1994). Reframing or positive interpretation techniques have proven effective for dealing with a wide range of adolescent behavioral and emotional problems (Alexander, Waldron, Barton, & Mas, 1989; Furman & Ahola, 1992; Minuchin, Rosman, & Baker, 1978; Sommers-Flanagan & Sommers-Flanagan, 1997).

Since families are often locked into a problem simply because they see the problem only from one rigid perspective (Brown & Christensen, 1986), family therapists use reframing techniques to:

1. Diffuse or deflect the open conflict that tends to characterize these families and offer hope for a resolution.
2. Change the family's perspective by introducing positive or nonblaming themes to describe problem behaviors or potential solutions.
3. Avoid escalating the cycle of pessimism and blame that can be exacerbated if the therapist encourages family members to dwell on the negative perceptions of the youth's behavior or motivation.

While reframing is a tool often attributed to strategic family therapists, several authors have asserted that the common denominator of all successful therapeutic approaches is the process of reframing (Barker, 1994; Nichols & Schwartz, 1991). Minuchin and Nichols (1993) observed that "in every case, success comes with a change in perception" (p. 113). This is true for all professionals who work with challenging youth.

Teachers, group home workers, and other front-line professionals may not be trained or expected to offer significant reframes for families; however, they can utilize a variety of reframing techniques to alter their own perceptions, reduce their defenses, and better connect with troubled youth. Certainly, professionals like Tobin are going to interact differently with these youngsters than someone with a more pessimistic, adversarial perspective. I agree with Tobin (1991) that most all misbehavior can be imagined to have a positive function. No child has a need to create a life filled with turmoil; they are always trying to accomplish something else. Through positive connotation and reframing, professionals can allow optimistic descriptions to guide their responses.

The following are just a few alternative labels that can be subscribed to challenging youth:

Common Frame	Reframe
1. Attention seeking	1. Attention/Encouragement needing
2. Hostile	2. Scared
3. Antisocial	3. Lonely
4. Demanding	4. Needing
5. Stubborn	5. Determined
6. Lying	6. Self-preservation
7. Impulsive	7. Creative
8. Resisting	8. Protecting
9. Abnormal	9. Unique
10. Antagonistic	10. Hurt

For each of these common frames, think about the picture that comes to mind. Do you see a different kid when the behavior is reframed? There are a number of other ways we could reframe these pictures. In some ways, each lesson in this book involves reframing.

Reality therapists try to change the youth or family's frame by facilitating a process in which the youth or family members take more responsibility for their emotional "re"sponses and stop viewing them as some uncontrollable, stimulus-response reactions (Wubbolding, 1988). Reaction is reframed as action. When a youth says, "He *makes* me mad," a reality therapist might offer any of the following:

1. "Wow. Do you always give him that much power over you?"
2. "What are you *choosing* to do?"
3. "So whenever he does that, you choose to get mad. What different choice will you make next time?"
4. "When you choose to get mad, does that help you get what you want?"

Solution-focused therapists are always searching for different, more positive explanations that will make solutions seem more palatable for all parties involved. Furman and Ahola (1992) shared the case of the Teenage Social Worker:

Nina, a 16-year-old girl began dating Rick, an 18-year-old boy with a history of behavior problems. When Nina's mother, Silja began to put boundaries upon the relationship, Nina ran away and moved in with Rick. After traditional efforts (i.e., threatening, cajoling) to bring Nina back home seemed to make matters worse, Silja consulted Furman and Ahola. The therapists helped Silja view her daughter's behavior in a different light:

"Tell me, does your daughter have a big heart? Does she care for others and like to help people with their problems?"

"Yes, she's always been that way. She is a very caring girl, that's why I can't understand her behaving this way."

"I understand that Rick has had a number of problems?"

"Yes, that's right. His parents even kicked him out some time ago."

"You know, I've noticed that sometimes girls of a certain age find someone who has problems and devote themselves completely to that person. Could it be that this is what has happened with Nina? Has she, perhaps, taken Rick under her wing? Nina, who seems to be well liked by Rick's parents, has actually succeeded in helping Rick by improving the relationship with his parents, hasn't she?"

"That's true. Also, according to his parents, both Nina and Rick are presently attending school. So maybe she is actually taking care of him."

"Perhaps when teenagers take the role of social workers they commit themselves so profoundly that they put the mission before their family. And your daughter probably knows that guys come and go but mothers stay forever. (Furman & Ahola, 1992, pp. 75–76)

Furman and Aloha recommended that Silja discuss the situation with Nina from this new perspective. Silja told Nina that up until now she had not appreciated how much it meant for Nina to help Rick. That conversation was the beginning of a reconciliation between mother and daughter. Although Nina continued to date Rick, she moved back home, respected the boundaries, and there were no more serious incidents.

These are only a few examples of how creative, constructive, and caring reframes can unlock doors. Remaining lessons in this chapter will offer a variety of new frames for old pictures. However, before reframing a youth's behaviors, it is important to keep the following guidelines in mind:

1. First, meet youth and families where they are. Eminent family therapists Jay Haley (1963) and Salvador Minuchin (1974) stressed that the first task is to understand the problem from the family's perspective(s). Once the family feels their perspectives have been understood and validated, the counselor can direct them to more constructive ways of viewing the problem.

2. Reframing is not traditional reverse psychology. You must be able to construct a frame both you and the family can perceive as plausible. While creativity is often rewarded, Cade and O'Hanlon (1993) emphasized that the frame be sufficiently congruent with the youth and family's experiences.

3. Viewing youth and their problems in a more positive light should not be mistaken as a naive, Pollyanna view of human nature. As Carl Rogers (1961) observed:

I am quite aware that out of defensiveness and inner fear individuals can and do behave in ways which are incredibly cruel, horribly destructive, immature, regressive, anti-social, and hurtful. Yet one of the most refreshing and invigorating parts of my experience is to work with such individuals and to discover the strongly positive directional tendencies which exist in them, as in all of us, at our deepest levels. (p. 27)

4. As always, if what we are doing or the frame we are suggesting is not working, we need to regroup, and try something different.

While this lesson focused on the importance of new ways of thinking, the next lesson emphasizes new ways of acting.

☐ Lesson 5.2: If at First You Don't Succeed, Try Again. If That Doesn't Work, Try Something Else

Only the supremely wise and the ignorant do not alter.

—Confucius

If you always do what you've always done, you will only get what you've always got.

—Unknown

During family counseling sessions, I sometimes interrupt a parent's lecturing or blaming monologue and ask, "When do you think she tuned you out?" Usually, on some level, they are aware the child is no longer paying attention; nevertheless, they frequently insist on finishing. I remember catching myself in similar predicaments when my son Carter was only 2 years old. I realized mid-lecture that even if he was listening (which he wasn't), he wouldn't understand. Yet, on several occasions, I found myself unwilling or unable to turn off the automatic pilot. Are we suffering from some gross cognitive deficiency? I don't think so. I think it is human nature to continue to do more of the same despite evidence that our behaviors are not productive—particularly with challenging youth. Why? I propose six interrelated hypotheses to explain this common cycle of futility:

Hypothesis 1. Over time, we learn and develop habitual patterns of perceiving and responding and neglect to make a connection between what we are doing and what we want. For example, we have learned to talk more slowly and loudly to people who do not speak English. Has this ever worked? Yet, people do it everyday.

Hypothesis 2. Too often, we focus our attention and emotional resources on defending the way things are rather than considering how things could be. Along the same lines, it is difficult to simultaneously assess blame and explore solutions. Opting for the former tends to blind parents and professionals to their role in the relationship. We tend to construct realities to support our preconceptions. Often, these perceptions lead to more of the same behaviors.

Hypothesis 3. We do not recognize when consistency is redundant. Most of the time, consistency is a desirable attribute for parents and professionals. Certainly, youth need clear expectations; they need to know which behaviors are acceptable and which are unacceptable. However, when what we are doing is not working, creativity is a more valuable commodity than consistency. Unfortunately, persons in the midst of conflict are not always objective.

Hypothesis 4. Our ineffectual efforts are supported by conventional wisdom and tradition. Since we were children, we have all heard the adage, "If at first you don't succeed try, try again." Persistence does not imply rigidity. I prefer the advice of the developers of brief problem-focused therapy, "If at first you don't succeed, you might try a second time—but if you don't succeed then, try something *different*" (Fisch, Weakland, & Segal, 1982, p. 18).

Hypothesis 5. We tend to evaluate interventions in terms of success and failure. If we view the responses of youth and families as merely helpful feedback, we are more likely to recognize when our behavior is not working and make the necessary adjustments (Bandler & Grinder, 1979; Walter & Peller, 1992).

Hypothesis 6. We want to help and assume that what we are doing is the only logical course of action. We do not see alternatives and we would rather repeat ineffective behaviors than do nothing. At least then, we can feel like we tried.

Brief problem-focused therapy developed around the notion that most problems are exacerbated or maintained by attempted solutions (Fisch, Weakland, & Segal, 1982; Weakland, Fisch, Watzlawick, & Bodin, 1974). These authors proposed that most problems stem from ordinary difficulties of life that are first mishandled and then made worse by more of the same solutions. The cycle escalates into a problem whose eventual size and nature may have little apparent similarity to the original difficulty. The following case example illustrates how a parent can easily become entrenched in behavior that is counterproductive.

Karen and Miles were distressed about their 12-year-old son Brock's continual acting-out behavior at home. Miles was a salesman who was away from home for long stretches. Karen, Brock's mother, had been the primary caretaker for the past six years. The behavior that was most distressing was Brock's reaction when given a directive. Specifically, Brock stomped, yelled, and gave dirty looks when given a directive by Karen. These incidents often followed suggestions or corrections regarding his homework. It should be noted that Brock almost always complied with the directive. In addition, his responses to his father were much more appropriate.

Karen, the most affected by the problem, appeared to be most concerned about it, as she made the most attempts to resolve it. She also initiated the discussions prompting the referral by the school counselor. Karen reported to me that she had repeatedly sought help from teachers and counselors but "nothing has worked," she was at her "wit's end," and was willing to "try anything."

Karen described a repetitive problem-maintaining cycle: Brock would misbehave or be given a directive by Karen, Brock would respond with some version of a temper tantrum, Karen would get angrier and demand compliance even more loudly, Brock would accelerate the tantrum behaviors, and so on. Although Karen reported that she had "tried everything," most of her responses had a central theme—trying to reach accord through opposition: I demand that you obey me and that you do so without snide remarks, dirty looks, or temper tantrums. I am not only demanding compliance but also respect, care, and appreciation that is due to me. If you fail to respond as I demand, I will get louder, angrier, and increase your punishment. If what I am doing is not working, I need to do more of the same.

Karen had been to parenting classes and prior counseling in the past. In addition, she had read numerous books to help her improve her parenting skills. She really wanted to improve her relationship with Brock and was doing her very best. However, as mentioned before, attempted solutions had been a variation of the same theme. Consequently, knowing what to avoid with this family was more important than knowing what to attempt. For instance, I would certainly not want to encourage or teach Karen how to become stronger in her efforts to demand compliance. It seemed imperative that to initiate positive change, I interrupt this cycle where Karen's attempted solutions (although well intended) were actually helping to maintain the behavior.

There are a lot of different routes a counselor could take here. Most importantly, I wanted the intervention to be a 180-degree shift from what had been tried before and found unsuccessful. I thought about intervening in a way that would shift more of the disciplinary responsibility to Miles; however, his frequent travel made that idea logistically suspect. I did not feel it would be sufficient for Karen to simply stop responding or quit giving directives. It appeared that the most complete shift from previous attempted solutions was to encourage Karen to take a one-down position. This is a variation of a technique sometimes used by problem-focused brief therapists to help parents regain control by ironically taking a position of weakness (Fisch, Weakland, & Segal, 1982). Knowing this would be difficult for Karen to accomplish, I needed to be careful to frame the suggestion in a way that validated her concerns so she did not feel she was losing further control. I told Karen:

I've given your predicament a lot of thought. Presently, Brock is in the powerful position. He knows what buttons to push and usually gets the reaction he wants—he makes you angry. Although what you are doing makes a lot of sense to me and would work with most kids, Brock has figured it out and it has become predictable. We need to think of something that puts you back in charge. To do that, you will need to become unpredictable. This is going to be difficult. I would not ask you to attempt it except you have done so much for Brock and deserve to be treated with respect. Since many of your arguments stem from your generous efforts to help Brock with his homework, I want you to use the excuse that you are not feeling well. This will be true because you've said that you start to feel sick when you help with homework because you know an argument is coming. Also, when you need to give Brock a time out or a directive which may lead to a conflict, I want you to develop a mild version of laryngitis to help keep from yelling. You won't need to yell because he is going to do what you tell him to do. Tell Brock in a raspy voice, "I'm sorry I have to ask you to _____ , because I know you are going to need to give me a dirty look or throw a tantrum. Since I'm not feeling well, I would appreciate it if you could cheer me up by giving me a really funny look or doing one of those really silly tantrums. Brock, I need you to _____ ." This will work best if you use a matter-of-fact tone, and not sarcasm. Okay?

We discussed this plan further and Karen agreed to try this strategy. Her relationship with Brock improved considerably. They continued to have occasional arguments, but the intensity and frequency lessened and they began to have more fun together. In future counseling, we agreed on two rules, 1) Continue to do what was working, and 2) When something does not work, try it again. If it still doesn't work, try something else.

Some may criticize this strategy for its paradoxical nature. A paradoxical intervention is one that, if followed, will accomplish the opposite of what it is seemingly intended to accomplish. During a 1975 interview, Richard Fisch defended the need to occasionally use paradoxical techniques:

> I don't see it as going around the back door. I think a more accurate way to look at it is, if I have to make choices of what to suggest, I will stay away from those efforts, solutions, positions, that the people have already taken that are not working. That I flag as poison. I don't know whatever else I will do, but I will not do that even though that might be regarded as direct, obvious, up front or anything else. I am not going to add to the agony that has already, in my view, made or escalated the problem. (Fisch, 1975, p. 25)

I agree with Fisch. It is important to note that thinking in terms of paradox is neither necessary nor helpful (Segal, 1991). The essence is knowing what to avoid—more of the same. Fisch, Weakland, and Segal (1982) argued that the term paradox is so overused it is "attributed loosely and casually to any intervention which strikes traditional therapists as novel, ironic, or contrary to 'common sense'" (p. 127). Successful counselors are pragmatists and ascribe no virtue to complexity or novelty for its own sake. I suggested what I did with Karen because traditional strategies had not been successful. If this new suggestion had not fit for Karen or not worked with Brock, we would have needed to come up with something different.

Reality therapy and solution-focused therapy are two other approaches that emphasize reading our audience and adjusting accordingly.

A common question asked by reality therapists is "Is what you are doing helping you get what you want?" (Wubbolding, 1988). Reality therapists recognize that this is also a question they need to regularly ask themselves. Subsequently, successful reality therapists also share the philosophy that a youth or family's ability and willingness to follow through with a behavior plan is merely helpful feedback for framing future plans or interventions.

deShazer (1985) and his colleagues have developed the Do Something Different formula task for families mired in repetitive responses that perpetuate the problem. The specific directive is adapted slightly to fit each specific case. deShazer offered the following message to the parents of a teenage girl:

> Between now and next time we meet, we would like each of you once to do something different when you catch Mary watching TV instead of doing what she needs to be doing, no matter how strange or weird or off-the-wall what you do might seem. The only important thing is that whatever you decide to do, you need to do something different. (deShazer, 1985, p. 123)

At first glance, this may seem illogical; although, how logical is it to continue to attempt something that is not working? Walter and Peller (1992) asserted that if we have done everything we can reasonably think of and it hasn't worked, the only things left to do seem to be the unreasonable or illogical.

The average troubled youth in counseling has gone through two or more past treatment experiences which usually took the form of more of the same approaches (Selekman, 1993; Watzalwick, Weakland, & Fisch, 1974). Creativity is especially important with these youth. "It's an understatement to say that therapy with children and adolescents often requires a departure from traditional talk therapy or contemporary behavior modification" (Sommers-Flanagan & Sommers-Flanagan, 1997, p. 5). It is important to remember that people have tried ordinary interventions with these kids for years and have been unsuccessful (Tobin, 1991).

These are important lessons for all of us who work with this population, not just for therapists. Anyone who has worked extensively as a teacher, counselor, or group home worker with challenging youth has fallen in the "more of the same" trap from time to time. We must continually assess our strategies and the assumptions that underlie these strategies. Tobin (1991) suggested that if our behaviors are not helping, we should write a new assumption and new interventions will come to mind naturally. As the next lesson demonstrates, a lack of creativity and flexibility on our part can propagate a belief system that is seldom helpful with this population.

☐ Lesson 5.3: Resist Using "Resistant" and Other Counterproductive Terms

Over 20 years ago, Bandler and Grinder (1979) offered a compelling argument that inflexibility on the part of mental health professionals was often mistaken as resistance on the part of clients:

> One of the operating procedures of most disciplines that allows a field to grow and to continue to develop at a rapid rate is a rule that if what you do doesn't work, do something else. If you are an engineer and you get the rocket all set up, and you push the button and it doesn't lift up, you alter your behavior to find out what you need to do to make certain changes to overcome gravity. However, in the field of psychotherapy, if you encounter a situation where the rocket doesn't go off, it has a special name; it's called having a "resistant client." You take the fact that what you do doesn't work and you blame the client. That relieves you of the responsibility of having to change your behavior. Or if you are slightly more humanistic about it, you "share in the guilt of the failure" or say he "wasn't ready." (p. 13)

Corey (1996) defined resistance as any "idea, attitude, feeling, or action (conscious or unconscious) that fosters the status quo and gets in the way of change" (p. 119). Armed with such broad definitions, many counselors do not have to look far to find resistance, particularly with this population. There are a number of behaviors we could characterize as resistant (i.e., when a parent or youth neglects to do what we suggest or direct, when they appear angry or indifferent through the entire session). Theoretically, this insight leads us to focus our energy on helping them uncover and work through the reasons for this resistance and begin to make positive changes. Sometimes this happens.

I have no doubt that psychoanalysts and other therapists could make some convincing theoretical claims that what we are seeing actually is a conscious or unconscious resistance to change. But validity is in the eyes of the theoretical beholder, whereas usefulness is in the eyes of the results. Hardy (1996) asserted that the term resistance carries powerful connotations that tend to prematurely shut down the helping process. A number of practitioner authors have reported more success with this population when they began to alter their views on resistance (deShazer, 1984; Newman, 1994; Selekman, 1993; Walter & Peller, 1992). My experience mirrors these perceptions. Over the years, I have heard youth and families framed as resistant many times, and it is hard to remember when this perception ever engendered progress in the form of more creative responses, more hope, improved relationships, or less resistance.

A variety of alternative frames have been presented that are more likely to help all human service professionals build and maintain therapeutic relationships with challenging youth and their families:

1. Resistance is not a very useful term to describe individuals; it speaks more to the relationship between helpers and helpees (deShazer, 1984; Hardy, 1996; Walter & Peller, 1992).

2. Clients really do want to change. Sometimes, however, our ideas about change do not fit for them. Their response is trying to communicate this mismatch and send a message regarding how we can be more helpful (Bandler & Grinder, 1979; deShazer, 1984, 1985).

3. Out of all the ways you have attempted to make contact and establish rapport, you have not found one that works yet. What you are seeing and hearing is merely feedback, not resistance. Utilize this feedback to increase your flexibility (Bandler & Grinder, 1979).

4. "We tend to view misbehavior as resistance because we understand where we want children to go. Children view misbehavior as protection because they know where they've been" (Tobin, 1991, p. 96).

5. What we see as resistant behavior in adolescents, particularly girls, may actually be a sign of strength and courage. In fact, the psychological health of teenage girls often depends on their willingness to resist or challenge cultural pressures to bear false witness to themselves (Gilligan, Rogers, & Tolman, 1991). These authors emphasize the need to respect and encourage healthy resistance.

Viewing a youth or family's responses as resistant tends to foster adversarial or overly hierarchal relationships. These alternative frames are more likely to lead to positive behavioral changes (both yours and theirs).

The next lesson identifies how reframing our assumptions can serve to alter our responses to aggressive behavior and subsequently deescalate the cycle of conflict.

☐ Lesson 5.4: Look Beyond the Behavior to Avoid Escalating the Cycle of Aggression

Look beyond the behavior. Practice decoding misbehavior into poor self-concepts, multiple stressors, overwhelming feelings, and unfulfilled needs. The reasons these children misbehave are seldom obvious. Again, no person has a need to create a life filled with conflict. They are always trying to accomplish something else, albeit unsuccessfully (Tobin, 1991).

Drawing from the work of Fritz Redl, Long (1991) developed the Conflict Cycle Paradigm to demonstrate how interactions between adults and challenging youth often follow a circular pattern in which the attitudes, feelings, and behaviors of adults are influenced by and in turn influence the attitudes, feelings, and behaviors of challenging students. Although each youth is unique, there is often a predictable pattern that leads to aggressive, acting-out behavior. Long (1991) asserted that challenging youth often share the following characteristics and behaviors:

1. poor self-concepts
2. multiple, intense stressors
3. "acting-out" as a way to deflect emotional pain

Poor Self-Concepts

Long (1996) remarked that "just as a primitive tribe can explain a tidal wave or an exploding volcano as something the tribe had done to offend the gods, troubled youth need to explain why they were abused, neglected, given away, or rejected" (p. 247). As humans, we all try to make meaning from our experiences. For too many kids, efforts to make sense of negative life experiences have resulted in self-fulfilling prophecies and extremely poor self-concepts (i.e., "I've been dealt a bad hand in life because I'm bad." "I don't deserve any better." "I'm not worthy of love."). Long (1991) observed that these seemingly irrational beliefs make perfect sense to the youth and provide them with a sense of security and control by bringing order to an unstable and chaotic world. They anticipate and expect the worst and then blame themselves. While their words and actions some-times suggest that they blame everyone but themselves for their misfor-tune, their internal critic tends to point the finger squarely at themselves. Unfortunately, they see this as just the way things are and thus fail to take responsibility for their behavior or see a reason to change. Long (1991) emphasized that a youth's self-concept is more important in determining a youth's behavior than any score on an objective test.

Multiple, Intense Stressors

The number and intensity of stressors also play a role in aggressive, acting-out behavior. Cross-sectional studies have shown a correlation between stressful events and emotional and behavioral problems in adolescents (Compas, 1987; Johnson, 1986). Stress is defined as "a state in which a strong demand is made on the nervous system" (*New Webster's Dictionary*, 1992, p. 980). Challenging youth are faced with the daunting task of jug-gling multiple, intense demands on their nervous system while struggling to make sense of their worlds.

While coordinating a treatment foster care program, I marveled at the resiliency of the kids. The typical child struggled daily to manage a plethora of intense stressors (i.e., separated from family, friends, school, and community; expected to adjust to new family, friends, school, com-munity, and various social service professionals; conflicted over physical, emotional, or sexual abuse). These ongoing stressors are magnified by the stressors all youth encounter on a daily basis (i.e., a poor grade on a test, peer pressure, accidents, lack of sleep, and hunger). Even self-confident, grounded adults who know they "choose their own weather" occasionally allow their mood and behavior to succumb to life events. For example, a teacher who was up all night with her child, is late for work due to traffic, and spilled coffee on her new dress may respond differently to the same situation if she had not experienced these stressors. Imagine how difficult it must be for challenging youth who regularly experience multiple, in-tense stressors.

Acting Out as a Way to Deflect Emotional Pain

The combination of poor self-concepts, multiple stressors, and low frustra-tion tolerance often results in conflicting feelings of loneliness, self-loath-ing, anger, and hurt. Many troubled youth also have learned that some feelings are unacceptable, and displacement and projection become regular defense mechanisms. In other words, the stressors and feelings become so overwhelming, they fail to distinguish feelings from behavior, and attempt to protect themselves by acting their feelings out in aggressive ways. These youth "have so few defenses, but they certainly perform wonders with those they have" (Minuchin & Nichols, 1993, p. 123).

Long (1991) stressed the importance of teaching challenging youth to distinguish between healthy feelings and unhealthy behavior. For example, it is healthy to feel anger when you believe you have been wronged, but it is unhealthy to act out your anger in aggressive ways. It is healthy to feel sad when you have been separated from your family, but is unhealthy to withdraw from all relationships. It is healthy to feel guilty when you hurt someone, but is not healthy to act out to increase your punishment. A variety of feelings are both normal and healthy. Too often, challenging youth become flooded by their feelings and subsequently lose control.

As adults, if we are not careful, our natural response often wins out over our professional response. In fact, youth experiencing stress can generate their feelings and behaviors in others. For example, aggressive behavior from youth often elicits hostile and counterproductive behavior from adults, and hyperactive behavior often yields impulsive, irrational adult responses (Long, 1991). This is human nature. Typically, when someone yells at us (whether we are stuck in traffic or intervening with a tough kid), few of us possess the inner peace to respond calmly without a conscious effort. Nevertheless, it is important that we recognize the potential impact of our reactions. Professionals who accept primary responsibility for acting in a calm, rational manner increase the probability of avoiding no-win power struggles and deescalating the cycle of aggression. I do not want to imply that adults accept total, or even most of the responsibility for a youth's escalating behavior. Sometimes, we can do and say all the right things and the youth, for whatever reason, is going to continue to spiral out of control. Nor am I implying that we disregard the behavior. Certainly, the behavior needs to be addressed to keep the youth's behavior from escalating further and causing the youth to hurt themselves, others, or property. Furthermore, kids need to learn their behavior leads to natural and logical consequences. So we cannot ignore the behavior.

It is easier said than done, but if we can see the acting-out as more than meanspirited or irrational behavior, we can help the youth in six distinct ways:

1. We communicate to them that we are sensitive to their internal struggles and open to talking about what is troubling them (Fagan, 1996).
2. We can focus attention on improving their self-concepts by challenging some of the understandable, but irrational meanings they've given

to their experiences. Simon (1988) identified an individual's belief that he or she does not deserve better as the primary roadblock to change. An improved self-concept may lead to greater internal motivation to change and positive self-fulfilling prophecies.

3. We can work with youth, family, and other professionals to eliminate, reduce, or reframe some of the stressors in their lives.

4. We can teach youth ways to recognize emotional triggers and subsequently prevent some of the acting out behaviors.

5. We can increase our likelihood of responding in a rational, empathic manner which deescalates rather than escalates the cycle of aggression if we see the kid as more than his or her misbehavior.

6. We can also model more appropriate ways to respond to stress by responding in a professional manner (Long, 1991).

In essence, we want to choose hurt over hate. This is especially important with youth who tend to react aggressively and those who are so easy to write off or label as impossible.

Tobin (1991), a master at reframing troubled youth's behavior, offered the following observation:

> He's violent you say. Perhaps. But imagine what it takes for a child to strike an adult—his only source of survival. Imagine the depth of terror behind this bravado—like a parachutist slashing at the very ropes that protect him. Imagine the depth of hurt. (p. 6)

Again, look beyond the behavior. Put yourself in the youth's shoes. Imagine the pain and confusion—the barrage of emotions that are battling inside. We would also do well to heed the advice of Rabbi Harold Kushner (1996), "Never attribute to malice what can be explained by human frailty or imperfection" (p. 109). Often, the aggressive behavior is masking deep, emotional pain.

☐ Lesson 5.5: Pay Attention to What You Pay Attention to

Try the following experiment on some of your friends: Ask them to close their eyes. Tell them that when they open their eyes, they will have 15 seconds to try to memorize everything in the room that is brown. After 15 seconds, have them close their eyes again. Now, ask them to tell you everything around them that is green. They will probably have great difficulty remembering many green items.

Lessons learned long ago from Pavlov's dog and Skinner's box about the potency of positive reinforcement sometimes get lost in the shuffle with challenging youth. We become so focused on what is brown and drab, we neglect what is green and alive. We become so focused on problem behaviors and perceived weaknesses, we neglect to recognize and build on strengths. During my first year as a residential counselor, I learned the importance of paying attention to what I pay attention to.

I found myself becoming more and more angered and frustrated by a kid named Scott. Nothing he did was right. My supervisor asked me to try the Penny Transfer Technique. It was really quite simple—the most memorable lessons often are. He asked me to start the day by putting five pennies in my left pocket. I was instructed to move a penny to my right pocket every time I commented on something Scott did right. I was also instructed to avoid phony or superficial affirmations (i.e., I like your clothes). My goal was to move all the pennies to the right pocket by the end of the day. I did this for one week. Although it felt somewhat contrived, two things began to happen. First, my relationship with Scott improved dramatically. Second, I began to automatically notice things Scott did right. Since that time, I have successfully used the Penny Transfer Technique to shift my focus and enhance my relationships with challenging youth.

In my Cross Cultural Counseling classes, the students are required to complete two Interaction Plans in which they conduct personal interviews, attend community meetings, attend social or political functions, and so forth with persons who are culturally different from themselves. One semester, several students chose to interview Reverend Damon Lynch III, a prominent African-American community leader in a neighborhood in Cincinnati called Over the Rhine. During their interview, the students learned that this valuable lesson should also be applied to communities as well as individuals. What follows are excerpts from one of those students' papers eloquently processing her experience.

> We discussed many times what we were going to ask Reverend Lynch. We wrote out questions we had thought of and felt we were pretty prepared for our interview. We each introduced ourselves and discussed our Multicultural Counseling class and the nature of our assignment. . . . We indicated that we hoped he would be able to give us a better understanding of the basic needs and concerns of this community. . . .
>
> Reverend Lynch paused reflectively then slowly began to explain that he did not want to talk about needs and concerns of the community; neither did he think it was a good place for us to start. He said he did not want to "label the community as deficient, and that's what has happened too long in communities like this. We would be labeling if we started there."

He explained that "this is a rich community. It is rich with resources, assets, people with gifts, institutions, and businesses. As a matter of fact, this is one of the richest communities in Cincinnati. There is no other community in the city that holds the promise that this community holds. When we talk about our children, we talk about the resource and the assets that they are, and the gifts they have. We need to spend some time on the focus that if the community is going to change, it is going to start with the strengths that we have."

He used the analogy of the glass that is half filled with water. "Is it half full or half empty?" he asked. In our attempt to show our optimism we answered that the glass was half full. He replied, "No actually, it is both, but, if you are going to rebuild the community with this cup, it is obvious that you need to start with what is half full. Traditionally, in communities like this, people start with the part that is half empty. I am just saying this to caution you two that when you go somewhere else to speak, instead of asking about their deficiencies, it would be better to ask about their strengths."

Needless to say, I felt I had just been to church, and learned a good lesson. I then felt all of the questions we had prepared were totally useless and inappropriate. We had a few minutes of silence. Then we rephrased our questions. "Reverend Lynch, could you please tell us about the strengths of the community?" [Reverend Lynch talked at length about specific strengths of the community.]

. . . . I started this experience thinking that I was empathic enough to the needs of the Over the Rhine community. I ended it with the realization that I have a lot to learn. I started the interview with the need to have someone confirm my concerns and beliefs about the community. Instead I was left exposed and ashamed by how stereotypical I was. I was embarrassed by my inability to perceive the positive aspects of the community. It is as if those of us who are the privileged majority cannot perceive the possibility of positive life outside our mode. We have a lot to learn.

This student should be commended for her willingness to entertain new ways of being and seeing. She should also be applauded for learning from her experiences. Too often, we opt for defending our own perceptions of the world at the expense of personal and professional growth. Reverend Lynch identified a common trap that many of us fall into, particularly when working with racial minority groups: rushing in and focusing on perceived individual, family, or community weaknesses rather than recognizing and building on existing strengths and potential. This is a difficult paradigm shift to make because the majority of counseling and helping approaches are deficit-oriented, focusing on what is supposedly wrong with the youth (Meichenbaum & Turk, 1987).

Shifting the focus helps us to see the youth and their problems in a new light and opens the door to new possibilities. Perhaps most importantly, we want to derail the negative self-talk and begin to improve the youth's own self-image. Sommers-Flanagan and Sommers-Flanagan (1997) described a relationship-building assessment procedure called What's Good About You? This technique can provide useful information about a youth's self-image and encourage a youth to recognize his or her own talents or positive attributes. The authors recommended the following format for introducing the game:

> "I want to play a game with you. I'm going to ask you the same question 10 times. The only rule is that you cannot answer the question with the same answer twice. In other words, I'll ask you the same question 10 times, but you have to give me 10 different answers." (Sommers-Flanagan & Sommers-Flanagan, 1997, p. 51)

Sommers-Flanagan and Sommers-Flanagan noted that many tough kids struggle to come up with positive responses. They suggested that if a youth says "I don't know," we should write it down the first time, but remind them in a humourous way that they must give ten different answers. If the assessment process includes the question, "What's bad about you?" the question should only be asked five times. This sends a symbolic message that the counselor is more interested in the positive qualities and attributes.

The next lesson will highlight some of the strategies used by successful coaches as well as solution-focused counselors to help counselors, youth, and families shift the focus.

☐ Lesson 5.6: Incorporate Strategies from Sports Psychology and Solution-Focused Therapy to Shift the Focus

To put it mildly, the 1988 season for our high school's Girl's Varsity Basketball team was an unpleasant experience for everyone involved. There was considerable friction and finger pointing and they finished the season with a record of 0 wins and 22 losses. Moreover, they did not come within 15 points of winning a game and the coach resigned at the end of the season. As a counselor at the school, I knew most of the players and decided to apply for the head coaching position. Several months later, the athletic director joked that there were two reasons he was offering me the job: 1) I had some prior coaching experience (I had taught tennis for years and organized and coached a makeshift team at a residential school); and 2) I was the only one naive enough to want the job.

With this strong vote of confidence, I hit the ground running. We won our first game by 22 points, finished the season with a record of 11 wins and 11 losses, and just missed upsetting the top team in the District playoffs. More importantly, the girls were able to adjust their attitudes, believe in themselves, and enjoy playing the game again. The fact that several students who had not played the previous year agreed to be a part of the 1989 team certainly improved the team's chances of success. However, I am convinced that the team's ability to shift their focus also played a major role in these drastic improvements in performance and attitudes.

Several experiences prior to the start of the 1989 season altered my approach to coaching. First, during my previous job at an inner city runaway shelter, I had been exposed to a solution-focused approach to helping youth and families. I watched gifted counselors utilize these techniques in creative, caring ways to alter the perceptions and habitual patterns of families. I also began to read books by deShazer and his colleagues and incorporate solution-focused techniques such as asking presuppositional questions, looking for exceptions, and focusing on strengths in my counseling practice and personal life. Second, I worked during the summer at Stan Kellner's Yes I Can Basketball Camp and learned about Basketball-Cybernetics, a revolutionary mind-training program. Mr. Kellner was a highly successful basketball coach on the high school and college levels who developed techniques to harness the potential of the subconscious. While his camps teach specific basketball skills, they were unique in their emphasis on also helping youth acquire the psychological tools necessary for optimal performance. Basketball-Cybernetics has been utilized and extolled by a number of collegiate coaches including Dean Smith, the most successful coach in the history of college basketball.

While Basketball-Cybernetics and solution-focused approaches have different origins and were developed for different populations, they share some common philosophies I have found useful for working with a wide variety of youth and families:

It Is Often More Productive to Focus on Strengths and Abilities Than on Weaknesses and Deficits

Success breeds success. Unfortunately, failure and negativity can also be contagious. Coaches love to use videotapes as teaching tools; however, I know of many coaches who are reluctant to let a player watch videotape of particularly bad performances. They worry that the player will focus more on what they need to stop doing rather than on what they need to start doing. As both a tennis instructor and a basketball coach, I typically only used videotape when I wanted the individual or team to see something I wanted them to repeat. For instance, while teaching tennis, I would physically move the pupil's arm into the proper back swing and repeat the motion over and over until it was stored in their subconscious memories. Then I would use videotape to instill confidence and strengthen the memory.

Similarly, counselors need to help families and youth shift the goal statement to what they want rather than what they do not want. Focus on the solution more than the problem (Walter & Peller, 1992). This might be difficult at first as the gatekeeper of the subconscious has received instructions over the years to give priority to negative imagery. We must use techniques to retrain these gate-keepers. When a parent says, "I want Johnny to stop being so damn moody all the time," there are a number of questions we could ask that might shift the focus. We could ask the parent, "Moody usually means back and forth. Tell me about the times when Johnny is in a good mood." Then to Johnny, "How do you put yourself in a good mood?" These questions presuppose that 1) Johnny is some times in a good mood, and 2) that Johnny has control over his moodiness. We need to ask these questions in a tone which does not discount the parents' frustration. We could also ask the parent (or Johnny), "How would you know that Johnny was beginning to turn his mood around? What would that look like?" Again, these questions elicit a different mental picture of Johnny.

Normalizing Common Struggles and Developmental Concerns Can Help Open the Door for Change (O'Hanlon & Weiner-Davis, 1989; Walter & Peller, 1992)

"As long as certain ball players had negative self-images, progress was going to be more than difficult. It was going to be impossible" (Kellner, 1989, p. 16). Negative self-images come from a variety of sources, but one is a tendency to pathologize mistakes everyone makes. These normal mistakes become a part of who they are rather than a normal developmental transition.

At the Yes I Can Basketball Camp, a teenage boy mumbled "I'll never get this right" as he missed shot after shot.

Stan Kellner said, "Son, all good shooters were once poor shooters who practiced. You practice hard so you too will be a good shooter."

The boy asked, "Michael Jordan was once a poor shooter?"

Mr. Kellner responded, "Sure, he was cut the first year from his high school team, but he knew all good shooters were once poor shooters who practiced so he kept practicing. It took time, but you know the rest."

I could actually see the boy's self-image begin to change.

Solution-focused therapists are trained to view many problems of challenging youth as ordinary difficulties of life rather than reflective of some underlying emotional disturbance or character disorder. When we complain to our doctors about headaches, we feel reassured if tumors or CAT scans are not mentioned (O'Hanlon & Weiner-Davis, 1989). Similarly, counselors can have a calming effect on parents (and youth) when the counselor appears to be unruffled by the description of the problem. When parents are reporting common behaviors they feel are atypical or pathological, O'Hanlon and Weiner-Davis recommend such responses as "Naturally," "Of course," "Welcome to the club," "So what else is new?" and "That sounds familiar." For example:

Parent: I put him on restrictions for one week and he bitched and moaned the whole time.

Couns: Of course. But did he follow your restrictions?

Parent: Yes.

Couns: Good. (Changes subject)

Parent: Sheila was out drinking with her hoodlum friends last weekend.

Couns: Some things never change do they?

Parent: What do you mean?

Couns: When we were kids, it seemed like half the kids or more were abusing alcohol.

Parent: Yeah, but that doesn't make it right.

Couns: No, you're right. Just because she's normal doesn't mean she's not breaking the rules or placing herself at risk. (This response normalizes the behavior while also validating the parent's concern and expectation for change.)

Again, gifted counselors are able to normalize parents' struggles in a way that doesn't trivialize their concern. They can do this through appropriate timing, empathic body language, and a mixture of normalizing and empathic responses.

The Mind Does Not Always Know the Difference Between a Real and Imagined Experience (Kellner, 1989)

The mind and the nervous system cannot always distinguish between an actual experience and one that is vividly imagined. Both the synthesized and the actual physical experience can be equally recorded in the mind's memory banks. Numerous experiments have affirmed this assertion by Kellner. Hypnotized subjects who are told that the temperature of the room is 100 degrees actually feel hot and sweat. Their subconscious mind does not know the difference. Kellner (1989) shared an experimental study on free throw shooting which also illustrated this point. Subjects were placed into three groups. One group practiced every day for 20 minutes, the second group did not practice at all, and the third group spent 20 minutes a day imagining one successful shot after another (all in their minds). The group who did not practice showed no improvement, the first group improved 24% and the visualization group improved 23%. Similar results have been found in other visualization studies. Clinical researchers have also noted significant physiological muscle reactions for athletes who were visualizing themselves performing their favorite sport.

Recognizing that the best way to eliminate negative thoughts is by focusing your thinking on a positive expectation, successful coaches, sport psychologists, and solution-focused therapists have mastered the art of utilizing positive imagery and hypothetical solution frames (Walter & Peller, 1992). Players are taught to repeatedly picture the ball going through the basket, the serve going into the court, the puck going into the net. For athletes who have been struggling, these techniques are especially important because they are always capable of imagining successful experiences. The same is true for challenging youth who have been struggling; however, many have become so entrenched in habitual negative patterns and problematic behaviors, they (and their families) may initially have difficulty visualizing a worldview that contains improved patterns and solutions. Solution-focused therapists utilize a number of questions to help challenging youth and families begin to see a better future. Three of the more common types of questions to encourage a hypothetical solution frame include presuppositional questions, the "miracle question," and exception-oriented questions.

Presuppositional Questions

O'Hanlon and Weiner-Davis (1989) used the term presuppositional questions to describe questions that are designed to influence clients' perceptions regarding change. Rather than asking if change is possible, these
questions are carefully worded and presuppose that change is inevitable
or already occurring. The authors note that these questions tend to have a
similar, but opposite effect as the question, "Have you stopped beating
your wife?" by directing clients to responses that are self-enhancing and
strength-promoting. These questions should be open-ended (i.e., What
went well at school this week?) rather than close-ended (i.e., Did anything go well at school this week?). The question should presume that the
youth or family is engaging in solution-oriented behaviors. The following
are examples of different types of presuppositional questions and statements I have used as a coach and a counselor.

> "After Debbie makes the second free throw, make sure you get
> back and play good defense."
> "After we win tonight, I know everyone is going to show good
> sportsmanship."
> "What did you do over the past week to work on your backhand?"
> "What did you do over the past week to work on your relationship
> with your mom?"
> "If you did know, what would you say?" (Can be effective when
> youth habitually responds, "I don't know.")
> "Suppose we were to run into one another in one month at the
> store after we successfully completed counseling together, and you pro-
> ceeded to tell me the steps you took to make things better, what steps
> would you tell me you took?"
> "This weekend when you are communicating successfully with
> your mom, what will that look like?"

The Miracle Question

The miracle question is a specific presuppositional question (or series of
questions) designed by deShazer (1988) to help clients better define what
they want and begin to visualize a future without their problem:

> "Suppose that one night, while you were asleep, there was a miracle
> and this problem was solved. How would you know? What would be differ-
> ent?"

Selekman (1993) noted that the miracle question is best utilized if it is expanded. Although we will need to read our clients and adjust our questions based on the specific situation and responses of the clients, Selekman (1993) recommended these possible follow up questions for family sessions:

"What else will be different between the three of you?"

"Who will be the most surprised when you do that?"

"Who next?"

"If I were a fly on your living room wall watching the three of you after the miracle occurs, what kinds of things will I see you doing differently?"

"If your sister were here, what would she say that is different about how you and your mother are getting along after the miracle?"

"I'm curious, are any of these miracles happening a little bit already?" (p. 63)

Contemplating these questions often makes a problem-free future more realistic and therefore more likely to occur (O'Hanlon & Weiner-Davis, 1989). These questions can also help the youth and his or her family articulate what it is they actually want and identify specific steps they can take (or are taking) to create a solution.

A word of caution is warranted. The miracle question can be an effective strategy for changing perceptions and clarifying goals; however, solution-focused therapy involves much more than asking the miracle question. Too many beginning counselors, desperate to find interventions that work, latch onto the miracle question as if it actually caused miracles, and neglect other tools in their toolbag. Do not be confused by the name; seldom does this question spontaneously produce miracles. Also, do not forget one of the main tenets of solution-focused therapy: If what you are doing is not working, try something else.

Exception-Oriented Questions

"He always acts that way." "She never listens." It is not uncommon to hear statements such as these which reflect the parent's frustration, anger, or exasperation. Unfortunately, these types of overstatements may inadvertently contribute to the downward spiral and cause parents and counselors to disregard important, but subtle changes. No matter how severe the problems seem, there are occasions when the problems do not occur. Challenging youth are not always challenging. There are many times when they listen and there are situations when they act appropriately. While we want to convey empathy for the parent's strong emotions, we can also convey hope by asking questions which encourage a more rational, less dogmatic examination of the problems and solutions. Unfortunately, we often write off these exceptions as anomalies of little therapeutic value.

> Most people, therapists included, consider these problem-free times to be disconnected from or unrelated to the problematic times and so little is done to better understand or amplify them . . . exceptions to the problem offer a tremendous amount of information about what is needed to solve the problem. Solutions can be unearthed by examining the differences between times when the problem has occurred and times when it has not. Clients often simply need to do more of what is already working until the problem no longer exists. (O'Hanlon & Weiner-Davis, 1989, p. 82)

While the miracle question encourages youth to envision a future when the problem is no longer occurring, exception-oriented questions can be used to help youth and families search the *present and the past* for times when the problem has not occurred or the goal is already being achieved, even though it may not be to the full extent or in the exact way they may want (Walter & Peller, 1992). In a survey of families at the McHenry County (Illinois) Service Bureau, two thirds of all families reported they had already begun to make positive changes in the problem area before their first appointment (Weiner-Davis, deShazer, & Gingerich, 1987). While many would view these changes as insignificant, a solution-focused counselor would likely place considerable emphasis on what they were doing right and encourage more of it. deShazer (1985) stressed that "just because the complaint is complicated does not mean the solution needs to be complicated" (p. xvi). There are a variety of ways we can seek out exceptions. Selekman (1993) offered the following examples of exception-oriented questions for challenging adolescents:

> "You have given me a fairly good picture of the problem you are concerned with, but in order to have a more complete picture about what needs to be done here, I now need to know, when this problem does not happen, what's happening instead?"

> "What are you (the parents) doing differently around Bill (the son)?"

> "If Bill were sitting here today, what would you say he would want the two of you (the parents) to continue doing that was helping you get along better?" (p. 58)

Again, timing is critical. Parents who feel the counselor hasn't taken the time to hear their story or understand their perspective are not likely to give adequate consideration to exceptions to the problem. If the first thing a parent says is "My daughter broke curfew five days last week," it is unlikely they want to hear, "Can you tell me about the other two days?" These other two days may or may not contain keys to the solution; however, if you rush the process, you will never know.

All effective approaches recognize the need to help youth and families shift their focus. While the concepts identified in this lesson are often linked to the work of Milton Erickson and the early proponents of solution-focused therapy, they have been integrated into a variety of counseling approaches. For example, presuppositional questions have been recommended by reality therapists such as Bob Wubbolding and family therapists such as Virginia Satir.

Lesson 5.7: Use Reality Therapy Principles to Help Youth Make the Connection Between What They Want and What They Are Doing or Thinking

> Self-evaluation is to reality therapy what interpretation is to psychoanalysis, the directive is to strategic therapy, and disputation is to rational emotive behavior therapy.
>
> —Bob Wubbolding **(in press)**

A person using reality therapy principles spends considerable time building a relationship by helping the youth explore and identify what they want and whether what they want is realistic and attainable (Wubbolding, 1988). This sounds simple, but many professionals are so focused on what the adults want for the youth, they neglect to fully investigate what the youth wants.

Exploring what a youth really wants serves at least four purposes:

1. It communicates to the youth that you care enough to learn about his or her world.
2. It enables youth to focus and visualize on what they really want. (Too often, we focus on what they do not want.)

3. It gives you a better understanding of the youth's perception of the problem and what he or she feels can be done to make things better. Does the youth feel that getting what he or she wants is more dependent on his or her behavior or the behavior of others? To what degree?

4. It allows you to begin to assess the youth's motivation for change.

One of the primary goals of reality therapy with challenging youth is to get them to start making the connection between what they want and what they are doing or thinking. Knowing that she can only control her own behavior, an effective counselor is reluctant to evaluate the behavior of a youth (Glasser, 1998a; Wubbolding, 1988). She understands that too often, this is a lose/lose proposition. Even when she is right, she is wrong. In fact, when the adult is right, the youth's reaction is often even more resentful. The youth tends to focus on the process of being judged rather than their own misbehavior or irrational thought process. The message itself gets distorted, lost in the translation, or abruptly returned to the sender.

While I truly believe adults often know what is best for adolescents, I also understand and appreciate that many challenging youth do not share my perspective. As Mark Twain remarked, "When I was a boy of 14, my father was so ignorant I could hardly stand to have the old man around. But when I got to be 21, I was astonished at how much the old man had learned in seven years" (Twain, 1939, p. 22). Adolescence as a culture needs to be respected. It is important that we meet kids where they are, not where we want them to be. Therefore, we may initially allow the youth to share their perspective regarding what others are doing to cause their problems, and then shift the focus to his or her own behaviors.

Two of the most common questions a counselor using reality therapy asks include:

1. What are you doing?
2. Is your behavior helping you get what you want? (Wubbolding, 1988)

Reality therapy professionals will use a combination of humor and a variety of creative techniques to focus on what the youth is doing and thinking, lessen the youth's defenses, and enhance self-evaluation. Glasser (1998b) asserted that the ability and willingness to effectively self-evaluate is the primary differentiator between happiness and unhappiness. "Happy people spend their lives evaluating their own behavior while unhappy people spend their lives evaluating the behavior of others." All of us need to learn to evaluate our own behavior and adjust when what we are doing is not working. Unfortunately, challenging youth are so used to having others evaluate their behavior for them, they neglect to learn this crucial life skill. Furthermore, many challenging youth who have grown up in abusive or otherwise dysfunctional families have often received conflicting messages about what works and what doesn't. The rules change from day to day. One day, they are praised by a parent for fighting with their sibling. The next day, they are beaten for the same behavior. They are taught not to trust their own judgment. Additionally, the adult models for these youth often have a long-standing pattern of externalizing responsibility for their problems. The youth learns to avoid responsibility by blaming others. Subsequently, professionals who work with challenging youth must recognize that they may initially lack the skills to effectively self-evaluate.

The process of self-evaluation is designed to help the youth recognize for themselves that their behavior is not working and begin to take ownership for positive change. "Why?" questions tend to be effective in helping youth clarify what they really want and ineffective in helping them self-evaluate. Too often, adults try to get students to evaluate their behavior by asking "Why?" or "How come?" There are two reasons these questions seldom illicit contemplative self-evaluation. First, while most kids can recognize whether their behavior is working, they may have more difficulty deciphering why they do what they do. In short, they may not know. Second, when you ask kids why they misbehaved, you are likely to get a barrage of externalized answers (i.e., "He made me mad." "I didn't want to come here in the first place." "Because the rules are stupid." "The dog ate my homework."). These responses just serve to magnify their sense of powerlessness to change their situation. Questions such as, "Did that help you get what you want?" empower youth by reinforcing that they make choices that directly impact their lives.

While youth are evaluating their behavior, the counselor is also helping them to develop a plan for new behaviors. Preferably, to increase commitment and as much ownership as possible, the plan should originate from the youth. At a minimum, the plan should be mutually agreed upon. The counselor should help frame the plan to ensure that it will help meet an unfulfilled need or a need that is being fulfilled irresponsibly. Wubbolding (1988) uses the acronym SAMI^{2}C^3 to remind counselors of the primary characteristics of a good plan:

SAMI^{2}C^3

Simple: Many challenging youth expect to fail. They may also set themselves up by making the plan too difficult.

Attainable: The counselor should help the youth make the plan simple and attainable so they can build on small successes.

Measurable: Can the youth tell if they achieved their goal? In order to feel and know success, the plan should be measurable.

Involved: Again the youth needs to be involved in developing the plan.

Immediate: A youngster might say, "I will not fight for the next six months." The counselor may help the youth revise his plan so that they can see more immediate results. "That's a great idea. What if you did not fight for two days and then we can meet again to see how you are doing?"

Controlled: A good plan should be entirely dependent on the behavior of the youth.

Consistent: Again, keep things simple. The plan should involve repetitive behaviors that the youth can remember and can be easily reinforced.

Committed: If the previous characteristics are adhered to, the chances of the youth making and keeping their commitment are much greater. Before the youth leaves the session, it is the responsibility of the counselor to assess the level of commitment (sometimes by asking, "On a scale of 1 to 10, how committed are you to following through on this plan?"). If the youth is unable to make a significant commitment, the plan should be adjusted or scrapped.

Another important characteristic of a good plan which captures the essence of reality therapy is that the plan be process-oriented rather than product-oriented. A process-oriented plan is entirely dependent on the action of the youth while a product-oriented plan is geared to achieve a certain result which may be dependent upon the reactions and behaviors of significant others. This is particularly true of challenging youth whose environment and social supports are often unpredictable and unreliable. For instance, Michael, a 12-year-old boy who struggles to constructively express his anger, is highlighted in the next lesson. Michael assesses that losing his temper and fighting with peers is not helping him get what he wants (move to a higher Level where he will receive more privileges). Together, we develop a process-oriented plan for him to choose a more need-fulfilling response when he feels himself start to become angry (i.e., ask to go shoot basketball or journal in a designated quiet area). Michael has control over whether or not he follows this plan. On the other hand, if his plan was to stop others from irritating him or improve his relationship with a particular youth, the success of the plan would also be dependent on external factors.

Joe, an 11-year-old boy, understands choice theory and the importance of making process-oriented plans. Joe left early one morning to go fishing in a lake near his house. When he returned late that afternoon, the following conversation occurred with his mother:

Mom: How was the fishing Joe?

Joe: Great Mom.

Mom: How many did you catch?

Joe: None.

Mom: But I thought you said it went great?

Joe: I did. It was my job to fish. It was their job to bite (adapted from Wubbolding, 1998, p. 54).

Joe knew better than to tie his contentment and satisfaction to the behavior of unpredictable fish. If only us adults could be as smart as Joe.

It is essential that we follow up and revisit the plan. Reframe whatever choices the youth made as useful feedback—information to help you be a better helper. If they followed the plan, offer praise and encourage them to extend the plan for a longer time or add new need-fulfilling behaviors. If they were unable or unwilling to follow the plan, label them as resistant delinquents and move on. Just kidding. Use this information to encourage more self-evaluation—both yours and theirs. Reassess and reexplore the relationship, the plan, and the commitment. Does something need to be changed or added? If they again do not follow the plan, take a step back, and entertain new approaches, new interventions, and new plans. They will expect you to lecture or give up. Do the un-expected.

☐ Lesson 5.8: Use Metaphors and Anecdotal Stories to Plant Seeds and Facilitate Growth

Consider the following story about a boy who always complained about his lunch:

I once knew a 12-year-old boy named Billy. Every day at noon, he would sit down with the same friends at the same table to eat lunch. Without fail, when Billy opened his lunch box, he would start to complain.

"This sucks, peanut butter and jelly again! I hate peanut butter and jelly!" Day after day Billy would complain about having to eat peanut butter and jelly sandwiches. Understandably, Billy's friends grew tired of hearing his constant complaining.

Juan, his best friend, had finally heard enough, and yelled, "Damn it, Billy. If you hate peanut butter and jelly so much, why don't you just ask your mom to fix something else for lunch?"

Billy, stunned by Juan's question, said "What do you mean? My mom doesn't make my lunch. I make my own sandwiches."

Can you think of ways the previous story could be utilized with challenging youth (or adapted for the adults who work with them)? How might this story help plant seeds for future growth? Can you think of other stories which might help individuals reframe their behavior, take responsibility for their actions or try new approaches for getting what they want? I shared the peanut butter and jelly story for two reasons. First, it has been useful in helping both challenging youth and counselors see things differently. Second, I once read a similar story (Millman, 1984) which helped me recognize my own pattern of irrational complaining. When I begin to fall back into this trap, I remind myself that most of the time, I make my own sandwiches.

For many adults, direct questions such as "Is that helping you get what you want?" enable us to view our behavior in a different light (to reframe) and begin to make better decisions. Sometimes, direct approaches can help motivate youth to develop new plans; however, metaphors and anecdotal stories are often the most effective ways not only to plant the seeds for change, but also to develop a theme which can be easily visualized and recalled by youth. Recognizing the need to use more creative strategies to reach tough kids, solution-focused counselors (Furman & Aloha, 1992; Selekman, 1993), reality therapists (Wubbolding, 1988), eclectic counselors (Sommers-Flanagan & Sommers-Flanagan, 1997), and others have advocated the therapeutic use of storytelling. Stories and metaphors offer a variety of potential benefits including:

1. Providing an alternate route when the direct routes are blocked. Therapeutic stories are best used when traditional behavioral and cognitive interventions have not proven successful (Sommers-Flanagan & Sommers-Flanagan, 1997).

2. A way to discuss values without directly referring to values in a man-

ner that might seem overbearing or judgmental. Subsequently, youth are less likely to resist these approaches (Sommers-Flanagan and Sommers-Flanagan, 1997).

3. Helping youth grasp a difficult subject more easily by providing some imagery rather than using strictly rational language (Furman & Aloha, 1992).

4. The ability to be recalled by the youth and utilized to increase the chances of long-term benefit (i.e., you might remember the importance of letting go from Chapter 2 because you remember the story about the two monks).

5. Injecting humor into the session and making the counselor seem more real in the eyes of the youth. Stories also have the potential to minimize the psychological distance between the counselor and the youth (Kottler, 1993).

Case Example: Using Blue Gill and Bass to Help a Challenging Youth Make More Constructive Choices

The following case example illustrates these benefits by demonstrating one way I used creative stories and silly metaphors to help a challenging youth reframe and evaluate his own behavior. In utilizing therapeutic stories, it is important to remember the adage, "Meet youth where they are." Stories should not be disguised lectures or introduced with phrases such as "When I was your age." To illustrate the importance of timing, I will first share some of the relationship-building dialogue that increased the chances Michael would be receptive to the metaphorical story.

Michael is a 12-year-old African-American boy who was placed in a group home after being arrested for assaulting another student at the bus stop. This arrest followed numerous suspensions from school for fighting with peers and cursing teachers and principals. His parents communicated to the judge "we've tried everything; we're at our wit's end." The judge ordered Michael to spend a minimum of four months at the group home. Since he arrived at the group home two weeks earlier, he had been placed on restriction several times for fighting with other boys and cursing cottage counselors. He had continued to externalize responsibility for his problems. The following is a transcript between Michael and myself using a variety of the strategies recommended in this book. The importance of confidentiality and the limits of confidentiality have already been discussed with Michael. It should also be noted that successful treatment with youth

in residential facilities almost always involves the youth's family. However, to highlight the value of therapeutic stories, this session will be limited to Michael (M) and his counselor (C).

C: Hey, Michael, good to see you again. How are things going for you?

M: All right. How long do we have to talk? I got things to do, man.

C: I know you do and I appreciate you taking the time to stop b   y   .
      We'll spend 40 to 45 minutes together on Mondays and Thursdays at
      this time. How's that sound?

M: All right, I guess. I'm not making any promises. What do we have to
      talk about?

C: Well, that's one of the things we're going to try to figure out today.
      Have you ever been to a counselor before?

M: Lots of them. And social workers and caseworkers.

C: How was that for you?

M: Some of them were all right. Most were just punching their clocks as
      part of The System—trying to get into my business.

C: Sounds like you have to get to know someone before you tell them
      your business. Is that true?

M: Yeah.

C: I don't blame you. I'm that way too. You really don't know me so I
      would encourage you to take your time and, down the road, I hope
      you will trust me with at least some of your business. All right?

M: Whatever.

C: Now, is there anything I shouldn't ask about until we get to know
      each other a little better?

M: I'll let you know if you get too much in my business.

C: I would appreciate that. I mean it. In order to help you figure out
      what's working and not working for you I'll need to ask some ques-

tions. But, if it feels like I'm getting too much in your business, you'll be sure to let me know?

M: Okay.

C: Great. Do you have any questions of me?

M: Not right now.

C: Okay, let me know if you think of anything. I have a question which will help me understand your situation a little better. Can you tell me why you were sent to live here for a while? [This should help me understand Michael's perspective as well as perceived locus of control.]

M: I'm sure you got all the records from my judge or the caseworker.

C: That's true Michael. To be honest, I've only had time to glance at what was sent. And besides, I would rather hear your story.

M: Here's my story. I don't know why I'm here.

C: If I asked your parents that question, what do you think they would say?

M: Well, mom would probably say she wasn't sure either.

C: And your Dad?

M: He would probably make up some lies about me.

C: What lies would he tell?

M: Probably something about me stealing stuff and having an attitude at school.

C: Michael, is there at least a kernel of truth to some of the lies he might tell?

M: Yeah, I'm no thief, but I guess some people might say I have an attitude sometimes.

C: What would Michael say?

M: Well, I don't mess with no one until they mess with me. But I ain't taking no crap off nobody.

C: I believe you.

M: Since I've been here, I've stood up to much bigger guys. People will learn not to mess with me.

C: I'm not so sure. People can be slow learners.

M: What do you mean?

C: Well you were in a bunch of fights in school, right?

M: Yeah.

C: And how many fights have you been in here?

M: Three.

C: Wow, three fights in only two weeks? Like I said, people can be slow learners.

M: Yeah, I can't wait to get out of here.

C: I can see why. What else do you want, Michael?

M: What do you mean?

C: Well, if I hear you correctly, you would rather be somewhere other than this cottage.

M: Yeah, anywhere would be better than here.

C: Right. Where do you want to be, Michael?

M: I want to be home.

C: I hear you. It's my understanding that you're going to be here at least four months. Is that what they told you?

M: I guess.

C: At least four months. So it could be longer? Is that right?

M: I guess. They said if I work the program, I could get out of jail free after four months and go home.

C: Do you know what that means Michael—work the program?

M: Well, I have to follow the rules and stay out of trouble. And I have to work my way up to Level 4.

C: How's it going so far?

M: The rules here are stupid.

C: So, have you been breaking the stupid rules?

M: I'm doing my chores and keep my stuff straight.

C: That's great Michael. Sounds like that comes pretty easy for you.

M: Yea, I'm no slob like some of these guys.

C: How are you doing with the other stupid rules?

M: These rules are so unfair.

C: I bet it feels that way, Michael. Which rules are you having the hardest time with?

M: Well, I'm still on Level 1 with restrictions.

C: Ouch.

M: I told you, I'm not taking crap off any of these guys. Plus, this no cursing rule is for the birds.

C: Do you fish, Michael? [A cottage counselor had already told me that Michael liked fishing.]

M: Yeah, I used to go with my uncle all the time.

C: You know how some fish are easy to catch and some fish are hard to catch?

M: Yeah, blue gill will bite anything and some fish, like bass just sit there and look at the worms.

C: Can I ask you a really silly question, Michael?

M: Yeah, I guess. Do I have to answer it?

C: No, not unless you want to. If you were a fish, Michael, which would you rather be—a blue gill or a bass?

M: This is stupid.

C: Yeah, I warned you it was pretty silly. What do you think? Blue gill or bass?

M: Well, I'm glad I'm no stupid fish, but if I had to be a fish, I would rather be a bass.

C: Why?

M: Because blue gill are stupid. All they see is the worm. You'd think they would learn to look for the hook.

C: Interesting, so if you had to choose, you would choose to be a bass?

M: That's right.

C: Maybe the blue gill wants to make sure the other fish don't think he's a punk so he always takes the bait and doesn't care about the hook?

M: Maybe, but he still gets eaten.

C: Yeah, it doesn't seem worth it. Can I tell you another silly story, Michael?

M: Yeah, whatever.

C: There was this lake not far from here where people could fish but they weren't able to keep the fish. They had to throw them back. Have you ever heard of a place like that?

M: Yeah, I know of a few places, but they don't make much sense to me.

C: Yeah, me either. Anyway, there were these two best friends. One was a bass and one was a blue gill. They liked to do everything together. They played on the same basketball team.

M: Fish, playing basketball. Come on, man.

C: I told you it was silly. Well, one night they were scheduled to play in the biggest game of the year, but the bass was very worried about his best friend, the blue gill. Because he kept getting himself hurt. You see, the bass had told his friend not to take the bait. Yet every time the fishermen teased the blue gill with a worm, you know what he did?

M: He bit the worm and the hook.

C: Right, you're pretty smart. That's what confuses me.

M: What?

C: Well, you say you want to get out of here. And to get out of here you have to work the program. But to work the program, you have to know when to stay away from the hook. Not let other kids bait you. You tell me you would rather be a bass than a blue gill. Yet, since you've been here, have you acted more like a bass or a blue gill?

M: I'm no stupid blue gill.

C: You're definitely not stupid. If you were stupid you would think that the blue gill was better off than the bass. But you're too smart for that. In fact, I can tell from talking to you and glancing at your records, that you're pretty smart.

M: Yeah.

C: So we both agree, you're no stupid blue gill. But maybe you're a smart blue gill who sometimes does stupid things like keep getting yourself hooked. What do you think?

M: My situation is different from the blue gill's.

C: Yeah, I agree. Most blue gills don't get to learn from their mistakes. They make one mistake and they get eaten. They don't get second, third, and fourth chances to learn.

M: The blue gill in the story kept getting second chances.

C: Yeah, you're right. Maybe you're more like that blue gill. What do you think?

M: What do you mean?

C: Well, what did you tell me you want most?

M: To get the hell out of here.

C: Right, and would you rather get out of here in four months or eight months?

M: I ain't staying no eight months.

C: I hope you're right. So, if you had to choose, you would choose four months over eight months. Right?

M: Yeah, man.

C: Yet, to get out of here in four months, you said you had to work the program and you told me that a big part of that was staying out of fights, right?

M: That's right.

C: So you know if you keep taking the bait, you're not going to get out of here in four months, yet you keep biting. So, to help you get what you want, do you need to be more like a bass or a blue gill?

M: I could be a bass if I wanted to.

C: I'm not so sure. If it was that easy, you would already be doing it. Becoming more like a bass would take a lot of work. Are you willing to work hard to help yourself get out of here?

M: I'll try.

C: I see you're wearing Nike shoes.

M: Yep, my boys call me Little Penny.

C: I know I'm not one of your boys, but would it be okay to call you Little Penny?

M: All right.

C: Do you know the new Nike slogan, Little Penny?

M: Just do it.

C: Yeah, that's the old one. I believe they have a new one—I can. Not "I'll try" but "I can."

M: All right, I can.

C: I can what?

M: I can keep from taking the bait?

C: Great. Remember the bass in the story. His name was Buddha. He used to be . . .

M: Is this another silly story?

C: Yeah, I'll keep it short, all right?

M: All right.

C: Well, Buddha used to be like his best friend, the blue gill. Whenever any one teased him he would take the bait, because he didn't want the other bass to think he was a punk. But then he realized, that by taking the bait, he was actually acting like a puppet punk.

M: A puppet punk?

C: Yeah, a puppet punk. Everyone was pulling his strings so much he felt like a puppet. So he decided he wasn't going to take the bait anymore. It was hard at first but he got so good at ignoring the punks who tried to make him angry that all the other bass started looking up to him and copying him. Pretty soon, all the other bass were trying to be like Buddha. Next thing you know, bass were respected worldwide for their ability to refuse to take the bait.

M: All right, I said I could do it.

C: You don't want to feel like a puppet punk?

M: Yeah, whatever.

C: Okay, how long do you think you can keep from taking the bait? Keep from getting in a fight or cursing someone?

M: Until I get out of this place.

C: That's a pretty impressive goal. Let's see, today's Monday, do you think you could make it until we meet again on Thursday.

M: Piece of cake.

C: No, it's going to be real hard. You know why?

M: Why?

C: Because I doubt the other boys in the cottage are going to change between now and Thursday. They will continue to do things to bait you and the staff might still get on your nerves.

M: I can handle it.

C: Okay, so you are going to choose to respond in a different way when you feel you are being baited. What will you do?

M: I'll just ignore them.

C: What else?

M: I don't know.

C: Is there anyone in the cottage who might be able to help you?

M: I can handle it.

C: I know, just in case.

M: Well, Dave and Bill probably would.

C: Are those kids or staff?

M: Staff.

C: Okay, how might they help?

M: I'm no narc.

C: Right, no one wants to be a narc. What other ways might they help?

M: Well, whenever I get mad, I could ask one of them to shoot some hoops with me.

C: Great idea. Are there times when you wouldn't be able to do that?

M: After eight at night or early in the morning.

C: What could you do then?

M: I could go to the quiet area and draw.

C: Great. And if for some reason, you can't play basketball or draw, can you come up with some other way to keep from taking the bait?

M: Sure.

C: How bad do you want to get out of this place?

M: Real bad, man.

C: Okay, would you be willing to tell Dave and Bill how you are tired of taking the bait, and ask them if they will help you with your plan?

M: Yeah.

C: When will you talk to them?

M: Bill gets off around three today and Dave takes his place. I'll talk to them then.

C: Well, Little Penny, this is going to be hard at first. Would you be willing to keep a record of how many times you feel that you were offered bait?

M: Yeah.

C: Okay, here's a notebook. I'm going to make five columns. All you need to write down is the date, time, describe what bait was offered, describe what you did, and check whether you acted like a bass or a blue gill. Remember, acting like a bass could be just ignoring the bait, shooting hoops, or drawing in the quiet area. Do you understand the chart?

M: Yeah, piece of cake.

C: Would you be willing to keep this chart for a few days until we meet again on Thursday?

M: Yeah.

C: Great, I'll see you on Thursday.

Case Analysis and Discussion

Much of the early part of the session was devoted to beginning to develop a trusting relationship. Telling kids it is both understandable and okay not to share too much too soon often paradoxically reduces defenses and increases openness. However, this should not be confused with traditional reverse psychology. While I hoped Michael would want to talk to me, I was sincere in telling him to trust his instincts and take his time. Other ways I tried to connect with Michael was to use active listening skills (i.e. paraphrasing, checking in to make sure I heard him correctly) and to use his language whenever appropriate (i.e. "stupid rules," "your business," "What lies would he tell?" and "work the program").

Two basic needs that I felt surfaced during this session were Michael's need for freedom and his need for power. He expressed a desire to free himself from the stupid rules of the group home and return home. Rather than make a futile attempt to convince Michael that the rules were for his own good, I opted to use this information to help Michael evaluate his behavior and increase his commitment. Michael, like many challenging youth, felt that fighting and not taking any crap were ways to gain power. Merely explaining to him that he was losing both freedom and personal power by responding this way would probably have little or no effect. The story and various analogies of the fish helped Michael self-evaluate that his behavior was not meeting his needs or getting him what he wanted. Also, as long as Michael connects not fighting with being a punk, he will continue to fight. Therefore, I wanted to help Michael begin to reframe the meaning of punk behavior. Sometimes, simply asking, "Is that helping you get what you want?" will help motivate the youth to develop a new behavior plan. However, it has been my experience that illustrative stories are often the most effective ways to not only plant the seed for change but to develop a theme which can be easily visualized and recalled by the youth. A cottage counselor had already told me Michael liked to fish. If he had not, I might have tried other ways to help him evaluate that his behavior was not helping him get what he wanted.

Another analogy that has been useful for kids who have difficulty controlling their anger is driving a car. Kids are asked if they owned a car, would they be willing to let someone else drive it all the time. A connection could be made between allowing people to take control of your emotional steering wheel and allowing people to drive your car. This is particularly useful because most kids either drive a car or wish they did. Again, self-evaluation is a two-way street. Counselors need to be creative but also flexible enough to shift gears if the stories or techniques are not helping.

Michael was initially reluctant to agree that he was acting like a blue gill. However, once he made the connection, I felt he was too nonchalant about changing his behavior. His initial plan was to not fight for the next six months. It is not uncommon for kids who have experienced little success to set themselves up for failure by developing a plan that is virtually impossible. It was critical to help him revise his plan to make it more do-able and immediate so he could build upon his early success. In fact, reducing the time frame to three days may not have been enough. It may have been better to adjust my schedule to meet with Michael the next day to increase the likelihood of initial success. I tried to use what Michael brought with him (his Nike shoes) to increase his commitment. Also, encouraging an internal locus of control should not be confused with rugged individualism. Subsequently, I encouraged Michael to use social supports (Bill and Dave) to help him follow through with his plan.

I would want to approach the session on Thursday as information gathering. Whatever Michael reported would merely be useful feedback to help both of us further self-evaluate. Michael may have been able to follow through on all, some, or none of the plan. Usually, kids are able to at least make some initial positive changes. For instance, he may be able to resist the bait later that night but have more difficulty the next few days. We would want to focus and build on the new resisting behaviors rather than the old aggressive behaviors. Together, we would need to tinker with the plan and see if Michael would be willing to commit to a new plan for a shorter period of time. Even if Michael had successfully followed through with the entire plan, I would praise him, but I would also reiterate that continuing to engage in new, bait-avoiding behaviors will be very difficult. Regardless, we would want to reassess Michael's commitment to the plan. Michael's pattern of externalizing responsibility is longstanding. Silly analogies about fish are not going to change this pattern overnight, but hopefully, Michael will begin to recognize that what he was doing was not working and small successes will yield additional successes. Positive change with kids like Michael is often two steps forward and one step backward—another reason to reframe behavior as informative feedback.

I want to stress that the preceding case is just one way of approaching youngsters with similar problems. Each session will take a different form depending on the presentation of the client and the preferred style of the counselor. For instance, many challenging youth are not as verbal as Michael and many counselors may feel more comfortable using a more direct means of facilitating self-evaluation. Whenever possible, we want to use what the client brings. We want to help begin a process in which the youth identifies what he or she wants and evaluates whether the behavior is congruent with the goals. We may have to try several creative ways to get this process rolling. Whatever we try, we want to do something different.

In the next three lessons, I share how the stigma of educational and psychological labels can impact a youth's self-concept and foster negative self-fulfilling prophecies.

Lesson 5.9: When Kids Feel They Have Only Two Choices, They Will Choose Smart Ass Over Dumb Ass Any Day

Carlos was a good-looking, athletic, intelligent, and popular 15-year-old Hispanic boy who a year earlier could not read. In seventh grade, Carlos was diagnosed as having a severe form of dyslexia and was sent to a small, residential school that specializes in teaching students with severe learning disabilities. Carlos had managed to hide his reading difficulties from all his teachers until seventh grade. After a year of individualized instruction with reading specialists at the residential school, Carlos was reading on a sixth grade level. I asked Carlos how he managed to make it so long without anyone knowing he could not read. He replied:

Most of the teachers had us read in order so I could tell when my time was coming. Right before I was supposed to read, I would create a ruckus. I got so good at it that the teacher often blamed somebody else. Plus, I was good most of the time so the teacher never paid me no mind. I couldn't hardly read one word, but I could write all the letters and I was a master cheater. I would copy off a few friends so nobody would know. I was more funny than mean—everybody just thought I was sort of a class clown. Even the teachers would laugh. [Carlos was quite funny.] Inside, I felt like totally bogus, like the biggest idiot ever. I didn't want nobody to know. And very few of um did. They just thought I was a big time smart ass. *I'll choose smart ass over dumb ass any day.* A few times, my best friend would help me memorize what I was supposed to read, and I'd fake it. Well, one day, the teacher changed up and here I am pretending to read one page and what I'm reading is like three pages away. I was so humiliated I left school. Turns out, I may never have gotten help if I hadn't screwed up.

Carlos' story is a familiar one. The particulars change but "I'd rather be a smart ass than a dumb ass" is a common sentiment. It has been my experience that many of the so-called behavior disorders or emotional disturbances are merely symptoms of undiagnosed or untreated learning disabilities. Smith (1989) described a number of other creative strategies these students employ to mask the feeling of being stupid. She identified 18 common masks including the mask of not caring, the mask of boredom, the mask of contempt and cutting everything down, and the mask of being bad.

While many teachers and other helping professionals are aware that the majority of students with learning disabilities have at least average intelligence, most students are not. In many ways, because he was a popular athlete, Carlos was one of the lucky ones. Peer ridicule can often be relentless and vicious, but this ridicule is nothing compared to the internal dialogue that takes place every day (i.e., "I'm so dumb," "I can't do anything"). Although it can be difficult at times, it is important to continue to try to look beyond the symptoms (behavior) and try to identify the unmet needs or the real problem.

When I was a school counselor, I was asked to work with a student on time management, as she was consistently tardy for her third period class—a learning resource class—a very small class in which students with reading disabilities received individual reading assistance. Rather than calling the student to my office, I decided to follow a hunch and discretely observe her before class. On two straight days, she made it to the library with time to spare. However, she did not want her friends and peers to see her going into the library for classes so she pretended to be waiting outside another class down the hall. When the bell rang, she would sneak in the library, and slump down in her seat with her back to the large windows parallel to the hall. Later, she told me, "I feel like everyone who walks down the hall is looking to see what the zoo animals are doing."

The incidents with Carlos and this girl occurred in 1985 and 1988, respectively. Since then, much has been done to educate both adults and youths about persons with special needs. Early diagnosis is more likely and services are more often appropriate and inclusive. Unfortunately, helping the learning disabled often means a label, and despite a more educated public, these labels continue to carry a stigma. We have a responsibility to continue to educate youth, helping professionals, and ourselves so we can offer assistance and lessen stigmas. Above all, one must not forget that for the student who has just recently been diagnosed, this is entirely new territory. As illustrated in the next lesson, stopping at the diagnosis often does more harm than good.

☐ Lesson 5.10: Don't Underestimate the Power of Diagnostic Labels

> I learned to look at highly disturbed children's behavior, and to assign labels. Faced with chaos and pain, we fall back on the human impulse to label as a way of distancing ourselves while giving the illusion we are doing something.
>   —Salvador Minuchin (Minuchin & Nichols, 1993, p. 23)

Many of us in the helping professions have fallen in the trap Minuchin describes above. We desperately want to help the troubled youth but all our efforts seem futile. Then, we observe that their behavior, symptoms, or test scores match some psychiatric or educational diagnosis. We document this diagnosis and feel that we have accomplished something. In reality, we have only accomplished something if:

1. the diagnosis is accurate,
2. the diagnosis is the most appropriate and least restrictive,
3. we educate the youth and his or her family so the diagnosis feels helpful, not hurtful, and
4. a new treatment or educational plan is implemented that is helpful for the youth and his or her family.

As an assistant professor, I teach the course Diagnosis of Psychopathology in the post-master's clinical counseling program at Xavier University so I am not opposed to the process of diagnosing. However, at the risk of sounding cynical about the profession of which I am a member, I feel these four interrelated criteria are rarely met. Various studies as well as feedback from colleagues, parents, and clients over the years leads me to think I'm not alone in that assessment. Of course, if we don't accomplish #1, the rest are moot. What follows are brief synopses of several cases which unfortunately, in my experience, are not anomalies.

In 1987, Colleen was a bright 22-year-old African-American woman whose 8-year-old son, Brian, was exhibiting behavioral problems at home and school. Although very verbal, he could not read and often became very agitated and aggressive during class. These behaviors would continue at home whenever Colleen tried to intervene. Colleen became increasingly frustrated with Brian and sought help from the school counselor who referred her to a local psychologist who specialized in youth with educational and behavior disorders.

After two meetings with Brian and Colleen, Brian was given several educational and psychological batteries and diagnosed with educable mental retardation and severe emotional disturbance. These terms were described to Colleen and she was informed that the overall prognosis was poor. Brian and his mother took this information, created a self-fulfilling prophecy of failure, and ran with it. Brian's behavior and educational performance continued to deteriorate for several more years until Colleen was transferred to another state, and with the encouragement of a colleague, sought a second opinion from another psychologist.

Brian was retested and diagnosed with Attention Deficit Disorder (ADD), a specific learning disability, and average to above average intelligence. This was explained to Brian in a way that made him feel both hopeful and better about himself. Both Brian and Colleen were given considerable information and guidance about ADD and Brian's learning disability. His classes were changed and his educational plan adjusted. Almost overnight, his behavior, attitudes, and grades skyrocketed. At the time of this writing, he was a college senior scheduled to graduate in the spring with a double major in Dance and Drama. He has performed in numerous plays and musicals.

When I met Mary, a vibrant White female, she was apprehensive about her pending discharge from her 18th psychiatric hospitalization (in 13 different hospitals). Mary was only 11-years-old. During one of her early hospitalizations, her father, a prominent business executive, was caught sexually abusing her in her hospital room. When she came to my agency, I was able to ascertain records from most of her previous hospital stays. Over the years, she was given at least 17 different diagnoses including: Bipolar Disorder, Dysthymia, Major Depression, Borderline Personality Disorder, Conduct Disorder, Oppositional Defiant Disorder, Posttraumatic Stress Disorder, Overanxious Disorder of Childhood, Schizoaffective Disorder, Psychotic Disorder NOS, and many others. Can you imagine how confused this child and her mother were? One of the two adults Mary was supposed to trust the most had committed the ultimate betrayal. She had literally hundreds of professionals coming in and out of her life offering entirely different perspectives regarding what was causing her pain and ways to alleviate it. Undoubtedly, the vast majority of these professionals cared deeply about Mary and wanted to help her. Many did help her find temporary relief. Perhaps they should be commended for not assuming that the previous diagnoses were accurate. (Too often, a child is unable to shake a diagnosis despite years of contrary evidence.) But we have to question the system and facilitators of the system that can be so unreliable. How can this happen?

Again, research and experience suggest that these cases are not anomalies. Numerous scholars and professional advocacy groups have long asserted that minority students are disproportionately diagnosed with mental retardation and severe emotional behavior disorders (Trent & Artiles, 1995). Furthermore, in a study of managed care agencies, Goodman and his colleagues (1996) noted that reviewers frequently express frustration with multiple psychiatric diagnoses over time for the same patient.

While working as a Clinical Director of a mental health agency, we had two unrelated 8-year-old girls with the diagnosis of Borderline Personality Disorder referred to our agency in the same week by two different licensed therapists. Borderline Personality Disorder is characterized by "a pervasive pattern of interpersonal relationships, self-image, and affects, and marked impulsivity beginning by early adulthood and present in a variety of contexts" (APA, 1994, p. 654). Many troubled children and adolescents display these characteristics. Too many young children are diagnosed as having Borderline Personality Disorder or Bipolar Disorder. I agree with Herman's assessment in her 1992 book, *Trauma and Recovery* that Borderline Personality Disorder is often little more than a sophisticated insult to describe people we find difficult. It is one of the most stigmatizing disorders in the *Diagnostic and Statistical Manual of Mental Disorders (DSM-IV)* (APA, 1994) and should never be given to children. Many kids are misdiagnosed every day and the resulting damage is often extensive and long standing. Others might argue that these diagnoses are necessary to inform treatment; however, this is rarely (if ever) the case. I would argue that many challenging kids who have experienced significant trauma meet the behavioral criteria for both Borderline Personality Disorder and Bipolar Disorder; however, they do not meet the criteria for least restrictive or most appropriate diagnosis.

Assessment of mental illness is not an exact science, and those of us who have been in the field long enough have certainly missed the mark on more than one occasion; however, the cases noted above seem to go beyond human error. Again, we need to question the system and facilitators of the system that can be so unreliable or unhelpful. At first glance, it would seem that the only prudent course of action would be to discard the *DSM-IV* and other formal means of classification. However, when working with challenging youth, classification is often necessary. It is impractical to constantly reinvent the wheel—to develop an entirely new treatment and educational approach for each youth (Jongsma, Peterson, & McInnis, 1996). Classification of disorders (not people) also enables professionals from different backgrounds and theoretical orientations to speak a common language. It appears to be a necessary, but certainly insufficient, tool. Classification systems need to be considered always as works in progress, not final products. We must continually strive to improve both the system and facilitation of the system.

The *DSM-IV*, for instance, is a vast improvement over previous editions. The authors took great strides to improve the reliability of diagnostic categories and made major revisions to make the manual more culturally sensitive. Nevertheless, clinicians should remember that the diagnostic criteria is only a small fraction of what we might need to know to assist a troubled youngster and his or her family. Too often, "the DSM diagnosis has become the main goal of clinical practice" (Tucker, 1998, p. 159). As the *DSM-IV* cautions, "To formulate an adequate treatment plan, the clinician will invariably require considerable additional information about the person being evaluated beyond that required to make a *DSM-IV* diagnosis" (APA, 1994, p. xxv). Furthermore, we must never forget that it is an imperfect manuscript developed by imperfect human beings; it is not the bible of the mental health profession as commonly stated by attorneys in court. We should heed the advice of McWilliams (1998) and resist the human tendency "to endow prosaic and imperfect documents with more than there share of authority, perhaps in an effort to avoid the discomfort caused by the ambiguity and uncertainty and to reify and elevate provisional concepts to the status of unquestioned wisdom" (p. 198).

☐ Lesson 5.11: All Helping Professionals Have a Responsibility to Make the Assessment Process More Kid-Friendly

Most of us are not in a position to revise the *DSM-IV*, and many readers are not licensed to make diagnostic assessments; however, here are a few interrelated steps all helping professionals can take:

1. *Evaluate diagnostic assessments and assumptions using criteria highlighted in the preceding lesson:*
   Is it accurate?
   Is it the most appropriate *and* least restrictive?
   Is the picture we are painting helping or hurting?
   Knowing what we know now, how can we better serve this youth and family?

2. *Watch our language.* Try to say "student with a learning disability" rather than "LD student" or "person with schizophrenia" rather than "a schizo-

phrenic." It's more than just semantics. Our language tends to reflect our biases. Furthermore, the language of significant adults plays a role in forming the youth's self-image.

3. *Be cautious about interpreting all the youth's behavior via the diagnosis.* Kids are kids, with regular kid needs. A learning disability, for example, is only a very small part of who the child is. Also, we want to consider how a child's history of abuse plays a role in forming who they are, but we want to be careful about overcompensating and assuming that all their behaviors, feelings, and so forth are related to the abuse.

4. *Consider cultural variations and explanations before making any diagnosis.* Be careful about equating normality and abnormality with statistical frequency or cultural norms of the majority. Regularly entertain the possibility that diagnoses may be reflective of cultural bias or we may be disregarding important cultural considerations. For instance, if an African-American boy tells you that he hates going into music stores because everyone is staring at him, is he paranoid? It is more likely that he is expressing an unfortunate reality or, as some theorists have suggested, a "paranorm" (Sue & Sue, 1990).

5. *Whenever possible, reframe behavior, symptoms, and diagnoses in a positive way.* A former instructor of mine would not use the term Multiple Personality Disorder (now referred to as Dissociative Identity Disorder). Instead she would say Multiple Personality Talent, to reflect the incredible coping skills of persons who have experienced unthinkable trauma. Herman noted that "this understanding provides the basis for a cooperative therapeutic alliance that normalizes and validates the survivor's emotional reactions to past events, while recognizing that these reactions may be maladaptive in the present" (Herman, 1992, p. 127).

In his creative book, *Attention Deficit Disorder: A Different Perspective,* Thom Hartmann (1993) reframed ADD by describing it as a natural adaptive trait. He highlighted the unique gifts of individuals with ADD. These are just two examples of new ways to view old ideas.

6. *Remember tests can be valuable tools, but be cognizant of their limitations.* If we take the time to explain tests to youths and their families before, during, and after administration in a way that is straightforward and basically nonpathologizing, tests can sometimes be a useful piece to a much larger puzzle (Sommers-Flanagan & Sommers-Flanagan, 1997). However, we must not forget that tests are often just a snapshot, and a

fuzzy one at that. For example, imagine you gave a boy who just turned 13 years old a battery of tests. Keep those tests in perspective. Do not place more magical powers on numbers derived from the last four hours than what occurred in the previous 113,640 hours.

Lessons Learned: Valuing Systemic, Collaborative, and Preventive Approaches

☐ **Lesson 6.1: Appreciate Context—Don't Judge a Kid by His or Her Cover**

Since youth are greatly influenced by their families, communities, and social environments, it is imperative that helping professionals appreciate this context and attend to these systemic considerations (Lewis & Lewis, 1989; Nichols & Schwartz, 1991). Because of these multiple influences, youth are not always what they appear. Often, the simple cover reveals very little about the complex book.

Whenever I forget this lesson, a kid like Brad comes around to remind me. I was a school counselor and Brad was a second-year freshman. He was respectful and cooperative, but he always appeared disheveled, was chronically truant, and seldom socialized with peers. Because of his polite disposition and quiet manner, he often went unnoticed. When he was 17 years old, he approached me about withdrawing from school to help support his family. He had obviously given this considerable thought and was committed to his decision to leave school and begin a full-time job. I thought I knew most of the details about his family situation until I went with him to his house that day.

From the outside, the house appeared abandoned. When we walked in, dirt was coming through the rotting plank floor and Brad's obese mother and mentally disabled sister were sitting on a broken couch surrounded by eight mangy dogs. Across the living room, Brad's elderly grandmother, who suffered from emphysema, was hunched over the kitchen table, smoking a cigarette as oxygen tubes protruded from both her nostrils. Brad politely and respectfully introduced me to his family and walked them through his decision to withdraw from school. In front of my eyes, this disheveled loner transformed into a strong, proud, family provider. His mother, who was also proud, would only sign his withdrawal permission form if he agreed to reenroll for summer school. Brad and I both knew that realistically he would not come back to school (he was a 17-year-old freshman making $15 an hour in construction and his father had terminal cancer).

I kept in touch with Brad for about a year and I must admit that trip to his house gave me a far better understanding of his struggles than anything he could have said in ten weeks of counseling sessions in my office. I know I never looked at him in the same way again. Like most school counselors, I was responsible for many students (375). I was proud of the effort I put forth to know the vast majority of the students in the school. Certainly, no one would expect any counselor to know the home life of every kid. There is just not enough time in the day. Yet, I also wonder how effective any of my previous work with Brad had been considering how little I really knew about him. As Ken Hardy (1996) once remarked, "Unless we appreciate the context of others, we can only be marginally helpful."

☐ Lesson 6.2: Families, Particularly Parents and Guardians, Cannot Be Peripheral to the Therapeutic Process

A colleague once remarked:

> We need to start with just the youth and then gradually include the family. I compare the process to learning to juggle. You start by practicing with two balls. Once you've begun to master two balls, you move to three balls, and so on.

While I agreed this rationale made perfect sense for learning to juggle, my experience with families summoned a different analogy. If we start with four balls (the youth and his or her family), it is true that we might drop more balls and juggling will be more difficult in the early stages. However, involving the family early in the treatment process may be the only way to reach our ultimate goal of making all the balls move in concert. If we start with only two balls (counselor and youth), by the time we get around to adding more balls (the family), we often find that those balls have magically transformed themselves into heavy bowling balls that make juggling virtually impossible—unless you are a master juggler which most of us are not. If families are not involved in the early stages, we may actually be cultivating resistance.

The following comments are typical of what I have heard (and sometimes said) over the years to justify keeping family members peripheral to the treatment process:

"Involving the family will just muddy the waters and confuse her even more."

"Julio has been neglected for some time. Bringing his parents into the process will dilute the attention Julio needs."

"While I know he will most likely be returning home, I think it would be counterproductive to include the family in the treatment process at this juncture."

"The only way she is going to learn more appropriate ways to manage her anger and communicate with others is by being exposed to healthy adult role models. This will require a long sabbatical from her parents."

Certainly, there are times when the emotional, physical, or sexual safety of the youth could be threatened by rushing parental involvement; however, experience suggests helping professionals are more likely to err on the side of exclusion rather than inclusion. The clinically prudent route is often the most difficult.

None of us lives in isolation. Bandura (1974) stressed that human beings are both products and producers of their environments. Family systems models contend that for youth to be best understood, they need to be viewed within the context of their environment. Fishman (1988) noted that of all the systemic influences, the youth's family is primary:

Out of the multifaceted context impinging on the adolescent—family, peers, school, idols, culture—the ecologically oriented therapist starts with the pivotal point, which is the family. The family is the social environment out of which the adolescent emerged. It is the source of the most enduring relationships and adolescent's primary financial support. And the family has the most resources with which to make changes. (pp. 4–5)

Glasser (1998b) contended that virtually all problems for which we seek counseling can be traced to an inability to satisfy a current relationship. He noted that most of these relationships are familial in nature. In a recent comprehensive study of at-risk youth, a strong sense of connection with parents and family members was revealed to be one of the most important protective factors (Resnick et al., 1998). Family systems approaches recognize that relationships cannot be satisfied and connections cannot be developed, or redeveloped, by keeping family members separate from one another.

Armed with hindsight and substantial research and literature that supports a family systems approach (Matthews & Roberts, 1988; McConkey-Radetzki, 1987; Minuchin, 1974; Schultz, 1991), residential facilities across the country have significantly revised their treatment protocol over the past two decades to require family participation in treatment and aftercare programs. These programs recognized that the interpersonal nature of many youth's challenging behavior could best be addressed interpersonally. While it was essential that the youth begin to make personal changes (i.e., better choices, less aggression) and develop trusting relationships with the treatment staff, these steps were not sufficient. Improvement strictly within the walls of the residential setting was seldom the best indicator of a successful transition back home or into the community. What was of primary importance was how well these improvements could be translated to future settings such as home and school. Subsequently, treatment should be geared to help foster successful transitions (Minuchin, 1974).

In addition to the benefits noted above and the obvious goal of helping challenging youth become less challenging, interventions involving the family have a number of other potential advantages. We demonstrate respect for family members when we communicate that they play an essential, ongoing role. Because some parents or guardians may initially equate our request for their participation as blame for the problem, it is important to explain why we feel it is necessary that they be actively involved (Sommers-Flanagan & Sommers-Flanagan, 1997). It is important for families to hear that, regardless of who or what is responsible for causing or maintaining the problem, no one is unaffected and everyone has unique insights that may help.

Family members can also share perspectives regarding the values and cultures of the youth's home and community that can and should be incorporated into the helping process (Garfat, 1990). It is imperative that we envision "the family not as an external encumbrance that is likely to disrupt therapy, not as a necessary evil, but instead as a resource to facilitate healing" (Fishman, 1988, p. 5). This requires considerable self-reflection because how we perceive the family will inevitably be communicated in some fashion.

Again, we are most likely to facilitate positive change if we first recognize and build on existing familial and cultural strengths. Virginia Satir's ability to see benevolent motivations and positive traits was one of the skills that made her so effective at connecting and intervening with even the most troubled families. Satir (1972) emphasized that by helping parents "raise their pots" (increase their own self-worth) we were likely to see a domino effect. Parents whose pots are raised tend to have a greater capacity to demonstrate patience, understanding, and nurturance with their children. All of us are better at caring for others when we show we can care for ourselves. Furthermore, by not assessing blame or identifying anyone as the primary problem, a family systems approach can spare the youth the potential negative self-esteem effects that are sometimes caused by such identification (Sommers-Flanagan & Sommers-Flanagan, 1997).

Karp (1993) noted that the children's mental health field as a whole has made tremendous strides in recent years in approaching and communicating with families: "Instead of 'we' and 'they,' professionals and families are gradually becoming partners in the therapeutic process" (p. 21). Families are less likely to be viewed as sponges who must soak up the counselor's expertise. Both have areas of expertise that should be respected and utilized.

However, stressing that many professionals have not heeded the call to form partnerships with families, Karp (1993) offered a number of questions that professionals can ask to assess their own beliefs and practices regarding collaboration. Embedded in these questions are a number of subtle, but important ways we include (or exclude) families:

1. Do I really believe that parents are my equal, and, in fact, are experts on their child?

2. Do I show the same respect for the value of families' time as I do for my own time by educating myself about an individual child's case before appointments or group sessions?

3. Do I speak plainly and avoid professional jargon?

4. Do I actively involve parents in developing a plan of action and then review, evaluate, and revise the plan with the family?

5. Do I make appointments and provide services at times and places convenient for the family?

6. Do I share information with other professionals to ensure that services are not duplicated and families do not expend unnecessary energy searching for services and providers? (p. 21)

As the next several lessons attest, working collaboratively with families may also include helping them recognize and change counterproductive communication and structural patterns.

☐ Lesson 6.3: Families with Challenging Youth Often Display Characteristic Structural Patterns That Tend to Limit Growth and Maintain or Exacerbate Problem Behaviors

Professionals often misperceive families as being "dysfunctional" when these families are, in fact, experiencing normal reactions to the serious lack of appropriate affordable accessible community-based services and supports. It is service systems that are dysfunctional when they do not respond to families' needs. (Karp, 1993, p. 22)

We need to respect families' healthy resistance to unreasonable, inadequate, or inappropriate services or directives. When we forget that all families are unique, we tend to want to pigeonhole them into some narrowly constructed definitions of functional and dysfunctional. In fact, there is considerable structural diversity among functional families (Colapinto, 1991; Minuchin, 1974). Nevertheless, family theorists have made strong arguments that:

1. families with challenging youth often display characteristic structural patterns that limit flexibility, restrict members' growth, and maintain or exacerbate problem behaviors;

2. these patterns can best be addressed by viewing the family, not the individual youth, as the primary consumer (Colapinto, 1991; Fishman, 1988; Minuchin, 1974; Tolan & Mitchell, 1990).

I focus on two prominent, interrelated patterns that tend to be highly problematic for families with challenging youth. These patterns may have been handed down from previous generations or developed from unsuccessful attempts to curb youths' behavior, and they can be addressed through family counseling and parent education:

Youth Have Learned How to Play Authority Figures Against One Another

Parents' ability to respect and support each other is tested by most children and adolescents. It is common for parents of challenging youth to have different philosophies regarding discipline. These kids possess a unique capacity to recognize, magnify, exploit, and even manufacture these differences. Minuchin and Nichols (1993) described a metaphorical approach which has been useful in highlighting the importance of avoiding triangulation when disciplining challenging youth.

When the counselor suspects the child has learned to play parents against one another, he or she asks, "Who is the sheriff in the house?" Typically, both parents can agree on who tends to play that role.

Then the counselor asks the other parent, "So, are you the deputy sheriff or are you the attorney for the defense?"

The parent will often admit that he or she openly disagrees with his or her partner and defends the youth. Further exploration will often reveal that the sheriff is not very competent while the defense attorney is quite good at his or her job. Minuchin noted that "this is the worst arrangement that exists" (p. 169).

Thomas Gordon (1975), a pioneer in parent education, argued that a united parental front is overrated because this advice is often unrealistic and encourages parents to present a false front. At the risk of sounding contradictory, I agree, and I think Minuchin would also. It would be ludicrous to expect parents to always agree. *Whether* parents disagree is not nearly as important as *how* they disagree. Different perspectives can be advantageous. The cliché "two heads are better than one" is true only when the two heads have something unique to offer. Furthermore, since it is easy to lose both our temper and our objectivity with challenging youth, a checks and balances system can reduce the possibility of one parent saying or doing something he or she will later regret. Therefore, we want to normalize and validate the right and need for parents to disagree from time to time. But we also want to facilitate a process where the parents can evaluate whether or not an open triangulation pattern is helping them achieve their desired outcome or pushing them further apart from each other and their children. Some additional questions which might help parents assess their negotiation skills include:

1. Do you take the time to entertain each other's perspective?
2. Are you respectful with each other?
3. Do you tend to disagree over smaller, strategical decisions or bigger, philosophical matters.
4. Are you modeling that negotiation and compromise are important values?

Based on answers to questions such as these, family members can be taught how to recognize when they are falling into unproductive triangulation patterns and practice using better times, places, and strategies for negotiating discipline. Parents who have had poor models themselves and tend to answer "no" to most of these questions may initially want to negotiate privately. Once parents learn the art of respectful negotiation, they may want to actually discuss options in front of the child while requiring the child to listen quietly without interrupting (Minuchin & Fishman, 1981; Tolan & Mitchell, 1990).

It is common in some families for one parent (often the father) to attempt to support his spouse by taking over and angrily demanding that a youngster comply with the mother's directive. Unfortunately, this response often inadvertently circumvents his partner's authority and drives a deeper wedge between himself and the child. One intervention that can be used to disrupt such patterns is called Passing the Baton (Biever, Jordan, Franco, Nath, & Yee, 1993). Parents are given a baton (actually a rolled up piece of paper), and instructed to pass the baton whenever they need assistance disciplining the children. The parents are also given the option of holding the baton jointly to communicate a joint message to the children. Parents can be encouraged to relinquish the baton whenever they feel themselves losing control. The authors noted that this technique has been successful in helping parents avoid triangulation patterns.

Family counselors often struggle with how much attention should be given to the quality of the marital relationship and the ability of parents to meet their own psychological needs. Minuchin (1974) argued that a two-parent family could only be as strong as the marital dyad. He felt that too often a youth's misbehavior was a metaphor for marital conflict. If parents and other key members of the youth's family are unable to meet their own needs, they are not likely to be sensitive to the needs of the youth. They are more likely to try to increase their control which often only works to magnify or contain the problem.

William Glasser frequently quotes Father John, a Chicago priest, who, understanding this phenomenon, once said, "The best thing parents can do for their children is to love each other." This is true, first, because parents who love (active verb) each other are modeling effective need-fulfilling behaviors for their children. Second, since they are able to meet their own need for love and belonging, they can be more attuned to the needs of their children. Third, parents who have appropriate channels to meet their need for power and achievement are more likely to recognize the difference between discipline (which focuses on the needs of the youth) and punishment (which focuses on the power needs of the adult). Fourth, parents who actively support one another are less likely to fall into the triangulation trap.

Nevertheless, it is important for counselors to follow the parents' lead and tread lightly when addressing issues seemingly unrelated to the presenting problem. When counseling has been initiated because of the behavior of the youth, some counselors may be tempted to delve into the underlying marital problems. Initiating discussions on marital issues rather than the presenting problem before a therapeutic relationship has been developed tends to make parents distrustful of the counselor and often leads to premature termination (Haley, 1980; Tolan & Mitchell, 1990). It is also important to remember that the strengths of the parental dyad may be shadowed by the stress of the youth's acting out behavior and demoralization of the family. Furthermore, as Freud use to say, "sometimes a cigar is just a cigar." The youth's behavior may not be related to marital problems. Unless mutually agreed upon, the primary goal is not to resolve marital disputes, but rather to help the parents become allies in providing logical and reasonable consequences to the child for desired and undesired behaviors (Tolan & Mitchell, 1990).

It should be noted that the phenomena discussed in the paragraphs above are not limited to two-parent or two-guardian households. Challenging youth are masters at triangulating teachers and parents, parents and grandparents, aunts and uncles, and so forth. What's important is that the adults in positions of authority use assertive, empathic, and age-appropriate discipline, and communicate to the youth that they are on the same team—even when they disagree.

Hierarchal Boundaries Are Out of Balance

Well-functioning families are sometimes described as democracies. This is true if we remember that well-functioning democracies also have reasonable, flexible, just, and fair people in positions of power. Regardless of culture, well-functioning families have hierarchal arrangements in which the parents are positioned above their children. "They are 'in charge'—not in the sense of arbitrary authoritarianism, but in the sense of leadership and protection" (Colapinto, 1991, p. 424). On the other hand, hierarchal arrangements in families with challenging youth tend to share one or more of the following characteristics:

1. Rules are not enforced because it is not clear that the parents are in charge.
2. Rules are not enforced because erratic, autocratic directives are made out of anger and are virtually unenforceable (i.e., "You are grounded for a year.").
3. Rules do not change over time in response to changing contexts. For instance, rules are not renegotiated to acknowledge an adolescent's increasing need for freedom and autonomy (Fishman, 1988).

Counselors can work with parents to achieve a hierarchal arrangement that puts the parents back in charge, strengthens generational boundaries, enforces reasonable rules, adjusts to changing contexts, and provides for both mutual support and autonomy of the youth (Colapinto, 1991; Fishman, 1988; Minuchin, 1974; Tolan & Mitchell, 1990).

From the outside looking in, solutions sometimes appear readily apparent and simpler than they really are. We must remember that these patterns are typically longstanding and make sense on some level to the family members. Otherwise, they would change on their own. Minuchin cautioned counselors not to engage in premature problem-solving or circumvent the authority of parents:

> Working with difficult children and ineffective parents, I always need to restrain my impulse to take charge. It seems so easy to say, "Johnny, don't do that," and he'll stop. But I know that *my* ability to make other people's children respond tells me nothing about *their* daily drama of helplessness and despair. It only tells me something about my skill with the children of strangers. . . . The more a therapist takes over and demonstrates his competence, the more likely he is to make the parents feel incompetent by comparison. (Minuchin & Nichols, 1993, pp. 147, 152)

Rushing in and offering quick fixes are seldom helpful—particularly if we are right. Oscar Wilde once said, "It is always a silly thing to give advice, but to give good advice is absolutely fatal." I learned this lesson from experience—several times. One possible strategy to begin to restore the balance is to encourage the adults to negotiate a rule for the youth while requiring the child to listen without interrupting (Tolan & Mitchell, 1990).

Triangulation and hierarchal distortions are two types of structural arrangements within families that limit growth and flexibility; however, many problems, including these, can trace their roots to unproductive communication patterns. In fact, each of the unhealthy communication patterns described in the next lesson are both a cause and effect of unhealthy structural patterns. They tend to be a package deal.

Lesson 6.4: Families With Challenging Youth Are More Likely to Use Habitual Communication Patterns That Tend to Limit Growth and Maintain or Exacerbate Problem Behaviors

Parents often find ways of getting out of difficult situations with their children, but sometimes they get stuck and repeat the same useless solutions again and again, with the same useless results, until everyone is exhausted. (Minuchin & Nichols, 1993, pp. 111–112)

Parents do not want to feel stuck with their children. They reap no benefit from ongoing conflict. They've grown weary of the arguments, the dirty looks, the anger, and the tears. Most can recall a time when things were better—a gentle hug, a subtle smile, a shared laugh, a long walk. Parents want to reconnect with their children. Some remember where they want to go; they just don't know how to get there. Sadly, others have never even seen the map so they assume the only way to go is the direction they are going.

Challenging youth do not want to feel stuck with their parents and siblings. They reap no benefit from ongoing conflict. They've grown weary of the arguments, the dirty looks, the anger, and the tears. Most can recall a time when things were better—a gentle hug, a subtle smile, a shared laugh, a long walk. Children want to reconnect with their families. Some remember where they want to go; they just don't know how to get there. Sadly, others have never even seen the map so they assume the only way to go is the direction they are going.

Virginia Satir (1988) noted that "Once a human being has arrived on this earth, communication is the largest single factor determining the kinds of relationships she or he makes with others and what happens to each in the world" (p. 51). At the risk of oversimplifying complex family dynamics, much family conflict can be traced to habitual communication patterns that limit growth and maintain or exacerbate problem behaviors. Actually, there is nothing simple about the interaction patterns of families in conflict. Intended messages get distorted. Words and looks take on new meaning. Messages within messages carry added significance. Frustration levels run sky high. The sense of hopelessness and helplessness is often palatable.

Even most healthy families struggle to communicate effectively, so unless we grade on a curve, we all would probably fail. Nevertheless, communication patterns in families with challenging youth tend to be more problematic than in other families. These families often share a combination of the following six characteristics:

1. Empathic Listening Is Not Valued and Is Rarely Used

Covey (1989) shared the following conversation with a father who was struggling to connect with his teenage son:

Father: I can't understand my son. He just won't listen to me at all.

Covey: Let me restate what you just said. You don't understand your son because *he* won't listen to *you*?

Father: That's what I said.

Covey: I thought that to understand another person, *you* needed to listen to *him*.

Father: Oh! . . . Oh! . . . Oh yeah! But I do understand him. I know what he's going through. I went through the same thing myself. I guess what I don't understand is why he won't listen to me (p. 239).

While this father's attempt to understand via talking might seem both odd and irrational, it is quite common. Very few families have developed a pattern of seeking first to understand and then to be understood. Empathic listening takes a back seat to talking and waiting to talk. Most of us, on occasion, have fallen victim to the following unproductive mind set:

> I have something I want to say and, by god, I'm going to say it. Who cares if I've already said it over and over and failed to get the outcome I was hoping for. This time it will work. Besides, I have to say it. My automatic pilot is already engaged.

Many family members, like the father in the earlier example, have become so entrenched in these behaviors, they fail to recognize the role they played (and play) in getting and staying stuck.

Because families are often unaware of how they habitually show disrespect for each other by not listening, the counselor may need to be very systematic and directive in his or her facilitation. One of the most common ways to encourage empathic listening is by asking family members to communicate back to the other person what they were saying (and possibly feeling), before responding. Family members can also keep a daily log of how many times they were able to communicate understanding of another's perspective prior to presenting their own. In Chapters 3 and 4 , I identified a number of other behaviors and beliefs that tend to thwart or enhance empathic listening. Parents often feel relieved and empowered when they recognize that they can be empathic, and still hold their child accountable for his or her behavior, and maintain their own perspective on the problem.

Active, empathic listening is one of the most important, yet most underutilized strategies for bringing or keeping family members connected. In fact, if we were to stumble upon a family who consistently displayed empathic communication skills, we might find this behavior even more peculiar than those families who consistently talk over or around one another. Perhaps we should work to develop more peculiar families.

2. Communication Time Is Dominated by One or Two People With an Implicit or Explicit Unwillingness to Compromise (Tolan & Mitchell, 1990)

There are a number of possible reasons why communication may be dominated by one or two family members. This may be a sign of an overly authoritarian parenting style that stresses obedience and respect for traditional values. There is little give-and-take with the children because the parent believes that the child should always accept the parent's position as right (Baumrind, 1971). This style of parenting may seem effective with younger children less likely to challenge parental authority; however, adolescents are more inclined to assert their own autonomy and question rules they perceive as unfair. Rather than adjusting to the developmental changes of adolescents, these parents fear that compromise and negotiation may open the flood gates to anarchy. Authoritarian parents often express concern that efforts to open the lines of communication in the past have "only made things worse."

Although this domineering style of communication is often reflective of an overly authoritarian parenting style, this is not always the case.

One parent's efforts to monopolize discussion may also reflect his or her best effort to avoid the unhealthy triangulation that was discussed in the last lesson. He or she may reason, for example, "If I step in and take charge, my child will not have time to play us against one another." Sometimes, this works. In many families with challenging youth, communication time may be dominated by one or more of the children. This may be a sign of a permissive parenting style in which there are few boundaries, rules, or consequences or it may simply reflect exhausted parents who are desperately trying to maintain their sanity in a chaotic environment.

Tolan and Mitchell (1990) offer a number of suggestions for helping the family realize a more productive sequence of problem solving. First, it is important to remember that there is considerable variation among healthy families, and any new plan should be culturally relevant and mutually agreed upon. Second, it is often best to first encourage discussion and negotiation between the parents by asking them to identify the primary concern(s) they want to communicate to their children. This may help create allies of parents who may be at odds over how to help their children and may serve to model negotiation skills for the children. Third, parents may need to be educated regarding graduated rules by asking them to discuss what behaviors and freedoms are expected and accepted at which ages. Fourth, the counselor may want to structure the interaction time by allowing family members three to five minutes to share their concerns and perspectives. This could also be accomplished in a less systematic manner by encouraging quieter members to share more while politely blocking those who monopolize communication time.

3. Communication Consistently Conveys Unrealistic Expectations That We Can Control Others and Others Can Control Us

In Chapter 4, I noted that believing we can control and change others is so embedded in human behavior and relationships, we often don't recognize how futile it is. This is never more apparent than in the interaction patterns of troubled families. The belief system that drives this behavior often reflects the following dualistic perspective:

> As a parent, I need to be in charge. Being in charge means being able to control those I'm in charge of. I will force you to abide by my rules. If I acknowledge that you have the power to make both good and bad choices, I am relinquishing my own power.

Frustrated parents indulge in fantasies of ownership that only serve to increase their frustration (Glasser, 1998a). These fantasies are reflected in desperate statements such as "You will not drink alcohol," "You will stop hanging out with Joe," and "You will listen to what I have to say."

The following is a more empowering and realistic philosophy parents might want to adopt:

> As a parent, I need to be in charge. Being in charge means establishing clear, age-appropriate expectations and rules and providing leadership and protection. I cannot force you to abide by the house rules, but I will follow through with natural and logical consequences if you choose to break the rules. By acknowledging that you have power to make good and bad choices, I am also acknowledging my own power to make choices.

Family members also relinquish personal power by believing that others have direct control over them. They fail to acknowledge that they are choosing to respond in a certain way. Therefore, they frequently engage in popular, but counterproductive, "Youisms" such as "You make me angry," "You made me hit you," "You caused everyone to get upset," and, "You are tearing this family apart." If family members believe that others have the power to control their feelings, they are more likely to allow others' behaviors to frustrate or agitate them. In this case, parents can be encouraged to examine their own perceptions and statements (i.e., "When I am frustrated, do I make threats that I am unable or unwilling to carry out?" "How can I communicate clear expectations, rules, and consequences in a way that respects my child and myself?" "Am I giving my child too much power to dictate my emotions?").

Many parents (and other adults) who struggle with challenging youth believe they must choose between empathy and dis-cipline. This belief is regularly conveyed in their interaction patterns. Parents can be taught the advantages of consequencing with empathy:

1. Parents model and teach self-control.

2. Parents model and teach youth that understanding does not necessarily mean agreeing.

3. The youth is more likely to focus on the poor choice he or she made rather than the parent's anger.

Consequencing with empathy is not an easy task with challenging youth, particularly for parents who live with the acting-out behavior evcıy day. Parents can be taught the SET (Support, Empathy, Truth) model, described in Chapter 4, a three-step strategy that reinforces boundaries, limits, and consequences while also diffusing conflictual communication patterns.

4. Communication Conveys High Levels of Suspicion and Mistrust (Satir, 1972; Tolan & Mitchell, 1990)

One of the most characteristic patterns of troubled families is the heightened tendency to assume the worst in each other and attribute aggressive or hostile motivations to relatively neutral questions (i.e., "What time is dinner?" "When will you be home?" "Have you seen my keys?"). Unresolved conflict, prior misunderstandings, and fear serve to sabotage family members' ability to trust each other and communicate effectively. Simple questions are often interpreted as attempts to get a family member out on a limb—only to have it sawed off. The primary goal of communication becomes self-preservation. Feeling threatened, family members respond with defensive questions (i.e., "What's that supposed to mean?" "What did I do wrong this time?"). The defenses remain on full alert as the protective armor is seldom removed. Reiss found (as cited in Tolan & Mitchell, 1990) that families with low levels of trust are more likely to view problem-solving opportunities as competitive rather than a joint challenge. This pattern of assuming intentional aggression often leads to an emotional stalemate and therapeutic dilemma.

Tolan and Mitchell (1990) recommended that the counselor help determine who in the family has the greatest motivation to make minimal movements to begin to end the stalemate. The parents may be demoralized while the youth may be willing to take the first steps to regain trust or privileges. It is often advantageous to help the youth evaluate how less defensive communication and more responsive behaviors can lead to tangible benefits such as restored privileges. Initially, they may find it hard to focus on more abstract goals such as family harmony, better relationships, or improved trust. One common theme which may warrant discussion is respect. Parents often complain that youth do not respect their values or authority and children complain that parents do not respect their struggles, positive attributes, and decisions.

> Youth can be coached to speak in a way that does not sound disrespectful, and parents can be coached to appreciate that a difference in opinion is not to be equated with disrespect or lack of affection. The focus on respect rather than being happy or liking each other is important; the positive effect will follow. (Tolan & Mitchell, 1990, p. 37)

5. Communication Is Vague or Indirect (Satir, 1988)

When family members trust one another and feel few threats to self-esteem, communication tends to be more open and direct. Subsequently, the message that is intended is more likely to be the message that is received. Unfortunately, many troubled families, in an effort to protect themselves from further pain, develop unrealistic assumptions that lead to vague, indirect, and counterproductive communication patterns.

Virginia Satir identified two communication traps that are common among struggling families: the hint method and the mind-reading method (Satir, 1988).

She shared the following dialogue between Tom, a 16-year-old boy, and his father to illustrate the first communication trap, the hint method:

Tom asks, "What are you doing tonight, Dad?"

Ted, his father replies, "You can have it!"

Tom, the son, answers, "I don't want it now."

With irritation Ted snaps, "Why did you ask?"

Tom responds angrily, "What's the use?"

What was this discussion about? Tom wanted to know if his father was planning to watch his basketball game; however, fearful that his father might say no if he asked directly, he used the hint method. Ted knew that his son was hinting and incorrectly assumed that he wanted to borrow the car. Tom thought his Dad was putting him off and Ted thought his son was being ungrateful. Both ended up angry and believing that the other did not care (Satir, 1988, p. 76).

A related communication trap is the assumption that others can and should read our minds. Family members tell themselves the following:

If you really care about me, you will know what I'm thinking and feeling with minimal prompts. I should be as transparent to others as I am to myself. When I ask you to "Cut *that* out!" you should know exactly what *that* is. When I tell you to improve your behavior, you should know exactly what I'm looking for.

When family members believe that others can and should read their minds, they feel little impetus to communicate clearly. Furthermore, because they expect mind reading from others, they also believe they too should possess this psychic ability. Therefore, they are reluctant to seek clarification and simple misunderstandings spiral into hurt feelings and confusion. Many harmful reactions could be avoided or minimized if family members remembered to be more specific about what they are saying and sought clarification from one another. Counselors can ask questions to encourage this specificity:

"What exactly would you like Jane to do differently?

"When Jane is beginning to show the improvement you are looking for, what will she be doing?"

"You say you want Jane to start talking more freely. Can you tell Jane exactly what you mean by 'more freely'?"

Counselors can also help family members recognize when they are relying on mind reading or guessing and encourage them to evaluate whether this style of communication is bringing them closer together or pushing them further apart.

Family members often tend to be vague and indirect as a way of avoiding conflict or confrontation. Counselors can encourage family members to evaluate the long-term ramifications of this style of communication, reframe confrontations as a way to develop closer, more genuine relationships, and teach them more productive ways to address concerns and level with each other (i.e., "I" messages, SET method). It can be very liberating to learn that "one does not have to approach something negative, negatively" (Satir, 1988, p. 77).

6. Familial Interactions Lack Playfulness and Humor

As a high school counselor, I remember enrolling two brothers who were accompanied by their mother. They had just moved 1,000 miles away from their home and were understandably apprehensive about a new school. Throughout the interview, the boys drew upon their excellent sense of humors to alleviate some of the anxiety. What struck me about their interaction was how much they seemed to enjoy each other. Several times, the boys had their mom laughing so hard she was in tears. How heartwarming and refreshing! I knew they would be okay.

There's an old saying, "Families who play together, stay together." Laughter and humor have incredible powers to bring people closer together. Troubled families who are able to maintain their perspectives and sense of humors seem to have more energy to make productive changes. It is sad to witness a family who never learned or, who forgot how, to have fun together. Faber and Mazlish (1980) observed that:

> [T]here's nothing like a little humor to galvanize children into action and to perk up the mood in the household. The problem for many parents is that their natural sense of fun fizzles out from the daily irritation of living with kids. (p. 78)

Minuchin frequently informed parents who were fixated on learning strategies to alter their child's behavior, "You don't need techniques for dealing with the kids. What you need are techniques for having fun with each other (Minuchin & Nichols, 1993, p. 160). Glasser (1984) listed *having fun* as one of the five basic psychological needs of all human beings. He asserted that both children and adults use play as a catalyst for learning. In fact, it would be virtually impossible to learn without it. These authors realized the powerful domino effect that enjoying one another can have on all families.

This section identified some common interaction patterns for families with challenging youth. By outlining a handful of possible directions for intervention, I do not mean to imply that change is easily attained. These patterns were developed and learned over a number of years (and probably generations). Decoding and changing such patterns can be a monumental task.

Fortunately, family therapists have developed a number of creative ways to begin to disrupt these patterns. Facilitating family therapy requires a unique set of skills. Professionals who have not been specifically trained in family therapy should refer families to a licensed mental health professional. Parents can also be encouraged to attend parent education programs (i.e., Active Parenting, Parent Effectiveness Training) and read books such as *How to Talk so Kids Will Listen and Listen so Kids Will Talk* (Faber & Mazlish, 1980), *The New Peoplemaking* (Satir, 1988), and *Choice Theory* (Glasser, 1998a) which will provide more detailed information and training for improving the family's interaction skills.

☐ Lesson 6.5: Take Time to See the Big Picture—Empathize With the Families of Challenging Youth

All in all parenting is an almost impossible task, and all parents fall short in some ways.

—Salvador Minuchin (Minuchin & Nichols, 1993, p. 111)

The importance of empathizing with challenging youth has been highlighted throughout this book. We maximize our effectiveness when we are not only able to empathize with the youth but with his or her family as well.

Gail was a social worker who often worked with my agency. Her primary responsibility was to supervise and teach parenting skills to parents who had been convicted of child abuse. Often, the goal was reunification. I was always impressed by her compassion, her ability to see beyond the obvious, and her effectiveness in facilitating positive changes in these families. Gail could be tough, set firm limits, and make unpopular recommendations when warranted, but she was more focused on empathizing with their daily struggles and teaching new strategies than she was in assessing blame and shame. She strived to help them increase their own sense of self-worth. The parents did not feel judged by Gail; they saw her as a genuine ally, and she was. She looked at problems and solutions systemically in an effort to see the big picture. She knew she could take a hardline, judgmental approach and likely encounter opposition or take a more balanced approach. She was a pragmatist and knew that except in extreme cases, the child would eventually return home. Certainly, these parents tended to be more open and honest with Gail because she saw them as more than child abusers. In short, she took the time to understand their world—not excuse it, but understand it. Once she communicated this understanding, positive change was easier to come by.

Again, as a traditional therapist, it's relatively simple for me to be empathic and nondefensive with a child or adolescent in the confines of a one hour therapy session. Rather than immediately reframing the youth's behavior for the parents, I must first communicate some understanding of how they see the behavior. To increase my empathic understanding of troubled families, I often use the *24/7 rule*. I imagine how I might view (or react to) this behavior if I were faced with it 24 hours a day, 7 days a week. Tobin (1991) asserted that child abuse can never be condoned, but sometimes it can be understood:

Imagine yourself as a young parent with a child who recoils from physical touch, never wants to be held, screams and cannot be comforted. Think of the maturity it would require to recognize this as the child's disposition and not your failure as a parent. Now imagine being in the house all day with this child for five years. . . . The abusive parent lacks skills, support, and direction; and needs healing as badly as the child. Condemnation heals no one. (p. 146)

I have also found it helpful to make a distinction between stressed, uninformed parents and evil parents. While I've seen parents whose ritualistic acts of abuse could be described as malicious and evil, the vast majority of parents who struggle with their children are simply overwhelmed by life's stressors or are unprepared for the parental role. It is certainly easier to empathize with parents I view as stressed or uninformed than those I frame as evil.

Furthermore, if we scapegoat the family as the sole cause of the youth's problems, we are likely to alienate one of our most valuable resources (Morse, 1996a). Phyllis and David York, authors of the popular book *Tough Love* (York, York, & Wachtel, 1982), were counselors who admitted that they used to judge parents until their own teenage daughter's behavior began to spiral out of control. They made a strong argument for empathizing and appreciating the struggles of parents as well:

We do not exaggerate when we say that many people, hidden safely behind their desks, forget they are seeing the parents after they've gone through hell and high water. Their perceptions are probably accurate: the parent's behavior is often very "nutsy." . . . We're all used to thinking that parents' behavior affects their kids, not the reverse. . . . People do not live in a vacuum. Their behavior is a product of interaction with their environment, and when their environment, which includes their offspring, changes drastically so do they. (pp. 72–73)

The Yorks are not making a case for accepting or excusing inappropriate or abusive behavior from parents. They merely want helping professionals to recognize that parents are people too. The Yorks have learned through personal and professional experience that for someone to help them get where they wanted to go, the helpers had to first meet them where they were. Otherwise, how would they find them?

☐ Lesson 6.6: Recognize, Appreciate, and Use Group Work and the Power of Peer Culture

Most comprehensive programs for challenging youth recognize and appreciate the power of the peer culture and view group work as an essential therapeutic component. It is beyond the scope of this book to provide a detailed description of group work with this population; rather, I will discuss the rationale for using small groups, share some potential pitfalls and disadvantages of group work, and briefly discuss a multifaceted intervention model designed specifically for angry and aggressive youth.

There are a number of logistical and theoretical reasons why researchers and experts have highly recommended the small group as a means of connecting and intervening with challenging youth.

Groups are more efficient and cost-effective than dyadic treatment approaches because they enable the counselor to work with more youth (Conyne, 1997; Corey & Corey, 1997; Rose, 1998) and have been found to be at least as effective as individual counseling in facilitating positive changes with troubled youth (Rose, 1998; Sleek, 1995; Towberman, 1993). Studies have shown groups to be effective in helping challenging youth in a number of important areas including reducing school dropout (Blum & Jones, 1993), improving interpersonal relationships (Towberman, 1993), improving self-esteem (Omizo & Omizo, 1988), reducing delinquent behaviors (Dryfoos, 1990), improving relationships with parents (Dinkmeyer, Dinkmeyer, & Sperry, 1987), and enhancing self-control and anger management skills (Feindler, Marriott, & Iwata, 1984; Larson, 1992; Omizo & Omizo, 1988). Groups also give the practitioner flexibility to address preventive, educational, or remedial goals (Corey & Corey, 1997; Gladding, 1999) and are often preferred by adolescents themselves (Ohlsen, 1983; Towberman, 1993). Since groups designed for youth tend to be relatively brief, problem-focused, and more cost-effective, they may be more likely to be supported by administrators and funding sources (Corey & Corey, 1997; Sleek, 1995). In an international review of the literature, Zimpfer (1992) found group work to be one of the most common treatment modalities for delinquent and at-risk youth.

Developmentally, groups meet youth where they are. Since much social learning occurs in the context of both formal and informal groups (i.e., family group, classroom group, social group, gangs, sports teams), most adolescents find small groups to be a natural and attractive setting (Gazda, 1984; Gladding, 1999; Rose, 1998). Ohlsen (1983) observed that many adolescents are more likely to share their concerns with peers in group counseling than individual counseling because they believe their peers will more readily accept their deficiencies and understand their perspectives. Furthermore, "the therapy group more nearly stimulates the real world of most clients than the situation consisting solely of a high-status adult and a low-status youth, as one finds in a treatment dyad" (Rose, 1988, p. 17).

As noted earlier, the youth's family is often the counselor's most valuable resource. However, Fishman (1990) recognized that there are times when the youth has been removed from the family or the family structure has been so damaged, that the youth's peer group may be the best prospect for learning more about what makes the youth feel good about him or herself:

> We must assume that even in situations of chronic delinquency, where moral development has been severely impaired, there exists a nascent, better self that can be reached within a context that allows an expression of competence. . . . Tapping into this, however, is often a struggle because it may be that the delinquent peer community is the only place where the adolescent is perceived as competent. . . . Often, to discover what nurtures and enlivens the self, the therapist must search the garden where the delinquent has been watered: the world of the delinquent's peers. Working with this external, second family may be more effective than treating the family that shares room and board with the adolescent. (p. 33)

In addition, groups provide for numerous role players and multiple sources of ideas, enabling the counselor to structure creative and entertaining activities. At a psychiatric hospital where I worked as an adolescent therapist, we recognized the need to experiment with creative group techniques to prevent or reverse therapy fatigue—a common malady of residential facilities where youth are required to participate in several therapeutic modalities every day. One of the most memorable, entertaining, and thought-provoking groups I facilitated there was an impromptu mock court session. Suspecting that several members were simply telling the staff what they wanted to hear or not taking their recovery process seriously, I asked one of the boys if he wanted to take his case to court. Needing a change in the routine and always up for a challenge, he readily agreed. The defendant selected his attorney, I chose the prosecuting attorney, a judge was elected, and, to make things easier, the jury was already sequestered. While each of the members had lots of fun with their roles, they remained focused on the presenting problem. After a forceful but fair cross examination, the defendant was found guilty, and, for the first time in many days, acknowledged he had a drinking problem, and began to take his treatment more seriously. The boy who played the prosecuting attorney received such positive feedback that he began to research the legal profession as a future career. Groups provide us with unique opportunities to do something different and creative.

Yalom (1985) identified a number of other potential therapeutic advantages of group work including universality, installation of hope, altruism, interpersonal learning, social skill development, and catharsis.

Yalom (1985) noted that many people entering counseling share common secrets:

> The most common secret is a deep sense of inadequacy—a feeling that if others really knew the person, they would discover his or her incompetence and see through his or her intellectual bluff. Next in frequency is a deep sense of interpersonal alienation. (p. 9)

My experience leading groups suggests that many challenging youth believe that few of their peers share their feelings of alienation and inadequacy and few, if any, have experienced similar injustices. They tend to mask their feelings through expressions of apathy or various acting-out behaviors. The relief is often palatable when a youngster hears others express similar concerns, fears, and life experiences. While adults can inform the youth that they are not alone, the group process allows them to actually experience a sense of universality with their peers.

Similarly, challenging youth often express hopelessness that their situation will ever improve. Yalom (1985) stressed that he had heard numerous patients share how important it had been in their own recovery to hear directly about the improvements made by others. I have frequently witnessed this phenomenon with adolescents, particularly those who were sexually abused and those who were struggling with substance abuse or dependence. Feeling that others were in the same boat lessened their sense of isolation and gave them hope. A recent study (Chase, 1991) found that two of the most valued therapeutic factors for inpatient adolescents were hope and universality.

Groups also enable youth to see and feel the benefits of supporting and assisting others. Frank (as cited in Yalom, 1985) noted that it was common for tribal leaders in primitive cultures to encourage troubled individuals to prepare a feast or engage in community service. In fact, one of the most effective ways to boost a youth's self-esteem and self-confidence is to structure situations in which they can help others (Gladding, 1999). As a school counselor, my colleagues and I instituted a program in which tenth grade students were trained to go into fourth grade classrooms and lead discussions related to a number of topical issues such as substance abuse and peer pressure. We purposely recruited a number of marginal and at-risk students for this project. Although feedback from the fourth grade students suggested the project was a success, the tenth grade facilitators seemed to benefit the most. Practitioners who are reading this book can undoubtedly relate to the therapeutic value of feeling needed and helpful.

In a recent study of 148 middle school students in Israel, the most important benefits of groups as perceived by the adolescents themselves were interpersonal learning, improved social skills, and catharsis (Shechtman, Bar-El, & Hadar, 1997). Interpersonal learning and social skill development are two interrelated areas that are particularly important for challenging youth as they often lack the necessary skills to effectively communicate their needs to peers and adults (Rose, 1998). Group facilitators can structure opportunities for frequent and varied forms of peer reinforcement and feedback, which is typically more compelling than adult reinforcement. Groups can also help youth gain greater appreciation for diversity and learn to deal with the idiosyncrasies of other individuals (Rose, 1998; Rose & Edleson, 1987). Yalom (1985) stressed that for individuals who lack intimate relationships, the group process may be their first opportunity to receive accurate, interpersonal feedback. Youth can use this feedback to learn new strategies to meet their needs for power and belonging in more prosocial ways outside the group experience.

Corey and Corey (1997) described catharsis as the "expression of pent-up emotions" (p. 249). Perls (1973) and other theorists have written extensively about the interpersonal and psychosomatic ramifications of bottling up strong emotions. It is often a tremendous relief for youth to be able to get things off their chest and feel the support of others when they share their pain. However, research and experience suggest that of all the therapeutic factors noted above, catharsis may be the most delicate.

Antonio, an Italian-American 17-year-old with a steely exterior, had been at the psychiatric hospital for almost a week and only shared superficial feelings and basic facts related to his cocaine addiction. During a group psychodrama exercise in which members played Antonio's family, Antonio appeared to have a breakthrough. He sobbed uncontrollably as he talked about the pain he felt for disgracing his family. Counselors and peers commended Antonio for his willingness to open up. The following day we encouraged Antonio to share how the group experience was for him. Antonio made a minimal reference to the embarrassment he felt for crying in front of his peers, and other efforts to revisit the incident or further discuss his addiction were met with cold stares. Antonio's subsequent progress in the hospital was minimal. Was his reluctance related to this experience, his own ambivalence regarding change, or something else? I'm not sure, but varied experiences with adolescent groups have taught me several valuable lessons regarding cathartic expression.

First, timing is critical as positive effects are more likely when group members have already developed strong bonds (Yalom, 1985). Second, cathartic expression is an intermediate step—not an endpoint. When physically restraining out of control children, it is imperative that the counselor allows time for the youth to process their experience as soon as they are calm. This cognitive reflection allows them to learn from the experience. The same is true of cathartic expression during group sessions. Everyone involved may benefit from taking the time to put the experience into perspective. "The cognitive component includes explaining, clarifying, interpreting, formulating ideas, and providing the cognitive framework for creating a new perspective" (Corey & Corey, 1997, p. 251). When this cognitive processing is neglected or downplayed, children and adolescents often create irrational and destructive meaning related to the experience. Third, overemphasizing this cathartic factor may inadvertently reinforce the myth that the only *real* work during group sessions involves the release of pent-up emotions. Corey and Corey have observed that members can be actively working on their issues and never experience catharsis. Fourth, while cathartic expression may be part of a healing process for many youth, some individuals and cultural groups place greater value on one's ability to restrain strong emotions (Sue & Sue, 1990).

Rose (1998) identified a number of other potential disadvantages of group work with troubled youth. Because youngsters are highly susceptible to peer pressure and the need for approval is so high, members may be overly coercive with one another or reluctant to trust their own instincts and judgment. Another common concern when large numbers of challenging youth get together is the potential to reinforce antisocial and antitherapeutic norms. However, peer pressure can also be used in positive ways to support one another and encourage more prosocial behaviors. A wilderness program in Virginia designed specifically for aggressive, challenging youth reported that they had gone over five years without one incident of physical aggression toward peers or staff. Administrators attributed this record largely to the powerful influence of a positive peer culture.

Another potential obstacle is the difficulty in balancing the need to pursue common goals with the need to structure the group to each individual's needs. Furthermore, many practitioners have not been specifically trained in group counseling and often operate under the mistaken assumption that group work requires the same skills as individual counseling. Successful group work requires specific skill acquisition and expertise (Corey & Corey, 1997; Rose, 1998). Also, group work presents a number of ethical and legal dilemmas. For example, confidentiality is difficult to maintain in group settings. While the individual counselor can assure clients of confidentiality (with certain exceptions), the group counselor cannot guarantee that members will not repeat confidential information. Counselors who work with groups should regularly review books such as *Group Process* by Corey and Corey (1997) to educate themselves regarding the vast array of important ethical and legal considerations for the group practitioner. These authors also underscored that a group's success is largely determined by adequate planning:

> We cannot overemphasize the importance of the preparatory period during which a group is organized. . . . A lack of careful thought and planning will show up later in a variety of problems that lead to confusion and floundering among participants. (p. 106)

Although group work can be more complicated, for the well-trained, well-prepared counselor, the benefits of group work clearly outweigh the disadvantages. Groups designed for challenging youth work best when they are structured around themes of related interest with preplanned activities to engender cohesion and generate discussion and participation. Although flexibility is warranted, most sessions include specific, structured learning objectives that build upon previous sessions (Corey & Corey, 1997; Gladding, 1999).

Goldstein and his colleagues (1987) developed Aggression Replacement Training (ART), a comprehensive model designed to facilitate growth in three areas in which many challenging youth are deficient: 1) interpersonal and social skills, 2) anger management, and 3) moral reasoning. Goldstein and his colleagues worked with small groups of 6 to 12 adolescent boys using a 10-week training format, involving weekly classes for each of the three components. The authors reported that participants have shown significant improvement in each area for groups conducted at schools and various residential facilities.

Goldstein et al. (1987) made a compelling argument that the goal of programs such as theirs should be habilation rather than the more commonly stated goal of rehabilitation.

> The goal of these programs is to enhance behaviors and attitudes not previously in the repertoires of the juveniles involved. "Rehabilitation" connotes efforts to reinstate learned qualities now in disuse. "Habilitation," in contrast, conveys teaching of that which was never previously learned. The interventions described above typically have as their dual goals the unlearning of antisocial attitudes and behaviors and the new learning of prosocial ones. Thus, our choice of the term *habilitation*. (p. 6)

ART consists of three coordinated interventions. The first component, Structured Learning, involves a series of social learning instructional procedures such as modeling and role playing, and is based on the social learning theory of Albert Bandura. For example, group participants are shown a specific social skill in which they are deficient, given guided opportunities to practice the skill, and taught ways to use this skill at home, school, and elsewhere. The second component, Anger Control Training, was developed by Feindler and her research group (Feindler, Marriott, & Iwata, 1984). This model trains youth to recognize triggers or antecedents to their anger as well as various proactive techniques to reduce their anger and generate alternative responses to provocation. The third component, Moral Education, is based largely on the pioneering work of Lawrence Kohlberg. To enhance the likelihood that challenging youth would use these newly developed skills, the authors exposed the youth to a series of moral dilemmas via a 10-week discussion group to advance the youth's moral reasoning to that of the higher level peers in the group.

Higher levels of moral reasoning have been correlated with greater empathy, lower incidents of delinquency, and a variety of other prosocial behaviors (Richardson, Foster, & McAdams, 1998). In essence, the first two components of ART were designed to teach youth *how* to respond in certain situations and the third component was designed to teach them *why*. Ideally, participants develop the necessary behaviors and values to meet their needs in more responsible ways. For a detailed explanation of how to implement this model, readers are encouraged to read *Aggression Replacement Training: A Comprehensive Intervention for Aggressive Youth* (Goldstein, Glick, Reiner, Zimmerman, & Coultry, 1987).

☐ Lesson 6.7: Even the Lone Ranger Never Rode Alone

Previous lessons in this chapter have emphasized the critical role played by families and peers in helping troubled youngsters. This lesson discusses benefits and challenges of developing formal and informal collaboration strategies with other professionals who serve this population. Selekman (1993) observed that "the difficult adolescent client has had frequent encounters with representatives from the juvenile justice system and local police departments, with school personnel, mental health and drug rehabilitation programs in the community, and some involvement with child protective services" (p. 108). As the following case attests, cooperation and communication among these various service providers may be more important for working with challenging youth than any other population.

John, an incredibly resilient 12-year-old White male, has been living with the Porters, an experienced treatment foster care family, for the past two years. When John was 5 years old, his kindergarten teacher, concerned about John's inappropriate touching of other students, convinced his parents to take him to a psychologist. His father fled the state when the psychologist called child protective services to report suspicions of physical and sexual abuse. The next year, John's mother was killed in a traffic accident and he was placed in an emergency foster home. Unable to make sense of these traumatic experiences, John's behavior problems became increasingly more difficult to manage. Since no relatives were willing or able to care for John, custody was awarded to the local department of social services.

For the next three years, several different foster families tried unsuccessfully to help John cope with his losses and manage his explosive temper and impulsive, hyperactive behaviors. Despite considerable efforts on his behalf by a number of caring adults, John's violent outbursts (i.e., attempting to stab his foster parent with a knife, pretending to sexually torture dolls, and several incidents of killing small dogs) necessitated his placement in a long-term residential treatment facility when he was just eight years old. After eight months and minimal progress in residential treatment, John was then moved to a facility which specializes in treating youth with histories of sexual trauma. Over the next two years, John made tremendous strides.

John was recommended for treatment foster care approximately one year before being placed, but several agencies and families were understandably worried about his placement history, extreme hyperactivity, and numerous psychotropic medications. A private treatment foster care agency agreed to pursue the placement after the Porters were identified as a potential foster family and the custodial funding agency agreed to an extensive preplacement process and considerable wraparound services to support the foster family.

Prior to John's placement with the Porter family (Mr. and Mrs. Porter have two adopted boys who were 12 years old), the Porters reviewed his records, met with his case manager several times, discussed his treatment needs with staff members at the residential facility, conferred with their adopted boys' therapist, and had six visits with him, including two weekend visits in the family home. His cottage counselors and therapist worked closely with the treatment foster care agency and the Porter family to develop goals and a behavioral plan to make the transition as smooth as possible. Throughout the preplacement process, John verbalized and demonstrated a commitment to succeed in the Porter home. The following services were offered initially: treatment foster care with intensive case management and crisis support; medical and dental services; weekly individual and family therapy; psychotropic medication management; intensive special education services via the public school; summer programing via the YMCA; and an in-home case aide to support and relieve the Porters up to 20 hours a week.

Since John was first considered for placement, the family and case manager have worked diligently to minimize two potential problems that can arise when so many service providers are working with one youth. First, regular informal communication and scheduled conferences have focused on making sure that everyone knew their role and were working toward common objectives. Second, steps were taken to normalize his familial experience as much as possible. Although John was monitored very closely, he was assigned regular chores, encouraged to participate in organized sports, and included in all family activities and vacations.

Over the last two years, John has made significant emotional, academic, behavioral, and social improvements as evidenced by his achievement of most of his Service Plan and Individualized Education Plan goals. With the support of caring, collaborative teachers and administrators, John's progression in school has been remarkable. His reading scores have gone up four grade levels, there have been no major behavior problems at school, and he has been mainstreamed for several classes. His hyperactivity (which had been infamous) has steadily declined as he has felt more comfortable and secure in his new home and school.

The Porters have accepted John as a member of the family and have dealt with minor setbacks such as lying and failing to follow house rules with appropriate discipline and nurturing. Self-reports and adult observations indicate that he is a much happier and self-assured child. There have been no incidents of acting out sexually and only four or five minor incidents in which John was physically aggressive with siblings and peers. Furthermore, he has become very attached to the family dog and has shown no signs of aggression toward any animal. In-home case aide services have been phased out and his medications have been reduced.

Overall, he has blossomed in his new environment. His therapist reports significant headway in dealing with his sexual trauma and abandonment issues and is supporting the decision by John, the agencies, and the Porter family to change the goal to adoption. His birth father's whereabouts were unknown until recently when he sent John a birthday present. Although John and his birth father have been estranged for years, the adoption process could be accelerated by six to eight months if the father signs a parental termination form.

The letter (Figure 2) written by John requesting that his father consented to the adoption only scratches the surface of the anguish and ambivalence felt by youngsters whose early experiences have been so twisted and traumatic.

After receiving John's letter, his father signed the necessary papers and John continues to thrive as a permanent member of the Porter family.

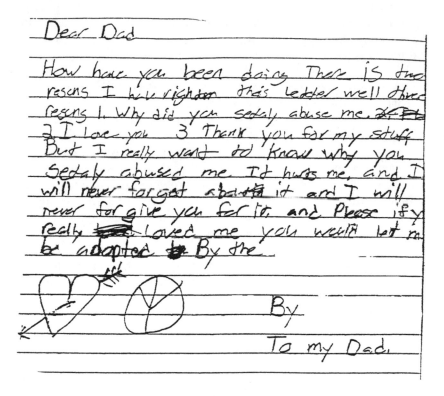

FIGURE 2. Letter by John (names deleted).

John's turnaround is remarkable, but not unparalleled. Early warning signs such as childhood exposure to, and propensity for violence, a fascination with weapons, and an inability to empathize with others are not always predictive of future psychopathy. Although some youth with early histories similar to John's grow up to be callous, violent, and antisocial adolescents and adults, many do not. Factors such as the resiliency of youth, nurturing environments, and early intervention by skilled, caring, and collaborative professionals and caretakers can sometimes help even the most troubled youth develop empathic skills and become responsible citizens.

In addition to illustrating the importance of never giving up on a troubled youth, this case highlights the importance of professional collaboration. Skilled professionals, such as those who have assisted John, know that the likelihood of successful outcomes for troubled youth are significantly increased when collaborative working relationships are culti-vated and a variety of community resources are utilized (Brabeck, Walsh, Kenny, & Comilang, 1997; Dryfoos, 1995; Morse, 1996b; Selekman, 1993). Like most challenging youth, John's case history supports the assertion by Goldstein et al. (1987) that "any and every act of juvenile delinquency has multiple causes, both within and external to the youth himself" (p. 13). Multiple causal factors necessitates a multifaceted, collaborative treatment approach. It is doubtful that John would have made these tremendous gains if the various professionals had not actively worked together.

Mental health professionals have long recognized the need for more collaborative approaches for working with at-risk youth (Selekman, 1993; Trieschman, Whittaker, & Brendtro, 1969; Yeh, White, & Ozcan, 1997). In theory, most, if not all professionals, would readily agree that teamwork is essential. Unfortunately, despite numerous studies demonstrating that collaborative approaches are most successful, many helping professionals continue to operate in a vacuum.

Collaboration is not easy; there are a number of obstacles. It requires considerable time, effort, and organizational support. Many professionals are understandably overwhelmed by paperwork requirements and the sheer numbers of their own case loads. Novice professionals may actually be unaware of many of the numerous individuals in agencies, schools, juvenile justice systems, churches, and so forth who are touched and chal-lenged by troubled youngsters. Some experienced professionals are aware of the larger systems, but have become frustrated and discouraged over a history of poor communication, disjointed coordination of services, role confusion, and territorial disputes (Brabeck, Walsh, Kenny, & Comilang, 1997; Morse, 1996b; Selekman, 1993). Although these frequently cited obstacles still exist, a number of individual, agency, and systemic changes in recent years have helped to bridge the gap between theory and practice. The following are some recommendations for enhancing collaboration among professionals and better serving troubled youth.

Regularly Solicit Feedback From Colleagues, Supervisors, and Other Professionals

Recognize that your perceptions of the youth, family, and situation are always influenced by your own experiences, biases, and projections. Also, remember the unique capacity of troubled youth to locate and push your emotional buttons. By actively pursuing other perspectives, you will be more likely to appreciate how others are approaching the problem, under-stand how you are being effected emotionally, and learn strategies for increasing your objectivity and responding more therapeutically.

Become Knowledgeable Regarding Professionals, Resources, and Policies Specific to Your Local Community

It is essential that helping professionals educate themselves regarding resources, referral sources, and roles and responsibilities of the numerous professionals in the community who regularly work with challenging youth. In addition, knowledge of laws, local ordinances, and organizational policies specific to this population will enhance both effectiveness and credibility. The following are reflective of various questions and dilemmas that might arise:

Jenny may need to be hospitalized for suicidal ideation and the guardians cannot be reached. Whom do I call? What steps will be taken?

Luis has been showing symptoms of Attention Deficit Disorder at home and school. His parents want him tested. Who is qualified to conduct an assessment?

Beverly has been arrested for shoplifting. Her parents want to know what might happen next.

Jermaine was just told that a guardian ad litem has been appointed to him and wants to know what that means.

Last night, Cindi reported that she was being abused by her parents and was placed in an emergency shelter. She wants to know what will happen next.

Professionals with experience networking in the local community would be able to answer many of these questions. While knowing the answers to questions such as these are helpful, no one can be expected to have the answer to every dilemma which arises. Those professionals who educate themselves about various resources and work to develop collaborative relationships will be more likely to know who to ask or where to look.

Take Proactive Steps to Foster Close Working Relationships

Asking the family or legal guardian to sign release of information forms will enable counselors and case managers to communicate freely with other service providers, advocate for the family and youth, and avoid more of the same interventions that have proven ineffective. Knowing that many professionals may feel overwhelmed with their case load or may have been frustrated by previous efforts at collaboration, it is also often advantageous to go out into the community and take proactive steps to foster close working relationships (Selekman, 1993). For example, visits to schools, residential facilities, and juvenile justice centers can give the counselor important insights, help them better understand the program's philosophy and procedures, and open the door for future collaboration. While it may be necessary to educate other professionals about your role or a particular youth, the primary purpose of these meetings should be to learn about their program and hear their perspective. It is also important to remember that challenging youth seldom say "thank you." I've found it helpful to take 10 or 15 minutes a week to convey appreciation by writing a brief thank you note or calling a colleague's supervisor to commend his or her work. By taking the initiative to seek out busy professionals, communicate that you value their role, and demonstrate that you are a team player, you are more likely to be given pivotal information and involved in key decisions.

Recognize the Unique Role Played by Schools and School Personnel

Because schools are embedded in the community, educate nearly all of society's children, and rely on a range of professionals, they increasingly are recognized as an opportune site for needed reforms in services delivery to children, youth, and families. In the midst of societal changes, schools will remain in the lives of our nation's poorest children, even after other institutions have collapsed or withdrawn. (Brabeck, Walsh, Kenny, & Comilang, 1997)

The role of schools and school personnel in assisting challenging youth cannot be overestimated. With the exception of parents and legal guardians, teachers spend more time with youth than any other adult and are often thrust into the role of front-line clinicians. Teachers, school counselors, and administrators can be instrumental in the early identification and intervention of learning disabilities, behavior problems, emotional difficulties, and social skill deficiencies. Students' self-perceptions regarding their ability to relate to other students and achieve academically impacts their development. Glasser (1998a) asserted that youth who are able to develop a successful identity in school are far less likely to develop behavioral and emotional problems.

Morse (1996b) observed that the need for a mental health–education liaison began in the 1920s. Attempts to develop effective partnerships between school personnel and other community professionals have had mixed results. Numerous challenges for developing effective partnerships have included disagreements over fiscal responsibilities, confusion regarding roles and goals, and various regulations and structures which make access difficult (Brabeck, Walsh, Kenny, & Comilang, 1997; Morse, 1996b). To address many of these obstacles, a number of communities have begun to develop full service schools which integrate a variety of educational, medical, legal, vocational, social, and human services. Services typically provided by the school are linked with various social services that can support the educational agenda. Although full service schools vary in their composition, each is designed to optimize community resources and interprofessional collaboration (Dryfoos, 1995).

Work to Develop and Enhance Community Models That Support Interagency Coordination and Cooperation

Recognizing both the inherent difficulties and value in developing partnerships for serving at-risk youth, Virginia was one of many states to pass recent legislation supporting and mandating comprehensive, community-based services. Starting in 1993, the Comprehensive Services Act (CSA) began requiring a new, coordinated approach to services for youth with emotional and behavioral difficulties. Funds from four state agencies were consolidated and community planning and assessment teams were developed. Each team consisted of parent advocates, individuals from the private sector, and representatives from the primary service delivery systems (i.e., school system, juvenile justice, mental health, social services, private agencies). The CSA included four basic tenets:

1. a full parental partnership with service providers in the determination of services

2. an independent financial base to ensure continuation of services

3. a community-based, child-centered, individually designed system that uses the least restrictive service delivery system

4. a reduction of the financial burden of state and local governments (Yeh, White, & Ozcan, 1997).

These four tenets reflect the struggles and desires of many states needing to explore less restrictive, more fully integrated, and less expensive alternatives to hospitalization.

Many states have recognized the importance of developing a system that includes a full range of mental health services tailored to the needs of individual children. This range of services, often referred to as a continuum of care, "aims to deliver coordinated services on an individualized basis using case management and interdisciplinary treatment teams to integrate and facilitate transition between services. The continuum is designed to be community-based, involving various agencies pertinent to children's needs" (Bickman, 1996, p. 689).

The CSA made it easier for many families to navigate through the various service systems. In essence, it created one-stop shopping, a point of entry where families had immediate access to a wide array of services. Service planning across agencies became more consistent which enabled reviewers to more easily assess outcomes. Perhaps most importantly, the emergence of community planning and assessment teams shifted much of the responsibility and incentive for making systemic change and enhancing the continuum of care onto community leaders who had more power to affect change. Previously, individual professionals and parents recognized that their community lacked the necessary programs and services for many at-risk youth, but felt powerless in effecting systemic change. These teams began to devise more comprehensive strategic plans to strengthen their continuum of care by developing or improving services such as intensive day treatment programs and crisis stabilization services.

Since many of these organizations and individuals were not accustomed to coordinating services, it is not surprising that many local planning and assessment teams experienced growing pains during the CSA's first several years. For example, some localities reported an increase in costs and some schools complained that special education students and programs were no longer being adequately served (Yeh, White, & Ozcan, 1997). Some of these early difficulties may have been a direct result of numerous providers trying to make sense of a new, evolving system; however, many struggles may have been more reflective of the new responsibility of one entity to acknowledge and address longstanding systemic problems (i.e., inadequate continuum of care, poor communication among providers). This mandate to cooperate may have heightened short-term frustrations by spotlighting existing problems in some communities, but it may also have provided the impetus for making important changes. Imperfect, formalized systems of collaboration appear to offer much more promise for helping troubled youth and families than fragmented, informal approaches where communication between providers is encouraged but not required.

☐ **Lesson 6.8: Follow the Lead of Activists like Mubarak Awad and Joseph Marshall— Advocate for Youth and Families**

Dr. Mubarak Awad had been taught that hard work pays dividends; yet, during much of the 1970s, as he worked tirelessly to meet the needs of troubled youth and families in Ohio, frustration became his greatest dividend. He believed that Ohio's current social services system was inadequate, unjust, and needed to be changed. As a child in Jerusalem, Awad had been forced to live in an orphanage after his father died, and he felt strongly that youth grow and develop best in a family setting—preferably their own. Too many youth who could succeed in home environments or community placements were being placed or kept in institutional settings because Ohio lacked alternative community placement options. In fact, Ohio ranked number one in the nation in 1978 in the number of youth held in secure facilities (National Youth Advocate Program, 1997).

With support of the Ohio Youth Commission (now the Department of Youth Services), the state agency responsible for finding placements for delinquent youth, Awad established the Ohio Youth Advocate Program, a private, not-for-profit organization designed to support and facilitate the development and operation of community-based residential and nonresidential services for at-risk youth and families. A variety of services such as therapeutic foster care, emergency shelter care homes, and respite care were crafted "based upon the belief that troubled youth should be surrounded by concerned, caring individuals within the community rather than the bars and walls of institutions" (National Youth Advocate Program Description, 1997, p. 1).

In 1983, due largely to the success of the Ohio program, the National Youth Advocate Program (NYAP) was incorporated. Over the years, NYAP has developed a reputation for creating innovative programs that utilize community resources and contain costs. By 1997, NYAP had expanded into a multi-state organization caring for approximately 1,350 youth and an international organization dedicated to advocating for the rights of youth around the world (National Youth Advocate Program, 1997). Although a number of dedicated and caring individuals are responsible for the growth and success of the National Youth Advocate Program, the fruits of their labor can be traced to the vision of Mubarak Awad. He saw a problem and created a solution.

Joseph Marshall became a teacher because he wanted to make a difference in the lives of African-American youth. Like Mubarak Awad, Marshall felt like much of his hard work was offset by systemic injustices, a culture of violence and drugs, and other ecological obstacles. In his book,

Street Soldiers (Marshall & Wheeler, 1996), Marshall recalls one of his most gifted students who kept having trouble staying awake during class because he didn't have a home. The boy worked nights to feed himself and slept in his aunt's basement several hours a night. Eventually, the youngster withdrew from school and Marshall ran into him several years later in the county jail, where he was serving time for selling drugs. Marshall shares how this and other tragedies eventually became so overwhelming that he had to try something new:

> As a teacher who had set out to make a difference—and I had plenty of company in that respect—it was not only tragic but also disillusioning to witness all that promise being laid to waste at such a tender age. The most frustrating part was that I was *trying* to help. I had dedicated my career to that purpose, but in the greater scheme of things it seemed almost fruitless. There were teenagers all around me drowning in an ocean of neglect, and I was frantically rowing out to save them in a crepe-paper lifeboat. There had to be another vehicle. (Marshall & Wheeler, 1996, p. 38)

Hard work is seldom the precipitator of burnout. It's the deadly combination of hard work, a sense of powerlessness to change inadequate systems, and the persistent feeling that your hard work is not reaping benefits which can be so paralyzing for so many professionals.

Fortunately, Joseph Marshall was able to harness his strong will and channel his frustration of losing too many young people to drugs and violence into the development of the Omega Boys Club. A grassroots organization started by Marshall and Jack Jacqua in the inner city of San Francisco, the Omega Boys Club was founded upon the belief that troubled teenagers *"want* a way out but just *don't know how to get out"* (Marshall & Wheeler, 1996, p. xxvii). In a 1987 letter to parents to garner support for their club, Marshall and Jacqua described the club's mission:

> The purpose of the club is to motivate boys to do their best in life and enjoy their achievements through academic and recreational activities. The Boys Club is basically an academic organization. We will ask each member to try to maintain the highest standards possible in school and their social lives. The Boys Club will make a strong effort to find out what it takes to help members develop to their greatest potential. (pp. 48–49)

Over the next 10 years, with the help of community support, the club grew to over 300 members who wore T-shirts proudly proclaiming they do not use drugs. The Omega Boys Club sponsored a weekly radio call-in program for inner city teenagers, developed peer counseling programs in several juvenile detention centers, and organized youth conferences where thousands of young people gathered to discuss strategies for improving their communities. Furthermore, the club placed over 100 members in various colleges, many of whom were former gang members and drug dealers. Amazingly, Marshall and Jacqua ran the Omega Boys Club at night on a volunteer basis (with the help of numerous other volunteers) while working full time as teachers during the day. The success of this club shows the tangible rewards that can be sown when passion triumphs over despair and people are inspired by a better way.

Cowen (1985) noted that a youngster's social environments can either restrict or facilitate their competence development. Professionals who work with challenging youth have to decide whether "to accept such effects as they fall randomly or to develop and apply bodies of knowledge designed to promote psychologically facilitative environments" (Cowen, 1985, p. 38). Proactive counselors recognize that problems derived from inadequate services or social systems need to be addressed systemically (Lewis & Lewis, 1989). While not everyone has the vision and organizational skills of Mubarak Awad and Joseph Marshall to make sweeping changes or develop large-scale programs, all professionals can utilize out of the box thinking to begin to reshape the youth's environment. Countless teachers, counselors, social workers, and coaches across America consistently make a difference by living the cliche, "If you are not part of the solution, you are part of the problem." These individuals challenge inadequate systems and advocate for youth and families whose rights may be in jeopardy. To help assess systemic influences on presenting problems, Lewis and Lewis (1989) recommended helping professionals, youth, and families work together to explore the following questions:

1. To what extent is the individual capable of resolving the issue through personal change?

2. What resources in the environment are available to help the individual grow?

3. To what extent does the solution depend on changing the environment, rather than on changing the individual?

4. How can the counselor, the client, or both bring about the necessary changes in the environment? (p. 8)

☐ Lesson 6.9: We Must Also Concentrate Our Efforts on Preventing and Addressing Problems Upstream

Every day, it feels like thousands of at-risk youth either get pushed or jump into raging waters before they are able to swim. Counselors and other trained lifeguards see these youngsters floating downstream and do their best to pull them out one at a time. Desperately trying to keep their heads above water and uncertain as to who or what is responsible for their predicament, many of these kids actively fight those who are trying to rescue them. Unfortunately, these struggles limit the number of youth who can be helped by any one lifeguard. Efforts to remedy this growing crisis need to consider a number of proactive and reactive approaches.

Throughout this book, a number of general principles and specific strategies have been offered to better train these lifeguards to maximize their rescue efforts. Enhancing self-awareness and empathic understanding regarding youth who feel they are drowning should help to build trust and reduce the intensity and frequency of these struggles. Discarding strategies that have not been effective and using multiple resources to develop more creative approaches should also help to pull more youth out of these turbulent waters. Many of the intervention strategies outlined in this book could also be characterized as secondary or tertiary prevention efforts. Secondary prevention is directed at early identification and prompt treatment of behavioral, emotional, and familial problems. Tertiary prevention is aimed at preventing long-term effects and reducing recidivism of delinquent acts or problem behaviors of challenging youth (Bartollas & Miller, 1998; Lewis & Lewis, 1989).

While these stopgap measures may help individual youth and families, communities need to continue to implement long-term, primary prevention programs to stem the tide of at-risk youth in America. Primary prevention focuses on proactive measures to lower the incidence of emotional, behavioral, and familial problems and is aimed primarily at high-risk groups not yet having special difficulties (Albee & Ryan-Finn, 1993). In essence, primary prevention programs concentrate their efforts upstream. They are designed to educate and strengthen communities and families, and prevent youth from jumping or being thrown into the rivers. Since few problems can be completely eliminated, primary prevention efforts also concentrate on supplying individuals with multiple life preservers and teaching them to swim.

Albee and Ryan-Finn (1993) contended that prevention "is the only feasible way to deal with the gap between the enormous number of individuals at risk for emotional disturbance and the limited availability of treatment resources" (p. 115). Sarason and Sarason (1996) proposed that the best treatment for conduct disorder is prevention. Since the inception of the Community Mental Health Centers Act of 1963, more communities have placed emphasis on primary prevention efforts. Examples of these efforts include Head Start, parent education programs, The Boys and Girls Clubs of America, the War on Poverty, and public service announcements on the dangers of drinking and driving (Orton, 1997).

Melton (1991) echoed the sentiments of many when he asserted that "prevention should be the cornerstone of child mental health policy" (p. 69). We sometimes expend so much effort getting kids out of the water, we forget that the problem can only be prevented or significantly reduced by also concentrating our efforts upstream:

> Although most human services professionals favor prevention over remediation, it is certainly fair to say that most investments in mental health services for children have been expensive reactions to problems that are already well developed and severe enough to attract attention. A more proactive and sensible response would be to expend existing resources on supports and interventions that would prevent problems or lessen their severity before they take their toll in human and economic hardship. (Orton, 1997, p. 356)

The primary purpose of this book was to offer practical strategies to help youth who had already been identified as challenging; however, to fully address the growing epidemic of at-risk youth and families in America, there must be sufficient allocation of resources to develop multifaceted, community-based, family-oriented models aimed at both prevention and intervention.

7

Revisiting the Six Principles

Each of the 47 lessons I have presented in this book contains a number of specific strategies, self-evaluation questions, and other considerations for working with challenging youth. The applicability of these recommendations will vary depending on your responses to the evaluation questions, your unique experiences, your personality and preferred style, and your roles, responsibilities, and expectations with this population. While I encourage you to make a deliberate effort to implement those recommendations that are most meaningful and useful for you, I want to reemphasize that our overall success in working with challenging youth rests largely on the attitudes, beliefs, and behaviors we display over time with a cross section of tough kids. Subsequently, I conclude by briefly revisiting the six interrelated principles that I propose are common denominators of the most successful practitioners and intervention models. When consistently applied, foundational principles become behavioral habits that enable fundamental transformations of individuals, relationships, and organizations (Covey, 1990).

    1. A therapeutic relationship is an essential ingredient for facilitating positive change with challenging youth. Specific techniques are relatively unimportant compared to therapeutic relationships, which are the result of a pattern of interactions over time. This principle is perhaps the most important because it is a necessary precondition for subsequent principles and techniques. Our belief (or disbelief) in this principle impacts most of our interactions and interventions with tough kids. Therefore, every lesson in every chapter has conveyed the importance of building and maintaining therapeutic relationships. As Irwin Yalom (1985) noted, "It is the relationship that heals" (p. 50).

2. Ongoing helper self-awareness and self-evaluation are critical for building and maintaining therapeutic relationships. Therapeutic relationships are absolutely dependent on our willingness and ability to regularly assess what we think and how we feel about specific youngsters and challenging youth in general. To keep this principle alive, I encourage you to review the self-inventory from Chapter 1 and the other self-evaluation questions presented throughout the book, and develop your own self-inventory based on those questions with the most personal and professional relevance for you. Schedule a time (by yourself or with a colleague, supervisor, or counselor) to regularly review your inventory and take concrete steps to keep moving in a positive direction along the continuum. Also, do not forget to notice the many ways you make a difference in the lives of troubled youth.

3. To help youth get where they (or you) want to go, you must first meet them where they are—individually, developmentally, and culturally. To meet youth where they are individually, we must take the time to find out what makes each youth unique. We do this by encouraging youth to share their stories and perspectives, listening empathically, and communicating through words and deeds that *they* are the real experts. To meet youth where they are developmentally, we periodically reflect back on our own adolescence, we ask questions to better understand how this period of searching and sorting is impacting today's adolescents, and we pay close attention to how each youth is attempting to meet their need for love and belonging (identity) and need for power and achievement (esteem). To meet youth where they are culturally, we embrace a model of cultural pluralism, we develop a clearer sense of our own cultural identity, and we strive to better understand and appreciate the racial, cultural, and individual uniqueness of each youth and family.

4. For relationships to mature, there must be a healthy balance between support and challenge. Challenging youth need to be supported and understood; however, they do not need or want to be coddled. In fact, the vast majority of these kids expect and want to be challenged by adults they feel close to. Many have difficulty managing and expressing their own emotions and look to adults to provide external control when warranted. Adults who fail to confront them or provide this structure are likely to be viewed as frightened, inadequate, or disingenuous. As helping professionals, we have a responsibility to help youth recognize discrepancies between their current behavior and their stated goals. Timely and effective confrontations can actually work to affirm the realness of the relationships and bring people closer together. Confrontations also serve to test the strength of the relationship. Those relationships (including those between adults and adolescents) that disintegrate under challenge are based on a false sense of connection. The key is balance.

5. Problems and solutions are best framed in creative, constructive, and caring ways. The success of various approaches, regardless of their theoretical framework, lies in the ability of counselors, youth, and families to begin to view the situation in a way that engenders hope and stimulates positive change. Counselors who are most gifted with this population possess both the creativity and the compassion to see these youth and their struggles differently than most other adults. They are able to sell new frames for old pictures. As pragmatists, they know to steer clear of previous ways of viewing and doing which have not been helpful. Because they pay attention to what they pay attention to, they are more apt to explore client strengths and adjust their approach to meet the needs of the youth and family. Furthermore, since they understand the mythical power of diagnostic labels, effective helping professionals take a number of proactive steps to make the assessment process more consumer-friendly.

6. Systemic, collaborative, and preventive approaches tend to be more fruitful than isolated or reactive approaches. Many of the earlier chapters emphasized ways counselors can engage youth who are unable or unwilling to ask for or accept help. These lessons focused on strategies for cultivating this one-on-one relationship. Later chapters highlighted the tremendous influence of families, communities, and social environments and the importance of appreciating this context and attending to these ecological considerations. As residential treatment facilities have learned over the years, the family is typically the most important influence and needs to be an integral part of the treatment process. Furthermore, since the typical challenging youth has had or will have extensive involvement with a wide array of community service providers, success is largely dependent on the ability and willingness of various professionals to communicate and collaborate. Counselors also have a responsibility to advocate for youth by working to impact inadequate or unjust systems and by actively supporting prevention efforts. Always be cognizant of the bigger picture.

I encourage you to take a minute to reflect on where you currently are regarding these six principles. Do you believe these principles capture the essence of effectively intervening with challenging youth? Are there any principles you would add to your list? Have you learned new ideas (or relearned old ones) for enhancing your ability to incorporate these principles? I encourage you to research and develop your own ideas and strategies, and keep a separate folder for each principle.

I have tried to paint a perceptive portrait of challenging youth and their struggles; however, brief narratives are seldom as heartfelt, messy, or fast paced as the real-life dramas that these youth engage us in. Because challenging youth do not always give us ample time to consider our options and rehearse our responses, we will continue to make mistakes and lose our way from time to time. Hopefully, these principles can serve as a compass to guide us in the right direction and keep us from straying too far from the path.

REFERENCES

Albee, G. W., & Ryan-Finn, K. D. (1993). An overview of primary prevention. *Journal of Counseling and Development, 72,* 115–123.

Alexander, J. F., Waldron, H. B., Barton, C., & Mas, C. H. (1989). The minimizing of blaming attributions and behaviors in delinquent families. *Journal of Consulting and Clinical Psychology, 57*(1), 19–24.

American Psychiatric Association. (1994). *Diagnostic and statistical manual of mental disorders* (4th ed.). Washington, DC: Author.

Anderson, B. S. (1996). *The counselor and the law* (4th ed.). Alexandria, VA: American Counseling Association.

Atkinson, D. R., Morten, G., & Sue, D. W. (1993). *Counseling American minorities: A cross-cultural perspective* (4th ed.). Madison, WI: Brown & Benchmark.

Bandler, R., & Grinder, J. (1979). *Frogs into princes: Neuro linguistic programming.* Moab, UT: Real People Press.

Bandura, A. (1974). Behavior therapy and the models of man. *American Psychologist, 29,* 859–869.

Bandura, A., & Walters, R. H. (1960). *Social learning and personality development.* New York: Holt, Rinehart, & Winston.

Barker, P. (1994). Reframing: The essence of psychotherapy? In J. K. Zeig (Ed.), *Ericksonian methods: The essence of the story* (pp. 211–223). New York: Brunner/Mazel.

Bartollas, C., & Miller, S. J. (1998). *Juvenile justice in America* (2nd ed.). Upper Saddle River, NJ: Prentice-Hall.

Baruth, L. G., & Robinson, III, E. H. (1987). *An introduction to the counseling profession.* Englewood Cliffs, NJ: Prentice-Hall.

Baumrind, D. (1971). Current patterns of parental authority. *Developmental Psychology Monographs, 4,* 1–103.

Beauchamp, T. L., & Childress, J. F. (1983). *Principles of biomedical ethics* (2nd ed.). Oxford, England: Oxford University Press.

Bickman, L. (1996). A continuum of care: More is not always better. *American Psychologist, 51*(7), 689–701.

Bienert, H., & Schneider, B. H. (1993). Deficit-specific social skills training with peer-nominated aggressive-disruptive and sensitive-isolated preadolescents. *Journal of Applied Developmental Psychology, 24,* 287–299.

Biever, J. L., Jordan, A., Franco, M., Nath, P. S., & Yee, E. F. (1993). Passing the baton. In T. S. Nelson & T. S. Trepper (Eds.), *101 interventions in family therapy.* New York: The Haworth Press.

Bing, L. (1991). *Do or die.* New York: Harper Perennial.

Blum, D. J., & Jones, L. A. (1993). Academic growth group and mentoring program for potential dropouts. *The School Counselor, 40,* 207–217.

Bond, J. (1999, February). *Civil rights: Now and then, Then and now.* Paper presented for Ethics/Religion and Society Lecture Series, Xavier University, Cincinnati, OH.

Brabeck, M., Walsh, E. W., Kenny, M., & Comilang, K. (1997). Interpersonal collaboration for children and families: Opportunities for counseling psychology in the 21st century. *The Counseling Psychologist, 25*(4), 615–636.

Brendtro, L. K., & Brokenleg, M. (1996). Beyond the curriculum of control. In N. Long, W. C. Morse, & R. G. Newman (Eds.), *Conflict in the classroom: The education of at-risk and troubled students* (5th ed., pp. 94–105). Austin, TX: Pro-ed.

Brendtro, L. K., & Ness, A. E. (1983). *Re-educating troubled youth: Environments for teaching and treatment.* New York: Aldine.

Brown, J. H., & Christensen, D. N. (1986). *Family therapy: Theory and practice.* Monterey, CA: Brooks/Cole.

Cade, B., & O'Hanlon, W. H. (1993). *A brief guide to brief therapy.* New York: W. W. Norton & Company.

Carkhuff, R. (1969). *Helping and human relations* (Vol. 2). New York: Holt, Rinehart, & Winston.

Chase, J. L. (1991). Inpatient adolescent and latency-age children's perspectives on the curative factors in group psychotherapy. *Groups, 15,* 95–108.

Cline, F., & Fay, J. (1990). *Parenting with love and logic: Teaching children responsibility.* Colorado Springs, CO: Pinon Press.

Colapinto, J. (1991). Structural family therapy. In A. S. Gurman & D. P. Knisken (Eds.), *Handbook of family therapy* (Vol. 2, pp. 417–443). New York: Brunner/Mazel.

Compas, B. E. (1987). Stress and life events during childhood and adolescence. *Clinical Psychology Review, 7,* 275–302.

Conyne, R. K. (1997). Group work ideas I have made aphoristic (for me). *Journal for Specialists in Group Work, 22*(3), 149–156.

Corey, G. (1996). *Theory and practice of counseling and psychotherapy* (5th ed.). Pacific Grove, CA: Brooks/Cole.

Corey, G., Corey, M., & Callanan, P. (1993). *Issues and ethics in the helping professions* (4th ed.). Pacific Grove, CA: Brooks/Cole.

Corey, M. S., & Corey, G. (1997). *Group process and practice* (5th ed.). Pacific Grove, CA: Brooks/Cole.

Covey, S. R. (1989). *The 7 habits of highly effective people.* New York: Simon & Schuster.

Covey, S. R. (1990). *Principled-centered leadership.* New York: Simon & Schuster.

Cowen, E. L. (1985). Person-centered approaches to primary prevention in mental health: Situation-focused and competence-enhancement. *American Journal of Community Psychology, 13,* 31–48.

deShazer, S. (1984). The death of resistance. *Family Process, 23,* 79–93.

deShazer, S. (1985). *Keys to solutions in brief therapy.* New York: W.W. Norton & Company.

deShazer, S. (1988). *Clues: Investigating solutions in brief therapy.* New York: W. W. Norton & Company.

Dinkmeyer, D. C., Dinkmeyer, D. C., Jr., & Sperry, L. (1987). *Adlerian counseling and psychotherapy* (2nd ed.). Columbus, OH: Merrill.

Dryfoos, J. G. (1990). *Adolescents at risk: Prevalence and prevention.* New York: Oxford University Press.

Dryfoos, J. G. (1995). Full service schools: Revolution or fad? *Journal of Research on Adolescence, 5*(2), 147–172.

Faber, A., & Mazlish, E. (1980). *How to talk so kids will listen and listen so kids will talk.* New York: Avon Books.

Fagan, S. A. (1996). Fifteen teacher intervention skills for managing classroom behavior problems. In N. Long, W. C. Morse, & R. G. Newman (Eds.), *Conflict in the classroom: The education of at-risk and troubled students* (5th ed.). Austin, TX: Pro-ed.

Feindler, E. L., Marriott, S. A., & Iwata, M. (1984). Group anger control training for junior high school delinquents. *Cognitive Therapy and Research, 8*(3), 299–311.

Fisch, R., Weakland, J. H., & Segal, L. (1982). *The tactics of change: Doing therapy briefly.* San Francisco: Jossey-Bass.

Fishman, H. C. (1990). *Treating troubled adolescents: A family therapy approach.* New York: Basic Books.

Frank, J. D. (1982). Therapeutic components shared by all psychotherapies. In J. H. Harvey & M. M. Parks (Eds.), *The master lecture series, Vol. 1: Psychotherapy research and behavior change* (pp. 9–37). Washington, DC: American Psychological Association.

Frankl, V. E. (1963). *Man's search for meaning.* New York: Simon & Schuster.

Furman, B., & Aloha, T. (1992). *Solution talk: Hosting therapeutic conversations.* New York: W. W. Norton & Company.

Garfat, T. (1990). The involvement of family members as consumers in treatment programs for troubled youths. In M. Krueger & N. Powell (Eds.), *Choices in caring: Contemporary approaches to child and youth care work* (pp. 125–143). Washington, DC: Child Welfare League of America.

Gazda, G. M. (1984). *Group counseling: A developmental approach* (3rd ed.). Boston: Allyn & Bacon.

Gilligan, C., Rogers, A. G., & Tolman, D. L. (Eds.). (1991). *Women, girls, and psychotherapy: Reframing resistance.* New York: The Haworth Press.

Gladding, S. T. (1999). *Group work: A counseling profession* (3rd ed.) Columbus, OH: Merrill.

Glasser, W. (1965). *Reality therapy: A new approach to psychiatry.* New York: Harper & Row.

Glasser, W. (1972). *The identity society* (rev. ed.). New York: Harper & Row.

Glasser, W. (1984). *Take effective control of your life.* New York: Harper & Row.

Glasser, W. (1998a). *Choice theory: A new psychology of personal freedom.* New York: HarperCollins.

Glasser, W. (1998b, January). *Counseling for the 21st century: Reality therapy/choice theory.* Presentation at Greater Cincinnati Counseling Association Winter Workshop, Xavier University, Cincinnati, OH.

Goldstein, A. P., Glick, B., Reiner, S., Zimmerman, D., Coultry, T. M. (1987). *Aggression replacement training: A comprehensive intervention for aggressive youth.* Champaign, IL: Research Press.

Goleman, D. (1995). *Emotional intelligence.* New York: Bantam.

Goodman, M., Brown, J. A., & Deitz, P. M. (1996). *Managed care II: A handbook for mental health professionals* (2nd ed.). Washington, DC: American Psychiatric Press.

Gordon, T. (1975). *Parent effectiveness training.* New York: Bantam.

Gordon, T. (1978). *Leadership effectiveness training.* New York: Bantam.

Gurian, M. (1998). *A fine young man: What parents, mentors, and educators can do to shape adolescent boys into exceptional men.* New York: Jeremy P. Tarcher/Putnam.

Haig, R. (1986). Therapeutic uses of humor. *American Journal of Psychotherapy, 40,* 543–553.

Haley, J. (1963). *Strategies of psychotherapy.* New York: Grune & Stratton.

Haley, J. (1980). *Leaving home: The therapy of disturbed young people.* New York: McGraw-Hill.

Hardy, K. (1996, September). *Family counseling from a multicultural perspective.* Paper presented at the meeting of Virginia Association of Marital and Family Therapists, Richmond, VA.

Hartmann, T. (1993). *Attention deficit disorder: A different perception.* Penn Valley, CA: Underwood Books.

Herlihy, B., & Corey, G. (1996). *ACA ethical standards casebook* (5th ed.). Alexandria, VA: American Counseling Association.

Herman, J. L. (1992). *Trauma and recovery.* New York: Basic Books.

Hoffman, M. L. (1976). Empathy, role-taking, guilt, and development of altruistic motives. In T. Lickona (Ed.), *Moral development and behavior: Theory, research, and social issues* (pp. 124–143). New York: Holt, Rinehart, & Winston.

Hutchins, D. E., & Vaught, C. C. (1997). *Helping relationships and strategies* (3rd ed.). Pacific Grove, CA: Brooks/Cole.

Johns, B. H., & Carr, V. G. (1995). *Techniques for managing verbally and physically aggressive students.* Denver: Love.

Johnson, J. H. (1986). *Life events as stressors in childhood and adolescence.* Beverly Hills, CA: Sage.

Jongsma, A. E., Peterson, L. M., & McInnis, W. P. (1996). *The child and adolescent psychotherapy treatment planner.* New York: John Wiley & Sons.

Jung, C. G. (1934). *Modern man in search of a soul.* London: Kegan Paul, Trench, Trubner & Co.

Karasu, T. (1986). The specificity versus nonspecificity dilemma: Toward identifying therapeutic change agents. *American Journal of Psychiatry, 14*(3), 687–695.

Karp, N. (1993). Collaboration with families: From myth to reality. *The Journal of Emotional and Behavioral Problems 1*(4), 21–23.

Kellerman, J. (1999). *Savage spawn: Reflections on violent children.* New York: Ballantine.

Kellner, S. (1989). *Taking it to the limit with basketball-cybernetics.* East Setauket, NY: Stan Kellner.

Kitchener, K. S. (1988). Dual role relationships: What makes them problematic? *Journal of Counseling and Development, 67,* 217–221.

Kottler, J. A. (1993). *On being a therapist* (rev. ed.). San Francisco: Jossey-Bass.

Kottler, J. A., & Hazler, R. J. (1996). Impaired counselors: The dark side brought into the light. *Journal of Humanistic Education and Development, 34,* 98–107.

Kreisman, J. J., & Straus, H. (1989). *I hate you—don't leave me: Understanding the borderline personality.* New York: Avon.

Kuhlman, T. L. (1984). *Humor and psychotherapy.* Chicago: Dow Jones-Irwin.

Kushner, H. S. (1986). *When all you've ever wanted isn't enough: The search for a life that matters.* New York: Pocket Books.

Kushner, H. S. (1996). *How good do we have to be? A new understanding of guilt and forgiveness.* New York: London, Brown.

Larson, J. D. (1992). Anger and aggression management techniques through the Think First curriculum. *Journal of Offender Rehabilitation, 18*(1/2), 101–116.

Lazarus, A. A., & Fay, A. (1984). Behavior therapy. In T. B. Karusu (Ed.), *The psychiatric therapies* (pp. 483–538). Washington, DC: American Psychiatric Association.

Lee, C. C., & Richardson, B. L. (Eds.). (1991). *Multicultural issues in counseling: New approaches to diversity.* Alexandria, VA: American Counseling Association.

Lewis, J. A., & Lewis, M. D. (1989). *Community counseling.* Pacific Grove, CA: Brooks/Cole.

Long, N. (1991). What Fritz Redl taught me about aggression: Understanding the dynamics of aggression and counteraggression in students. In W. C. Morse (Ed.), *Crisis intervention in residential treatment: The clinical innovations of Fritz Redl.* New York: The Haworth Press.

Long, N. (1996). The conflict cycle paradigm on how troubled students get teachers out of control. In N. Long, W. C. Morse, & R. G. Newman (Eds.), *Conflict in the classroom: The education of at-risk and troubled students* (5th ed.). Austin, TX: Pro-ed.

Long, N., Morse, W. C., & Newman, R. G. (Eds.). (1996). *Conflict in the classroom: The education of at-risk and troubled students* (5th ed.). Austin, TX: Pro-ed.

Magid, K., & McKelvey, C. A. (1987). *High risk: Children without a conscience.* Goldon, CO: M & M.

Maier, H. W. (1991). What's old—is new: Fritz Redl's teaching reaches into the present. In W. C. Morse (Ed.), *Crisis intervention in residential treatment: The clinical innovations of Fritz Redl* (pp. 15–30). New York: The Haworth Press.

Marshall, J., & Wheeler, L. (1996). *Street soldiers*. New York: Delacorte Press.

Maslow, A. H. (1954). *Motivation and personality*. New York: Harper & Row.

Matthews, W., & Roberts, J. (1988). The entrance of systems family therapy into a residential treatment center. *Child and Youth Services, 11*(1), 77–91.

McConkey-Radetzki, N. (1987). The development of a family therapy program within a residential treatment setting: Phases, issues, and strategies. *Journal of Strategic and Systemic Therapies, 6*(2), 3–15.

McWilliams, N. (1998). Relationships, subjectivity, and inference in diagnosis. In J. W. Barron (Ed.), *Making diagnosis meaningful: Enhancing evaluation and treatment of psychological disorders* (pp. 197–226). Washington, DC: American Psychological Association.

Meichenbaum, D., & Turk, D. (1987). *Facilitating treatment adherence*. New York: Plenum.

Meier, S. T., & Davis, S. R. (1997). *The elements of counseling* (3rd ed.). Pacific Grove, CA: Brooks/Cole.

Melton, G. B. (1991). Socialization in the global community: Respect for the dignity of children. *American Psychologist, 46*, 66–71.

Miller, G. A., Wagner, A., Britton, T. P., & Gridley, B. E. (1998). A framework for understanding the wounding of healers. *Counseling and Values, 42*, 124–131.

Millman, D. (1984). *Way of the peaceful warrior: A book that changes lives*. Tiburon, CA: H. J. Kramer.

Minuchin, S. (1974). *Families and family therapy*. Cambridge, MA: Harvard University Press.

Minuchin, S., & Fishman, H. C. (1981). *Family therapy techniques*. Cambridge, MA: Harvard University Press.

Minuchin, S., & Nichols, M. P. (1993). *Family healing: Tales of hope and renewal from family therapy*. New York: The Free Press.

Minuchin, S., Rosman, B., & Baker, L. (1978). *Psychosomatic families*. Cambridge, MA: Harvard University Press.

Mitchell, B, (1998). *Using humor in counseling*. Paper presented at National Youth Advocate Program National Conference, Columbus, OH.

Morse, W. C. (Ed.). (1991). *Crisis intervention in residential treatment: The clinical innovations of Fritz Redl*. New York: The Haworth Press.

Morse, W. C. (1996a). Knowing your students: The initial and ongoing dialogue. In N. Long, W. C. Morse, & R. G. Newman (Eds.), *Conflict in the classroom: The education of at-risk and troubled students* (5th ed., pp. 150–159). Austin, TX: Pro-ed.

Morse, W. C. (1996b). Mental health professionals and teachers: How do the twain meet? In N. Long, W. C. Morse, & R. G. Newman (Eds.), *Conflict in the classroom: The education of at-risk and troubled students* (5th ed., pp. 133–147). Austin, TX: Pro-ed.

Morse, W. C. (1996c). The role of caring in teaching children with behavior problems. In N. Long, W. C. Morse, & R. G. Newman (Eds.), *Conflict in the classroom: The education of at-risk and troubled students* (5th ed., pp. 106–112). Austin, TX: Pro-ed.

National Youth Advocate Program Description. (1997). Hilliard, OH.

Newman, C. F. (1994). Understanding client resistance: Methods for enhancing motivation to change. *Cognitive and Behavioral Practice, 1*, 46–69.

New Webster's Dictionary and Thesaurus of the English Language (rev. ed.). (1992). Danbury, CT: Lexicon.

Nichols, M. P., & Schwartz, R. C. (1991). *Family therapy: Concepts and methods* (3rd ed.). Boston: Allyn & Bacon.

Nicholson, M. L. (1991). A letter to Fritz. In W. C. Morse (Ed.), *Crisis intervention in residential treatment: The clinical innovations of Fritz Redl* (pp. 11–14). New York: The Haworth Press.

192   Working With Challenging Youth

Norcross, J. C. (1986). *Handbook of eclectic psychotherapy.* New York: Brunner/Mazel.
O'Hanlon, B., & Weiner-Davis, M. (1989). *In search of solutions: A new direction in psychotherapy.* New York: W. W. Norton.
Ohlsen, M. M. (1983). *Introduction to counseling.* Itasca, IL: F. E. Peacock.
Okun, B. F. (1997). *Effective helping: Interviewing and counseling techniques* (5th ed.). Pacific Grove, CA: Brooks/Cole.
Omizo, M. M., & Omizo, S. A. (1988). The effects of participation in group counseling sessions on self-esteem and locus of control among adolescents from divorced families. *The School Counselor, 36,* 54–60.
Orton, G. L. (1997). *Strategies for counseling children and their parents.* Pacific Grove, CA: Brooks/Cole.
Patterson, C. H. (1974). *Relationship counseling and psychotherapy.* New York: Harper & Row.
Patterson, C. H. (1996). Multicultural counseling: From diversity to universality. *Journal of Counseling and Development, 74,* 227–231.
Pederson, P. (1988). *Handbook for developing multicultural awareness.* Alexandria, VA: AACD Press.
Perls, F. (1973). *The Gestalt approach and eye witness to therapy.* New York: Bantam.
Pierce, R. (1985). Use and abuse of laughter in psychotherapy. *Psychotherapy in Private Practice, 3,* 67–73.
Pipher, M. (1994). *Reviving Ophelia: Saving the selves of adolescent girls.* New York: G. P. Putnam's Sons.
Prochaska, J. O., & Norcross, J. C. (1994). *Systems of psychotherapy.* Pacific Grove, CA: Brooks/Cole.
Rak, C. F., & Patterson, L. E. (1996). Promoting resilience in at-risk children. *Journal of Counseling and Development, 74,* 368–373.
Redl, F., & Wineman, D. (1951). *Children who hate.* New York: The Free Press.
Redl, F., & Wineman, D. (1952). *Controls from within.* New York: The Free Press.
Redl, F., & Wineman, D. (1957). *The aggressive child.* New York: The Free Press.
Resnick, M. D., Bearman, P. S., Blum, R. W., Bauman, K. E., Harris, K. M., Jones, J., Tabor, J., Beuhring, T., Sieving, R. E., Shaw, M., Ireland, M., Bearinger, L. H., & Udry, J. R. (1998). Protecting adolescents from harm: Findings from the National Longitudinal Study of Adolescent Health. In R. E. Muuss & H. D. Porton (Eds.), *Adolescent behavior and society: A book of readings* (5th ed., pp. 376–395). New York: McGraw-Hill.
Richardson, B. (1996). *The relationship between moral and ego development and treatment foster parent effectiveness and attitudes.* Ph.D. dissertation, The College of William and Mary, Williamsburg, VA.
Richardson, B., Foster, V. A., & McAdams, C. R. (1998). Parenting attitudes and moral development of treatment foster parents: Implications for training and supervision. *Child & Youth Care Forum, 27*(6), 409–431.
Richardson, T. Q., & Molinaro, K. L. (1996). White counselor self-awareness: A prerequisite for developing multicultural competence. *Journal of Counseling and Development, 74,* 238–242.
Rogers, C. (1957). The necessary and sufficient conditions of therapeutic personality change. *Journal of Consulting Psychology, 21,* 95–103.
Rogers, C. (1961). *On becoming a person.* Boston: Houghton Mifflin.
Rogers, C. (1977). *Carl Rogers on personal power: Inner strength and revolutionary impact.* New York: Delacorte Press.
Rose, S. D. (1998). *Group therapy for troubled youth: A cognitive-behavioral interactive approach.* Thousand Oaks, CA: Sage.
Rose, S. D., & Edleson, J. L. (1987). *Working with children and adolescents in groups: A multimethod approach.* San Francisco: Jossey-Bass.

Sarason, I. G., & Sarason, B. R. (1996). *Abnormal psychology: The problem of maladaptive behavior.* Upper Saddle River, NJ: Prentice-Hall.

Satir, V. M. (1972). *Peoplemaking.* Palo Alto, CA: Science & Behavior Books.

Satir, V. M. (1983). *Conjoint family therapy* (3rd ed.). Palo Alto, CA: Science & Behavior Books.

Satir, V. M. (1988). *The new peoplemaking.* Mountain View, CA: Science & Behavior Books.

Schultz, M. J. (1991). Program development and training in residential treatment: Integrating milieu and systemic models. *Journal of Strategic and Systemic Therapies, 10*(2), 6–20.

Segal, L. (1991). Brief therapy: The MRI approach. In A. S. Gurman & D. P. Knisken (Eds.), *Handbook of family therapy* (Vol. 2). New York: Brunner/Mazel.

Selekman, M. D. (1993). *Pathways to change: Brief therapy solutions with difficult adolescents.* New York: The Guilford Press.

Seligman, L. (1990). *Selecting effective treatments.* San Francisco: Jossey-Bass.

Shechtman, Z., Bar-El, O., & Hadar, E. (1997). Therapeutic factors and psychoeducational groups for adolescents: A comparison. *The Journal for Specialists in Group Work, 22*(3), 203–213.

Simon, S. B. (1988). *Getting unstuck: Breaking through your barriers to change.* New York: Warner Books.

Sleek, S. (1995). Group therapy: Tapping the power of teamwork. *The APA Monitor, 26*(7), 1, 38–39.

Smith, S. L. (April, 1989). The masks students wear. *Instructor, 27*–28, 31–32.

Sommers-Flanagan, J., & Sommers-Flanagan, R. (1996). Counseling difficult adolescents. *Directions in Clinical Counseling and Psychology, 6,* 1–16.

Sommers-Flanagan, J., & Sommers-Flanagan, R. (1997). *Tough kids, cool counseling.* Alexandria, VA: American Counseling Association.

Stiles, W. B., Shapiro, D. A., & Elliott, R. (1986). Are all psychotherapies equivalent? *American Psychologist, 41*(2), 165–180.

Sue, D. W., & Sue, D. (1990). *Counseling the culturally different: Theory & practice* (2nd ed.). New York: John Wiley & Sons.

Sullivan, H. S. (1953). *The interpersonal theory of psychiatry.* New York: W. W. Norton.

Target, M., & Fonagy, P. (1996). In A. Roth & P. Fonagy (Eds.), *What works for whom? A critical review of psychotherapy research* (pp. 263–320). New York: The Guilford Press.

Tobin, L. (1991). *What do you do with a child like this? Inside the lives of troubled children.* Deluth, MN: Whole Person Associates.

Tolan, P. H., & Mitchell, M. E. (1990). Families and the therapy of antisocial and delinquent behavior. *Journal of Psychotherapy and the Family, 6*(3/4), 29–48.

Towberman, D. B. (1993). Group vs. individual counseling: Treatment mode and the client's perception of the treatment environment. *Journal of Group Psychotherapy, Psychodrama, & Sociometry, 45*(4), 163–174.

Trent, S. C., & Artiles, A. J. (1995). Serving culturally diverse students with emotional or behavioral disorders: Broadening current perspectives. In J. M. Kaufman, J. W. Lloyd, D. P. Hallahan, & T. A. Astuto (Eds.), *Issues in educational placement: Students with emotional and behavioral disorders.* Hillsdale, NJ: Lawrence Erlbaum Associates.

Trieschman, A. E., Whittaker, J. K., & Brendtro, L. K. (1969). *The other 23 hours.* Chicago: Aldine.

Tucker, G. J. (1998). Putting DSM-IV in perspective. *American Journal of Psychiatry, 155*(2), 159–161.

Twain, M. (1939). *The Reader's Digest.* Sept. 1939, 22.

Van Bockern, S. (1996). Profiles of reclaiming schools. In N. Long, W. C. Morse, & R. G. Newman (Eds.), *Conflict in the classroom: The education of at-risk and troubled students.* (5th ed., pp. 126–132). Austin, TX: Pro-ed.

Wallbridge, H. R., & Osachuk, A. G. (1995). Therapy with adolescents. In D. G. Martin & A. D. Moore (Eds.), *Basics of clinical practice: A guidebook for trainees in the helping professions* (pp. 208–222). Prospect Heights, IL: Waveland Press.

Walter, J. L., & Peller, J. E. (1992). *Becoming solution-focused in brief therapy.* New York: Brunner/Mazel.

Watzlawick, P. (1976). *How real is real?* New York: Random House.

Watzlawick, P., Weakland, J. H., and Fisch, R. (1974). *Change: Principles of problem formulation and resolution.* New York: W. W. Norton.

Weakland, J. H., Fisch, R., Watzlawick, P., & Bodin, A. M. (1974). Brief therapy: Focused problem resolution. *Family Process, 13*(2), 141–167.

Weaver, G. R. (1990). The crisis of cross-cultural child and youth care. In M. Krueger & N. Powell (Eds.), *Choices in caring: Contemporary approaches to child and youth care work* (pp. 65–103). Washington, DC: Child Welfare League of America.

Wehlage, G., Rutter, R., Smith, G., Lesko, N., & Fernandez, R. (1989). *Reducing the risk: Schools as communities of support.* London: Falmer Press.

Weiner-Davis, M., deShazer, S., & Gingerich, W. (1987). Building on pretreatment change to construct the therapeutic solution: An exploratory study. *Journal of Marital and Family Therapy, 13*(4), 359–363.

Wrenn, C. G. (1962). The culturally encapsulated counselor. *Harvard Educational Review, 32,* 444–449.

Wubbolding, R. E. (1988). *Using reality therapy.* New York: Harper Perennial.

Wubbolding, R. E. (1991). *Understanding reality therapy: A metaphorical approach.* New York: Harper Perennial.

Wubbolding, R. E. (1996). *Reality therapy training: A comprehensive guide for learning reality therapy and choice theory* (10th ed.). Cincinnati, OH: Center for Reality Therapy.

Yalom, I. D. (1985). *The theory and practice of group psychotherapy* (3rd ed.). New York: Basic Books.

Yeh, J., White, K. R., & Ozcan, Y. A. (1997). Effective evaluation of community-based services in Virginia. *Community Mental Health Journal, 33*(6), 487–499.

Young, M. E. (1998). *Learning the art of helping: Building blocks and techniques.* Upper Saddle River, NJ: Prentice-Hall.

York, P., York, D., & Wachtel, T. (1982). *Toughlove.* Garden City, NY: Doubleday.

Zimpfer, D. G. (1992). Group work with juvenile delinquents. *Journal for Specialists in Group Work, 17,* 116–126.

INDEX